On
The
Trail
Of
The
Saucer
Spies

Other Books by Nick Redfern

Body Snatchers in the Desert
Three Men Seeking Monsters
Strange Secrets
The FBI Files
A Covert Agenda
Cosmic Crashes

ON THE TRAIL OF THE SAUCER SPIES:

UFOs and Government Surveillance

NICK REDFERN

ANOMALIST BOOKS
San Antonio • New York

An Original Publication of ANOMALIST BOOKS

Anomalist Books   **Anomalist Books**
5150 Broadway #108   **PO Box 577**
San Antonio, TX 78209   **Jefferson Valley, NY 10535**

For Alex and Gloria,
Keep on rocking, ladies!

CONTENTS

INTRODUCTION

I n 1992 in a privately published paper titled "Have You Checked Your File Lately?" Robert Durant, a UFO researcher and pilot, discussed the theme of an all-encompassing, Government-sanctioned-and-controlled operation designed to covertly monitor the activities of the public UFO research community:

"You, the reader, are among the approximately 4,000 Americans who subscribe to ufological journals or newsletters, buy UFO books through the mail, attend conferences, or spend time with others who engage in such activities. Not a large group. We are only 3 percent of the total number of citizens the government admits to watching with intense care. A very easy group to track. Building your file is so much easier than compiling one on a Russian spy or a Mafioso. There is a file on you at the Internal Revenue Service, the Social Security Administration, the driver's license bureau of the state in which you are licensed, the commercial credit card companies that do business with your bank and your lenders, your doctor's office, and so forth and so on. Is it really unreasonable to suspect that a UFO file would be created?" [1]

The answer to Durant's question is: it is not at all unreasonable to suspect that such a scenario exists. Indeed, as *On the Trail of the Saucer Spies* demonstrates, such a scenario most assuredly does exist. This book does not attempt to answer in detail the complex questions

of what UFOs are, where they are from, or why there are here—
there are countless titles available that focus upon these controversial
issues. Rather, it resolves the seldom-addressed questions of precisely
why and how the official world is keeping a close watch on those
individuals who engage in UFO research, or who are witnesses to
UFO activity.

The truth-is-weirder-than-fiction examples recounted in these
pages span more than half a century, and include all of the staple
ingredients of the most controversial aspects of the UFO puzzle:
crashed flying saucers, alien bodies held in cryogenic storage, black
helicopters, crop circles, alien abductions (by alleged aliens and by
elements of the military), underground bases, animal mutilations,
Government-sponsored disinformation campaigns, and even the
exploits of the nefarious Men in Black.

As will become apparent, however, the full story also incorporates
issues and organizations that—at first glance, at least—would appear
to be totally unrelated to the UFO mystery. Ultra-fascist political
organizations, the Irish Republican Army, communist-based
groups, animal rights activists, computer hackers, Chinese Military
Intelligence, and the North Korean Government ultimately prove
to be pivotal to both understanding and unravelling the full picture
of why a number of Governments take such a deep interest in the
activities of those who look skyward. Caveat lector: keep a close
watch over your shoulder. "They" may be watching you, too.

1

THE EARLY YEARS

The saga of the flying saucer began with Kenneth Arnold, the pilot whose 24 June 1947 encounter at the Cascade Mountains in Washington State, kicked off the modern-era of UFO sightings. At approximately 3:00 p.m., Arnold was searching for an aircraft that had reportedly crashed on the southwest side of Mt. Rainier. Arnold's subsequent flying saucer encounter attracted the keen interest of not just the public and the media, but also of the all-powerful Federal Bureau of Investigation (FBI). Arnold's verbatim statement of what happened appears in previously secret 1947 FBI records that confirm the Bureau's deep interest in his strange encounter:

"I hadn't flown more than two or three minutes on my course when a bright flash reflected on my airplane. It startled me as I thought I was too close to some other aircraft. I looked every place in the sky and couldn't find where the reflection had come from until I looked to the left and the north of Mt. Rainier, where I observed a chain of nine peculiar looking aircraft flying from north to south at approximately 9,500 feet elevation and going, seemingly, in a definite direction of about 170 degrees."

Arnold stressed that the objects were approaching Mt. Rainier very rapidly and he was puzzled by their physical appearance. "I thought it was very peculiar that I couldn't find their tails but assumed they were some type of jet plane. The more I observed these

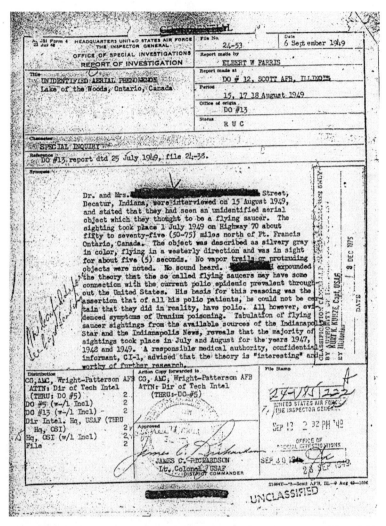

In 1949, the Air Force, FBI, and Atomic Energy Commission all carefully monitored the theories of a doctor from Indiana who was researching links between UFO sightings and outbreaks of viruses and diseases.

objects, the more upset I became, as I am accustomed and familiar with most all objects flying whether I am close to the ground or at higher altitudes. The chain of these saucer-like objects [was] at least five miles long. I felt confident after I would land there would be some explanation of what I saw [sic]."

No conclusive explanation for Arnold's sighting ever surfaced, and the mystery regarding what he did or did not see has raged for more than half a century. Even the FBI, which was monitoring UFO activity in the summer of 1947 on a somewhat ad hoc basis, came away impressed by the report: "It is difficult to believe that a man of [Arnold's] character and apparent integrity would state that he saw objects and write up a report to the extent that he did if he did not see them."[1]

As UFO sightings reached epidemic proportions across the United States in the summer of 1947, the military swung into action, and various studies and operations were formulated that ultimately unified into an official, investigative operation known as "Project Sign." In 1948 that project would be replaced by "Project Grudge" and then by "Project Blue Book," which continued until 1969. Collectively, the three projects concluded that no UFO sighting that was investigated officially ever had a bearing on national security, and there was no evidence to indicate that any UFO sightings represented alien visitations.[2]

Of course, numerous claims, counterclaims, arguments, and counterarguments have been put forth by a variety of authors and commentators on whether or not some UFOs are indeed alien spacecraft, and whether or not elements of the U.S. Government, military, and intelligence community have systematically hidden evidence in support of that theory.

Two weeks after Kenneth Arnold's encounter, Brigadier General George F. Schulgen, Chief of the Requirements Intelligence Branch of Army Air Corps Intelligence, met with Special Agent S.W. Reynolds of the FBI. Schulgen wanted to determine if the Army Air Force could solicit the assistance of the Bureau on a regular basis in its investigation of the UFO mystery. General Schulgen advised

Reynolds that, "every effort must be undertaken in order to run down and ascertain whether or not the flying discs are a fact and, if so, to learn all about them."

An examination of the FBI's relevant files demonstrates that, in the weeks following Arnold's encounter of 24 June 1947, the foremost thought on General Schulgen's mind was that the saucers were Russian in origin. He confided in Special Agent Reynolds that, "the first reported sightings might have been by individuals of Communist sympathies with the view to causing hysteria and fear of a secret weapon."

General Schulgen guaranteed the FBI "all the facilities of [my] office as to results obtained," and outlined a plan that would involve the FBI in both locating and questioning witnesses to UFO sightings to ascertain whether they were sincere in their statements, or whether their statements were prompted by "personal desire for publicity or political reasons."[3]

Similarly, in 1953, the Robertson Panel—a select group of consultants brought together by the Central Intelligence Agency (CIA) to look at the national security implications of the UFO controversy—recommended that a number of public UFO investigative groups that existed in the United States at the time, such as the Civilian Flying Saucer Investigators (CFSI) and the Aerial Phenomena Research Organization (APRO), should be "watched" carefully due to "…the apparent irresponsibility and the possible use of such groups for subversive purposes…"[4]

Indeed, the fear, paranoia, and concern (sometimes justified and sometimes not) expressed by the military, the CIA, and the FBI in the early formative years of official UFO studies was that many of those implicated in the flying saucer mystery possibly had "Communist sympathies" or were following a covert, political agenda—the intention of which was "causing hysteria" and subversion. This inevitably led to intense surveillance of practically anyone and everyone who delved into the subject, and particularly those who criticized the Government's handling of the situation, as now becomes apparent.

Next to the so-called Roswell Incident of July 1947, without doubt the most controversial UFO crash case is alleged to have occurred in the vicinity of Aztec, New Mexico, in 1948. According to data published in Frank Scully's best-selling 1950 book, *Behind the Flying Saucers*, as a result of a number of incidents in 1947 and 1948, the wreckage of four alien spacecraft and no fewer than thirty-four alien bodies had been recovered by U.S. authorities and were being studied under cover of the utmost secrecy at a variety of defense establishments in the United States. As Scully was willing to admit, the bulk of his information had come from two prime sources: Silas Mason Newton (described in a 1941 FBI report as a "wholly unethical businessman") and a Dr. Gee, the name given to protect the eight scientists, who had supposedly divulged various details of the crashes to Newton and Scully. According to Scully's sources, one such UFO was found in Hart Canyon, near the town of Aztec, in March 1948.

So the story went, after the Aztec saucer had crashed, it was located essentially intact by elements of the U.S. military that gained access to the object via a fractured porthole. Bodies of sixteen small, humanlike creatures, all slightly charred and undoubtedly dead, were found inside the craft. The UFO was then dismantled whereupon it and the bodies of the crew were transferred to Wright Field air base in Dayton, Ohio for study. At the time of its release, Scully's book caused a major sensation. In both 1952 and 1956, however, reporter J.P. Cahn authored two detailed exposés, which cast extreme doubt on the claims of Newton and Dr. Gee (identified by then not as eight scientists but as one Leo GeBauer—who had a background as dubious as that of Newton).

Did a UFO crash at Aztec, New Mexico? Were diminutive alien bodies recovered at the crash site? Was the incident successfully concealed by a concerned U.S. Military? Were the key players in the story all that they appeared to be? And if not, then exactly what did occur at Aztec, New Mexico, on the fateful day in 1948? To answer those questions, we have to turn—surprisingly—to the U.S. Government. While documentation pertaining to the allegedly similar events at Roswell nearly twelve months earlier is practically nonexistent; the exact opposite can be said about Aztec.

Born 25 February 1903, Frank Scully's mysterious Dr. Gee—Leo Arnold Julius GeBauer—is the subject of an FBI surveillance and investigation file that totals no less than 398 pages. Interestingly, of that file, fewer than 200 pages have been declassified under the provisions of the United States' Freedom of Information Act (FOIA). As the available papers amply demonstrate, GeBauer was, to put it mildly, a colorful character that was being closely watched by the FBI. He had numerous aliases, including Harry A. GreBauer, Harry A. GeBauer, Harry A. GreyBauer, Harry A. Barbar, Leo A. J. GeBauer, Leo Arnold Julius GeBauer, and Arnold Julius Leopold GeBauer. As a confidential FBI report of 19 December 1941 revealed, GeBauer had made some disturbing statements seven months prior: "What this country needs is a man like Hitler; then everybody would have a good job...It would be a God's blessing if we had two men in the United States to run this country like Hitler. The English people are nothing but a dirty bunch of rats. We should stay to home and tend to our own damn business and let Germany give England what they had coming."

Even more controversial, GeBauer went on to describe Hitler as a "swell fellow," adding that: "the guy who shoots President Roosevelt should be given a gold medal." As FBI Special Agent J.J. McGuire noted, "GeBauer is always pointing out the good points of the German Government over the English and our democratic form of government." To demonstrate that controversy continued to surround GeBauer, a memo dated 14 February 1969 prepared by the FBI's Denver office, referred to an unnamed source who "threatened to do bodily harm to GeBauer and demanded $50,000 as part of commissions due him." No wonder the FBI kept watch on the man.

Silas Mason Newton, Frank Scully's main source for the Aztec UFO story, attracted his own fair share of FBI interest – resulting in the creation of a file on the man that ran to more than 70 pages. An FBI document dated 30 September 1970 stated: "Newton was born on July 19, 1887, at Shelby County, Kentucky. He is divorced and is a college graduate. He has claimed his occupation was that of a geologist, who has an income of $500 a month. He claims to have a Bachelor of Science in geology from Baylor University and to have studied for six months at Oxford University." However, a further FBI report of 1970 reveals: "Silas Newton, presently under indictment [in] Los Angeles, California, for fraud, returned to Silver City, New Mexico, area January 1970, and began to organize what appears as a mining swindle."

Having established—thanks to the FBI's surveillance files – the shady credentials of Newton and GeBauer, what was it that brought them and crashed UFOs into the world of Frank Scully? The FBI took a very keen interest in the intricacies of the Aztec affair, and watched the activities of Scully, Newton, and GeBauer very closely. Their now-declassified files reveal that the FBI was fully aware of not just the alleged Aztec crash, but also the way in which Newton, Scully, and GeBauer came together, and the way in which the whole saga progressed. According to the FBI:

"Regarding the saucer story in July 1949 GeBauer, as a specialist in geomagnetics, became consultant to Newton, an alleged geophysicist, using instruments of his own design to make microwave surveys of oil pools. Newton had been a friend of Scully, who writes a weekly column for *Variety*; and in the fall of 1949, GeBauer discussed saucers with Newton and Scully at which time he claimed to have conducted secret inquiries with the government and other scientists on several saucers which had landed in New Mexico and Arizona.

"GeBauer claimed to have recovered from these saucers the tubeless radio, some small gears and small disks, all of which material had been secreted by GeBauer from the other scientists and government investigators. The three men agreed to publish a story of GeBauer's discoveries, but because of GeBauer's connections with the matter, he was to be identified only as Dr. Gee. To determine the reaction of the public to an unauthenticated story of the actual existence of flying saucers, on March 8, 1950, Newton, as Scientist X, appeared as a guest lecturer before a science class at Denver University. Newton told of Dr. Gee's findings, and the substance of the lecture leaked out to the newspapers. As a result, Scully wrote his book setting forth Dr. Gee's discoveries and revelations.

"After reading the saucer story, J.P. Cahn noted several inconsistencies, and he determined to make an investigation to determine whether the story was based on facts or a hoax. In the beginning he went to Scully, but was unable to obtain the identity of Dr. Gee, and Scully was reluctant to produce Newton. Cahn met Newton in Scully's home at which time Newton claimed to be a graduate of Baylor University and Yale University, and a post-graduate of the University of Berlin. Newton promised to discuss with Dr. Gee the proposition to disclose fully an authenticated announcement that space ships were landing on earth, together with photographs, metals, and other evidence.

"Newton exhibited a couple of gears, fine-toothed and about the size of pocket watches, and two disks of unknown metals, all being tied up in Newton's handkerchief. He alleged these items were obtained from one of the saucers. Newton also told Cahn of seeing secret detailed plans on the Airflow system of B-26s in Dr. Gee's laboratories in Phoenix on which the mysterious Dr. Gee was doing research for the government. Dr. Gee had developed a magnetic fog, rain and darkness dispelling screen to be fitted on the windshields of airplanes to enable the pilot to see through any weather.

"While in Scully's book, Dr. Gee was said to have degrees from the University of Berlin, GeBauer only claimed electrical engineering degrees from Louis Institute of Technology in Chicago in 1931 or 1932; that while the book claimed from 1943 to 1945 Dr. Gee had headed 1,700 scientists doing experimental work in the secret magnetic research, GeBauer was merely chief of laboratories of Air Research Company in Phoenix and Los Angeles, mainly in charge of maintenance equipment. Cahn talked with GeBauer and obtained a signed statement from him denying that he was Dr. Gee mentioned in Scully's book, and stating that he had no connection with Scully, his book, or statements, and had given Scully no authority to infer that he was Dr. Gee. GeBauer did state that he was acquainted with Newton."

On 8 March 1950 Newton delivered a lecture at Denver University where he was billed as Scientist X. If the lecture was not attended by agents of the FBI, it was certainly monitored by them. A teletype of 9 March 1950 from the FBI's Denver office confirms its awareness of Newton's talk: "Two sources advised today that Silas Newton has given at least one and possibly more lectures before classes at Denver University yesterday or today in which he discussed flying saucers which he allegedly personally observed. This person claims to have seen several such objects, one of which allegedly landed in New Mexico. He also claims to have observed occupants of saucers described by him as of human form, but about three feet tall."

Newton had been escorted to the lecture by George T. Koehler, a staff member at the Rocky Mountain Radio Station. Curiously, in *Behind the Flying Saucers*, Frank Scully reported that within two hours of Newton's lecture, U.S. intelligence agents were asking questions at the university about Newton and the nature of his talk, and what the general consensus of opinion was with respect to Newton's revelations. In addition, there is evidence to show that Koehler was "relieved" of certain audiotapes after he had the foresight to surreptitiously record an interview between himself and a representative of the U.S. Army. "We know you have been recording these interviews," Koehler was told. "Now hand them over."

Matters took an even more bizarre turn when a Kansas City car dealer named Rudy Fick began telling stories that Koehler had informed him that he—Koehler—had "crashed the gate" at a radar station near the New Mexico–Arizona border and had seen two flying saucers the military had in its possession. One of the crafts was supposedly badly damaged, while the other was relatively intact. Once again, officials took careful note of who was saying what and to whom, as the following FBI extract makes clear:

"According to the information given Koehler around 50 of these flying saucers have been found in the United States in a period of 2 years. Of these, 40 are in the U.S. Research Bureau in Los Angeles. Each of the craft had a crew of 3. The bodies in the damaged ship were charred, but the other ship's occupants were in a perfect state of preservation, although dead. All were uniform height of 3 feet, beardless and their teeth were completely free of fillings or cavities. They wore no under-garments but had their bodies taped and were dressed in a sort of wire. Mr. Fick feels that the security department of the military fear that the sudden shock of a surprise announcement that interplanetary travel is possible might cause mass hysteria. OSI District 13 will interview Fick. The editor of the *Kansas City Star* stated that while they were aware of this story they did not dare publish it in the paper because it is too fantastic."

A partially censored FBI document of 22 March 1950 shows a story very similar to that told by Fick was in circulation in Washington, D.C., too. A one-page report from Guy Hottel, the FBI Special Agent-in-Charge at Washington to J. Edgar Hoover, reveals that: "An investigator for the Air Forces stated that three so-called flying saucers had been recovered in New Mexico. They were described as being circular in shape with raised centers, approximately 50 feet in diameter. Each one was occupied by three bodies of human shape but only 3 feet tall, dressed in metallic cloth of a very fine texture. Each body was bandaged in a manner similar to the blackout suits used by speed flyers and test pilots. According to Mr. [Deleted], informant, the saucers were found in New Mexico due to the fact that the Government has a very high-powered radar set-up in that area and it is believed the radar interferes with the controlling mechanism of the saucers."

Although its contents are eye-opening, investigator William Moore (who, with Charles Berlitz, co-wrote the book *The Roswell Incident*) asserts that the document is largely worthless, since its origins can be traced from Fick to Koehler and ultimately to Newton—whose testimony has to be examined very carefully. Pro-Aztec researchers maintain that if Newton and GeBauer were in possession of information that was even remotely accurate, then the memo of 22 March 1950 should not be ignored outright.

Was the Newton-GeBauer-Scully story factually correct? Was GeBauer the elusive Dr. Gee? Or was the entire matter without foundation? Here things become decidedly murky. In 1953 both Newton and GeBauer received suspended prison sentences for their part in defrauding Herman Flader, a Colorado businessman who owned the Stay Put Clamp and Coupling Factory on the outskirts of Denver. And yet, for all of the faults of Newton and GeBauer, there are a number of intriguing pointers that continue to breathe life into the Aztec affair. As far as GeBauer was concerned, it is a proven fact that in the 1940s, he most definitely was employed as chief of laboratories at the Air Research Manufacturing Company in Phoenix.

It so happens that of the four alleged UFO crashes discussed in Frank Scully's book, one allegedly occurred north of Phoenix at Paradise Valley in 1947. Timothy Good, a UFO researcher, revealed in his 1987 book *Above Top Secret* that he had spoken with a pilot named Selman Graves who described witnessing aspects of an operation to retrieve a "large aluminum dome-shaped thing" in the Paradise Valley area, around which were "pitched buildings—tents—and men moving about." In the early 1940s, Leo GeBauer had been employed in the aerospace industry relatively close to where this event supposedly occurred; the possibility that he may have gleaned details of the alleged event from former colleagues at Air Research cannot be wholly dismissed. And with respect to GeBauer, there is one final point that should not pass without comment. In portions of his classified file, a number of pages are exempt from release "in the interest of national defense," according to the FBI.

Silas Newton, Frank Scully, and Leo GeBauer have long since gone to their graves; however, the extensive FBI files on the trio—as well as the Bureau's documentation on the Aztec affair in general—ensure that the case and its attendant controversies continue to live on.[5]

Nearly sixty years ago, a doctor from Indiana was certain that he had solved the UFO mystery. He was determined to warn the American Military and Government of the horrific truth: that the intelligences behind the UFOs were attempting to wipe out the human race with biological and radiological warfare. Despite the bizarre nature of the doctor's assertions, officially declassified documentation reveals that the controversy was addressed very closely by the FBI, the Aero Medical Laboratory, the Atomic Energy Commission (which intriguingly suggested that the doctor should be "watched for any political reason"), and the Air Force Office of Special Investigations, the latter having even made a specific visit to the home of the doctor to interview him about his theories.

This strange saga all began on 1 July 1949 when "Dr. X"—as I will dub him, since both the FBI and the Air Force have been very careful to delete his name from relevant, released documentation—and his wife had a close encounter of the distinctly unusual kind while vacationing in Canada. Special Investigations Agent Elbert W. Farris from Scott Air Force Base, Illinois, prepared a report dated 6 September 1949 that was marked for the attention of HQ AFOSI and the Director of Technical Intelligence at Wright-Patterson Air Force Base. "Dr. and Mrs. X of Decatur, Indiana, were interviewed on 15 August 1949, and stated that they had seen an unidentified aerial object which they thought to be a flying saucer. The sighting took place 1 July 1949 on Highway 70 about 50–70 miles north of Ft. Francis, Ontario, Canada, and near the east side of Lake of the Woods, Canada."

Farris's report continues that based upon an interview conducted with the doctor by Special Agent Clarence A. Trumble of the AFOSI at Offutt Air Force Base: "The object was described as silvery gray in color, flying in a westerly direction and was in sight for about 5 seconds. No vapor trails or protruding objects were noted...The object pursued a straight path of flight with an erratic motion comparable to that of an oblong object being thrown through the air.

"The aerial anomaly appeared to be faster than an airplane. It did not hover...and was likened to a small aircraft at two thousand feet. Dr. X observed no fins, no vapor trail and heard no sound. After passing across his line of vision, the object was lost from view behind the trees. The day was bright and sunny, and Dr. X emphasized that he had definitely observed an object in the air unlike any other known to him. Mrs. X corroborated her husband's statements..."

Meanwhile, on the same day that the Air Force became enmeshed in the controversy, the FBI Special-Agent-in-Charge (SAC) at the

Bureau's Indianapolis office advised J. Edgar Hoover much of the same. The SAC added that the FBI was keeping a close watch on Dr. X, too, and that when he returned to his home town of Decatur, Indiana, "…he found himself in the midst of a polio epidemic and that as a result he had read as much literature as possible with respect to polio, its symptoms, diagnosis, etc. Dr. X told that in his opinion, the cases which were thought to be polio in the vicinity of Decatur, Indiana, were not polio, but possibly the result of uranium poisoning and that he felt the presence of flying saucers had direct bearing on the polio epidemic."

The SAC at Indianapolis informed Hoover of Dr. X's unique line of thinking: "[He] pointed out that flying saucers were observed in the Carolinas in 1948 and there was a polio epidemic in the vicinity at that time. Dr. X stated he had consulted one of the physicians at the Benjamin Harrison Air Base and had also checked the records with reference to allegations concerning the sighting of flying saucers and had done a little research with respect to correlating the presence of flying saucers and any polio epidemic."

The SAC also noted that—according to their investigations— Dr. X was reporting his conclusions to "the proper Air Force authorities" and had also spoken with staff at the Indiana University Medical School, "where doctors treated the entire matter as a big joke." Interestingly, J. Edgar Hoover was further advised: "Dr. X had heard while in Canada that there had been some rather strange events somewhere in the interior with respect to finding what might have been remains of flying saucers."

Despite the nature of Dr. X's theories, the Air Force did not dismiss him as a crank. Indeed, Air Force Agent Elbert W. Farris undertook some detailed background investigations himself: "Tabulation of flying saucer sightings from the available sources of the *Indianapolis Star* and the *Indianapolis News*, reveals that the majority of sightings took place in July and August for the years 1947, 1948 and 1949."

More notable is Farris's next statement: "A responsible medical authority, confidential informant, CI-1, advised that the theory is 'interesting' and worthy of further research." In other words, the Air

Force actually appeared to take the idea that aliens were possibly engaged in a covert operation to poison the human species with biological or radiological warfare seriously. One might ask, what on Earth, or indeed off it, would prompt the Air Force to pursue this particularly novel (and, if true, highly disturbing) theory? Certainly Dr. X's background was a key and contributing factor, and was something that officials took very careful note of.

According to Air Force Agent Farris, "Dr. X produced membership cards which show him to be a member of the Masons, Scottish Rite, Knights of Pythias, Loyal Order of Moose and the Eagles. He served as a Naval officer for 14 months and also held a commission in the United States Public Health Service...he is an associate member of the Association of Medicine, Bloomington, Indiana, and he is an associate member of the Association of Military Surgeons. He is a physician and surgeon."

An illustrious and intriguing background, to say the least.

Agent Farris further advised his superiors that, in an attempt to gather additional background data on the doctor, he had visited the Chief of Police at Decatur—James Border—who had firmly vouched for the integrity of Dr. X, asserting that he was "reliable," "responsible," and "enjoys an excellent reputation in the community." And Agent Farris was still not finished. On 17 August 1949 he carefully perused the available UFO reports collected by the Air Force from the period 4 July 1947 to 26 July 1949 and prepared an official report that detailed the sightings and their exact locations. Farris's next step was to contact a person he described as a "reliable medical authority at Benjamin Harrison Air Force Base, Indiana," in an effort to "determine whether the possibility of uranium poisoning, as expounded by Dr. X, had any basis in fact."

According to Farris, "The authority, who preferred to remain anonymous, is hereinafter known as Confidential Informant CI-1. Informant CI-1 advised the writer that the Polio period extends from April to October, with the peak months of the disease being reached in July and August...Informant CI-1 was doubtful if the answer to the question of uranium poisoning could be readily answered, and he was of the opinion that the possibility and its connection with the Polio epidemic prevalent throughout the United States had never been explored."

As a result of this, plans were initiated to approach the Aero Medical Laboratory Research Department at Wright-Patterson Air Force Base for comment. "Does [the] uranium element produce any physiological reaction in human beings corresponding to symptoms applicable to many of the so-called Polio clinical and sub-clinical conditions?" asked Agent Farris, continuing, "Are topographical areas where so-called Flying Disc are predominantly seen (or known uranium deposits) pin points of endemic areas of clinical symptoms resembling Polio?"

In addition to forwarding these questions, inquiries were also dutifully dispatched to a source at the Indiana University School of Medicine who was described as "an authority on poison" and who was subsequently interviewed on 25 August 1949. The source advised that in his opinion, the "Flying-Saucers-are-poisoning-us-with-uranium" idea espoused by Dr. X was "negligible." The source added that while he did recall Dr. X as a student who had graduated from the Indiana University School of Medicine in 1941 and considered him to be a "good boy," he was also of the opinion that Dr. X was "not the best student Indiana University ever turned out" and was somewhat "imaginative."

Yet the same source recommended bringing the Atomic Energy Commission (AEC) into the controversy. He considered the AEC to be "the only Agency in the United States capable of answering this question once and for all." As a result—and in what was certainly a highly unusual and unique scenario—the FBI, the Aero Medical Laboratory at Wright-Patterson Air Force Base, the Atomic Energy Commission, and the Air Force Office of Special Investigations became deeply embroiled in the bizarre theories of Dr. X, his background, and questions concerning his motivations for digging into this strange aspect of the UFO mystery.

It transpired that the AEC was less concerned by the doctor's theories but more by the possibility that he was working with an unknown political agenda that involved the dissemination of "saucer hysteria." This statement was very similar to that of Brigadier General George F. Schulgen who had expressed his concerns back in the summer of 1947 that alleged UFO witnesses were "causing hysteria" for "political reasons." This would seem to suggest that, at the time, a number of agencies were in accord with Schulgen's theories, and that their reasons for taking an interest in UFOs had practically identical motivations.

On 6 October 1949 an answer was forthcoming to the mystery. In a one-page document titled "PROJECT GRUDGE—Incident at Lake of the Woods, Ontario, Canada—1 July 1949," Major D. Lynch, Acting District Commander of the AFOSI, revealed the results of an investigation prepared by Wright-Patterson's Aero Medical Laboratory. Signed off by Lieutenant Colonel A.P. Cagge of Wright-Patterson, the report read thus:

"While it is true that some of the clinical symptoms of poliomyelitis may be similar to uranium poisoning, the over-all clinical syndrome is quite different. Progress in the case of uranium poisoning is very dismal, with recovery unlikely. Besides the heavy metal poisoning effect of uranium poisoning, there is also the prolonged and continuous radiation effect of uranium which can be detected in the broad picture."

The report continued, "This is quite a distinctive clinical feature of uranium poisoning which any physician should readily be able to recognize. It is also a feature which does not diminish with time and, hence, the patient does not recover. This results because the uranium is a long-lived radioactive isotope, which becomes fixed in the body and cannot be eliminated to any appreciable extent. Because of the above considerations, it is the opinion of this office that there is little, if any, ground for the theory that the annual poliomyelitis epidemics are related to radioactivity in any way.

"It is also to be noted that the annual outbreak of poliomyelitis during the summer months has been prevalent for many years prior to flying saucers and the widespread use of radioactive isotopes."

This would seem to suggest that as ingenious as Dr. X's theories undoubtedly were, they were very wide of the mark when it came to providing a definitive answer as to what motivated the apparent UFO presence on our world. Nevertheless, as this now-declassified official documentation firmly reveals, during the early years of its flying saucer investigations, elements of the U.S. Military and Government were not only keeping a careful eye on the public's UFO theories—no matter how bizarre those theories ultimately proved to be—they were keeping an even closer watch on the motivations of those that dared to enter the strange arena of UFOs.

In the early 1950s two new UFO research groups surfaced. One such group was Civilian Saucer Investigation (CSI), which was formed in December 1951 by a group of engineers, scientists, and journalists. One prominent member was Walter Riedel, a former German rocket scientist. The fact that Riedel was dabbling in the saucer controversy would have caused the official world to sit up and take notice. The CSI's files were eventually turned over to another investigative group—the National Investigations Committee on Aerial Phenomena (which became the subject of deep CIA surveillance), and ultimately to the Center for UFO Studies, where they still reside.

According to investigator Richard Dolan, "Of more lasting impact was the Aerial Phenomena Research Organization (APRO), founded in Sturgeon Bay, Wisconsin by Coral Lorenzen in January, 1952. She soon began sending a periodical, the *APRO Bulletin*, to members. Early in the year, a man from Green Bay claiming an intelligence background became one of the group's most active supporters. He offered a number of suggestions to lead the organization into 'metaphysical areas of research.' Coral Lorenzen wrote that she gently parried these attempts."[6]

2

CONTACTS OF THE COSMIC KIND

Throughout the 1950s and 1960s, numerous people across the United States claimed face-to-face contact with eerily human-looking aliens who preached peace and love, who desired an end to all human conflict, and who demanded the complete disarmament of our nuclear arsenals. Thus was born the cult of the Contactee. Not surprisingly, as a result of the overtly political nature of their revelations, many of the Contactees were subjected to intense surveillance by the U.S. Government. Although the Government's spying on the Contactees was most intense during the height of the Cold War, declassified FBI files demonstrate that cases that seemed to fall into the realm of the Contactee had been circulating around Southern California—at an official level, no less—since the late 1940s.

As an example, on 9 July 1949 the columnist and broadcaster Walter Winchell (who was himself the subject of a massive 3,908-page Bureau file) brought to the attention of the FBI a report that he had received from a "Mr. Jones of Los Angeles," who had undergone a distinctly out-of-this-world encounter in the summer of 1947. Winchell stated that Jones had sent him a letter that—according to a memorandum to J. Edgar Hoover from FBI Assistant Director Ladd—was "very well written, obviously by a man of intelligence." As a result, the FBI dug deep into the man's story, as the following report from Ladd to Hoover reveals: "In this letter Jones stated that in August of 1947 he left Los Angeles for the mountains and started hiking through the mountains. About 10:00 a.m. he was laying on the ground when he observed about one-half block away from him a large, silver metal [object], greenish in color, shaped like a child's top and about the size of the balloons used at Country Fairs.

"He stated that there appeared to be two windows in the object and portions of metal appeared transparent and that he gained the impression that there was some life within this object although he saw no persons. The object appeared as though sealed as a pressure chamber. He stood up and waved toward this object and this so-called Flying Saucer was off the ground in a second, knocking Jones to the ground. In its flight he stated that its power was silent and he raised the question as to whether this was an inter-global landing on our planet. He thought that it might be a device to land [on] our planet because the occupants of another planet had become curious as to the reaction caused by the explosion of the atomic bomb causing trouble in an expanded universe. He asked the question as to whether it was possible that the occupants of another planet might have solved the theory of negative energy."

An unnamed source within the scientific arena asserted that Jones's letter indicated "a very good knowledge of physics," and stated that it would benefit the FBI to "check into" Jones's background and to secure a full interview with him to ascertain the complete picture. And so a systematic search to find Jones began. However, all attempts to do so ended in failure, and it was initially suspected that perhaps the whole saga was nothing more than a hoax. Nevertheless, claims of people who had seen UFOs at remote locations—such as mountains and deserts—and who asserted that the intelligences behind the UFOs were concerned about humankind's burgeoning atomic weaponry would soon become very familiar to the FBI. Just as Assistant Director Ladd had recommended that Jones's background be secretly examined and that the man be interviewed firsthand, now the Contactees were about to receive the same special treatment.

orn on 12 March 1910 in Jefferson County, Ohio, George
Wellington Van Tassel maintained that he experienced face-
to-face contact with very human-looking alien entities in
August 1953 near his Yucca Valley home in California. The complete
story of Van Tassel's exploits with apparent extraterrestrials involves
weird accounts of meetings with imaginatively named aliens including
Numa of Uni, Ah-Ming of Tarr, Rondolla of the Fourth Density, and
Zolton, the Highest Authority in the Sector System of Vela.

According to the now-declassified FBI records, before moving to
Yucca Valley in 1947 Van Tassel had been employed by the Douglas
Aircraft Corporation in Santa Monica and at Hughes Aircraft,
where he worked in an assistant capacity to Howard Hughes. He
also worked—the FBI learned—for both Universal Airlines and
Lockheed. Exactly what prompted Van Tassel to uproot his family
and transfer them to Yucca Valley is something now lost to history.
Yet, along with his wife and children, Van Tassel soon settled into his
new surroundings—his famous (or perhaps infamous) cave under
Giant Rock, an area leased from the Government.

The image of a twentieth-century family living in a cave situated
beneath a 60-foot-high rock, twenty-eight miles from Joshua Tree,
California, cannot fail to conjure up the scenario of a prehistoric
family struggling to live in less-than-friendly conditions. Always
resourceful, the Van Tassels soon began to earn a comfortable living
from an airstrip they rented at the Giant Rock Airport and by running
a small restaurant. As time passed, Van Tassel began to improve the
family's living facilities and the cave became a friendly environment.
Fully furnished, it was equipped with electricity, had its own supply
of water, a large library, and, as the journalist Ed Ritter noted in
1954, "a comfortable living room where [Van Tassel] studies and
entertains guests."

As a result of his alleged August 1953 encounter, Van Tassel
compiled the first issue of what he titled *The Proceedings of the College
of Universal Wisdom*, a small journal that served as a mouthpiece for
not only Van Tassel but for his supposed cosmic friends. In the first
issue, Desca, like Rondolla of the Fourth Density, urged Van Tassel's
followers (whose number would very quickly reach four figures) to

UNITED STATES DEPARTMENT OF JUSTICE

FEDERAL BUREAU OF INVESTIGATION

Los Angeles, California
April 12, 1965

Reply, Please Refer to
No.

GEORGE WELLINGTON VAN TASSEL
GIANT ROCK AIRPORT,
YUCCA VALLEY, CALIFORNIA

VAN TASSEL has been known to the Los Angeles FBI
Office since 1954. He is reported to be owner and operator
of the Giant Rock Airport, which is located approximately
18 miles from Yucca Valley, California. He has also been
reported to be a director of the College of Universal Wisdom,
Yucca Valley, California. Numerous complaints have been
received by the Los Angeles Office concerning VAN TASSEL
and his activities surrounding "flying saucers", "spacemen"
and "space craft."

VAN TASSEL was interviewed by Special Agents of
the FBI on November 16, 1954, and advised that he had pur-
chased a ranch in the vicinity of Giant Rock about seven
years prior to the interview and subsequently had leased
land from the government. He stated that the newly acquired
land was then known as Giant Rock Airport, having been
acquired under the "Airport Act", and was a certified Civil
Aeronautics Authority (CAA) emergency landing strip.

VAN TASSEL advised that in August 1954 he had been
awakened by a man from space. The spaceman had allegedly
invited VAN TASSEL to inspect a space craft, or flying
saucer, which was manned by three other male individuals
who were identical in every respect with earth people. VAN
TASSEL furnished detailed descriptions of an unarmed, bell-
shaped flying saucer and claimed the spacemen were mutes who
conversed with him through thought transfers.

VAN TASSEL stated that he advocates and follows a
metaphysical religion and research which is based on thought
transfers, and that through the thought transfer media he
has ascertained that there will be a third world war with a
destructive atomic explosion. He further stated the above
facts could be verified through the Bible, and that the peace-
loving space people would not enter or provoke a war.

/a - 1566 - 12

ENCLOSURE

*UFO contactee Goerge Van Tassel was extensively spied on by the FBI
from the 1950s to the 1960s.*

"remove the binding chains of limit on your minds, throw out the barriers of fear [and] dissipate the selfishness of individual desire to attain physical and material things."

In the *Proceedings* dated 1 December 1953, Van Tassel stated that in the previous month a "message was received from the beings who operate the spacecraft." There were also orders from Ashtar, "the Commandant of Space Station Schare" (pronounced Share-ee) to contact the office of Air Force Intelligence at Wright-Patterson Air Force Base. Van Tassel went on to advise the Air Force that, "The present destructive plans formulated for offensive and defensive war are known to us in their entirety...the present trend toward destructive war will not be interfered with by us, unless the condition warrants our interference in order to secure this solar system. This is a friendly warning."

Were Van Tassel's contacts genuinely of unearthly origin? Were they the rants of a sadly deluded mind? Or were they possibly a part of a sophisticated Communist-inspired intelligence operation designed to disrupt the internal security of the United States? This third possibility was definitely of concern to a Yucca Valley resident who, on 5 August 1954, wrote to the FBI suggesting that Van Tassel be investigated to determine if he was working as a Soviet spy. Seriously concerned that Van Tassel was either a witting or an unwitting player in an ingenious, but subversive, Communist plot, the FBI sought to ascertain the full picture. On 12 November 1954, Major S. Avner of the Air Force Office of Special Investigations (AFOSI) met with N.W. Philcox—who was the FBI's point-of-liaison with the Air Force—to discuss the growing controversy surrounding Van Tassel. Three days later, Avner re-established contact with Philcox and advised him that the Air Technical Intelligence Center (ATIC) at Wright-Patterson "has information on Van Tassel indicating that he has corresponded with them regarding flying saucers."

This probably was a reference to the letter Van Tassel wrote to ATIC at the request of the mysterious Ashtar, who had offered a "friendly warning" with respect to plans formulated for offensive and defensive war. As a result, the Air Force offered, "to furnish the Bureau with more detailed information."

The day after Major Avner spoke with Philcox, two Los Angeles FBI Special Agents met with Van Tassel at his Giant Rock home. In a memorandum to FBI Director J. Edgar Hoover dated 16 November 1954 the agents wrote, "Relative to spacemen and space craft, VAN TASSEL declared that a year ago last August, while sleeping out of doors with his wife in the Giant Rock area, and at about 2:00 a.m. he was awakened by a man from space. This individual spoke English and was dressed in a grey one-piece suit similar to a sweat suit in that it did not have any buttons, pockets, and noticeable seams. This person, according to VAN TASSEL, invited him to inspect a spacecraft or flying saucer, which had landed on Giant Rock airstrip. VAN TASSEL claimed the craft was bell shaped resembling a saucer. He further described the ship as approximately 35 feet in diameter and is now known as the scout type craft. Aboard this craft was located three other male individuals wearing the same type of dress and identical in every respect with earth people.

"VAN TASSEL claims that the three individuals aboard the craft were mutes in that they could not talk. He claimed they conversed through thought transfers, and also operated the flight of the craft through thought control. He stated that the spokesman for the group claimed he could talk because he was trained by his family to speak. The spokesman stated that earthmen are using too much metal in their everyday work and are fouling up radio frequencies and thought transfers because of this over use of metal. According to VAN TASSEL, these individuals came from Venus and are by no means hostile nor do they intend to harm this country or inhabitants in any manner. He declared they did not carry weapons, and the spacecraft was not armed. He mentioned that a field of force was located around the spacecraft which would prohibit anything known to earth men to penetrate. VAN TASSEL claims this craft departed from the earth after 20 minutes and has not been taken back since."

Van Tassel added that "through thought transfers with space men," he had been able to ascertain that a third world war, which was likely to be "large" and "destructive," was on the horizon. Much of this correlated directly with certain biblical passages, he said. Also, the war would not be "universal," and that the "space people are peace loving and under no circumstances would enter or provoke a war." To illustrate their benevolence toward humankind, Van Tassel told his FBI visitors that the aliens had bestowed upon him some remarkable data, including information relating how the human lifespan could be extended to anywhere between 300 and 1,500 years. "This principle was not developed by Van Tassel," said the FBI.

Van Tassel then described his newsletter to the FBI agents. J. Edgar Hoover was informed, "In connection with his metaphysical religion and research, he publishes bi-monthly a publication in the form of a booklet called PROCEEDINGS OF THE COLLEGE OF UNIVERSAL WISDOM, YUCCA VALLEY, CALIFORNIA. He declared this publication is free and has grown from an original mailing list of 250 to 1,000 copies. VAN TASSEL stated that he sends his publication to various individuals, Universities, and Government Agencies throughout the world. He declared this publication is forwarded to the Federal Bureau of Investigation at Washington, D.C. He stated that he has donated 10 acres of his ranch holdings to the college. He mentioned that many of the buildings will be made free of metal; which will be keeping within the request of the spacemen."

Particularly illuminating was the FBI's concern regarding the funding of Van Tassel's operations, on what was certainly a large scale. "[Van Tassel] declared that for the most part he secures money for his needs of life, for the furtherance of his religion, research, and college through the generosity of certain individuals, number [sic] about 100. He failed to identify any of these people. He also mentioned that he derives income from his airstrip and a very small restaurant that is located at Giant Rock.

"VAN TASSEL voluntarily stated that he is not hiding anything nor is he doing anything against the laws of this country in his research at Giant Rock. He voluntarily mentioned that he is a loyal American and would be available at any time to assist the Bureau. VAN TASSEL did not volunteer the names of any individuals whom he was soliciting for funds except his statement above that he sent his publications to various individuals, universities and Government agencies and also the Federal Bureau of Investigation in Washington, D.C."

At the conclusion of the interview, the two agents secured copies of Van Tassel's *Proceedings* that were then forwarded to Washington, D.C., for study. These became the subject of a confidential report that in part stated, "One of the pamphlets contains an article by Van Tassel claiming that Jesus Christ was born of space men and that the Star of Bethlehem was a space craft that stood by while Jesus was born."

As a result of his growing reputation as someone with detailed knowledge of alien intelligences, Van Tassel became increasingly in demand on the lecture circuit where he espoused at length on his dealings with extraterrestrials, their intentions for the human race, and their overall philosophy.

On 17 April 1960 Van Tassel gave a lengthy speech at the Phipps Auditorium in Denver, Colorado. He was invited by the Denver Unidentified Flying Objects Investigative Society. To ensure that the lecture was a success, the society advertised on local radio, which caught the attention of the Denver FBI. Subsequently, the FBI directed a special agent to report the details of Van Tassel's talk, which he did and in great detail: "The program consisted of a 45 minute movie which included several shots of things purported to be flying saucers, and then a number of interviews with people from all walks of life regarding sightings they had made of such unidentified flying objects. After the movie, GEORGE W. VAN TASSEL gave a lecture that was more of a religious-economics lecture than one of unidentified flying objects.

"VAN TASSEL stated that he had been in the 'flying game' for over 30 years and currently operates a private Civil Aeronautics Authority approved airfield in California. He said he has personally observed a good many sightings and has talked to hundreds of people who have also seen flying saucers. He said that he has also been visited by the people from outer space and has taken up the cause of bringing the facts of these people to the American people.

He said it is a crusade which he has undertaken because he is more or less retired, his family is grown and gone from home, and he feels he might be doing some good by this work.

"The major part of his lecture was devoted to explaining the occurrences in the Bible as they related to the space people. He said that the only mention of God in the Bible is in the beginning when the universe was being made. He said that after that all references are to 'out of the sky' or 'out of heaven.'

"He said that this is due to the fact that man, space people, was made by God [sic] and that in the beginning of the world the space people came to the earth and left animals here. These were the prehistoric animals which existed at a body temperature of 105 degrees; however a polar tilt occurred whereby the poles shifted and the tropical climates became covered with ice and vice versa."

Van Tassel then suggested that to ensure life on Earth following the Ice Age, his alien visitors populated the planet with various species of animals, and it was this action that became the legend of Noah's Ark. Van Tassel continued on other Biblical tales and legends as the FBI noted carefully: "After the polar tilt the temperature to sustain life was 98.6 degrees, which was suitable for space people, so they established a colony and left only males here, intending to bring females at a latter date on supply ships. This is reflected in Adam not having a wife. He said that Adam was not an individual but a race of men.

"[Van Tassel] said that this race then inter-married with 'intelligent, upright walking animals,' which race was EVE [sic]. Then when the space people came back in the supply ships they saw what had happened and did not land but ever since due to the origin of ADAM, they have watched over the people on Earth.

"He said that this is in the Bible many times, such as MOSES receiving the Ten Commandments. He said the Ten Commandments are the laws of the space people and men on earth only give them lip service. Also, the manna from heaven was bread supplied by the space people.

"He also stated that this can be seen from the native stories such as the Indians in America saying that corn and potatoes, unknown in Europe were brought here by a 'flaming canoe.' He said that this can be shown also by the old stories of Winged Chariots and Winged white Horses, which came from out of the sky.

"He said that JESUS was born of MARY, who was a space person sent here already pregnant in order to show the earth people the proper way to live. He said the space people have watched over us through the years and have tried to help us. He said they have sent their agents to the earth and they appear just as we do; however, they have the power to know your thoughts just as JESUS did. He said this is their means of communication and many of the space people are mute, but they train a certain number of them to speak earth languages."

Bringing matters more up to date, Van Tassel went on to suggest an ingenious explanation for both poltergeist and spectral phenomena, as the FBI carefully noted: "Van Tassel said that the space people here on earth are equipped with a 'crystal battery' which generates a magnetic field about them which bends light waves so that they, the space people, appear invisible. He said this has resulted in ghost stories, such as footsteps, doors opening, and other such phenomena."

The FBI was most likely worried that Van Tassel's warnings about atomic destruction would have an effect on the American population, which was then living under threat of nuclear war. "The space people are now gravely concerned with our atom bombs. He said that the explosions of these bombs have upset the earth's rotation and, as in the instance of the French bomb explosion in North Africa, have actually caused earthquakes. He said that the officials on earth are aware of this and this was the reason for the recent Geophysical Year in order to try to determine just what can be done. He said these explosions are forcing the earth toward another polar tilt, which will endanger all mankind. He said that the space people are prepared to evacuate those earth people who have abided by the 'Golden Rule' when the polar tilt occurs, but will leave the rest to perish.

"He advised that the space people have contacted the officials on earth and have advised them of their concern but this has not been made public. He also said that the radioactive fallout has become extremely dangerous and officials are worried but each power is so greedy of their own power they will not agree to make peace."

The FBI viewed Van Tassel as a potential troublemaker given the fact that he was openly and vehemently criticizing the U.S. Air Force's handling of the UFO subject. The Denver FBI office also made its observations known to the Air Force Office of Special Investigations at Lowry Air Force Base: "Van Tassel also spent some time saying that the U.S. Air Force, who are [sic] responsible for investigations on unidentified flying objects, has suppressed information; and as they are responsible only to the Administration, not to the public, as elected officials are, they can get away with this. He said that also the Air Force is afraid that they will be outmoded and disbanded if such information gets out. The Administration's main concern in not making public any information is that the economy will be ruined, not because of any fear that would be engendered in the public. He said this is due to the number of scientific discoveries already made and that will be made which are labor saving and of almost permanency so that replacements would not be needed."

In conclusion, the FBI report stated, "Throughout his lecture, VAN TASSEL mentioned only the U.S. economy and Government and the U.S. Air Force. He did refer to the human race numerous times but all references to Government and economy could only be taken as meaning the U.S. One question put to him was whether sightings had been made in Russia or China. He answered this by saying sightings had been reported all over the world, but then specifically mentioned only the U.S., Australia, New Zealand and New Guinea. He also mentioned that he was not advocating or asking for any action on the part of the audience because he said evil has a way of destroying itself. He did say that he felt that the audience, of about 250 persons, were the only intelligent people in Denver and he knew they had not come out of curiosity but because they wanted to do the right thing. He said that they were above average in intelligence and when the critical time came, the world would need people such as this to think and guide."

Perhaps the most interesting aspect of Van Tassel's character was his fascination with weird electronic devices. The most famous was the Integratron. For years Van Tassel worked on the machine, the purpose of which, he claimed, was to enhance our psychic powers and potentials and extend the human lifespan. Van Tassel never had the opportunity to see his project come to fruition; however, his reputation as someone who had a longstanding fascination with advanced technology was not lost on his followers. Nor was it lost on the FBI.

In April 1965 rumors circulated around the FBI's Miami office that Van Tassel had succeeded in creating a weapon that could cause blindness. The production and utilization of this weapon was related to an acquaintance of Van Tassel, described in FBI memoranda as "an ultra-rightist with tendency toward violence."

A two-page Teletype to FBI headquarters dated 9 April 1965 revealed the facts: "A source, who has furnished reliable information in the past, and in addition has furnished information which could not be verified or corroborated, advised that a secret device, which can be carried on a person and used to blind people, has recently been perfected. This device, also referred to by [censored] as a weapon, formerly developed to keep others from seeing operator of weapon. [Censored] reports no other details regarding description and use of device. However, he said his information was second hand.

"The source states that it has been determined the alleged device, was developed by GEORGE W. VAN TASSEL, Giant Rock, Yucca Valley, California, who reportedly owns or operates an airport some 20 miles from Yucca Valley in the desert area.

"Source stated VAN TASSEL claimed he worked over seven years in research and development of this device and the machine to make it. The weapon reportedly is of an electrical type, not further described. Any additional information can be obtained only by individuals who purchase the device and must be present at the time it is made."

Less than a week later, the FBI seemed far less impressed with Van Tassel and his claimed inventions. "Because of Van Tassel's apparent mental condition, as evidenced by his statements and apparent beliefs concerning interplanetary travel by men from Venus, and in view of his other highly imaginative and incredible statements concerning space travel and population, it is believed that no further inquiries need be conducted by the Miami or Los Angeles Offices concerning Van Tassel."

The FBI's interest in Van Tassel was now clearly on the wane. A 12 April 1965 FBI document referred to him as "an eccentric, self-ordained minister of a quasi-religious organization." And a three-page document from the Los Angeles FBI sent to Director Hoover wasted no time describing him as nothing less than a "mental case."

The last entry in the FBI's file on Van Tassel was a copy of a letter dated 17 August 1965. It was originally sent from a member of the public to the Information Office of the Air Force's UFO study program, Project Blue Book. The writer expressed that Van Tassel's position on UFOs was not exactly patriotic to the United States. "In my opinion, it is quite subversive and in conflict with the interests of the United States the way this gentleman uses the demoralizing of religion and also his accusations against our Government."

The FBI took no action with regard to this letter or with Van Tassel ever again. Van Tassel died 9 February 1978 at the age of sixty-seven. He would not be the only Contactee to interest the FBI.[1]

3

WHO GOES THERE?

Born in Poland in 1891, George Adamski had the distinction of being the most supported, celebrated, and ridiculed of those who claimed direct contact with humanlike extraterrestrials. The controversy essentially began on 20 November 1952 when, along with six other people, Adamski claimed that he witnessed a UFO land in the California desert. He said he then made contact with its pilot. FBI documentation, however, showed that Adamski's interest in UFOs preceded the 1952 date by at least two years. Timothy Good has noted that in Adamski's 1936 book, *Wisdom of the Masters of the Far East*, published by the Royal Order of Tibet, the alleged contactee claimed he had otherworldly encounters as a child and had received instruction from these beings in Tibet.[1]

At the start of George Adamski's surveillance, the FBI were apparently not aware of his earlier claims of contact, although a document dated 28 May 1952 references his 1950 encounters. It also reveals that—as with Van Tassel—the FBI considered Adamski to be a subversive. A study of the documentation shows that much of the FBI's initial data on Adamski came from a source (whose name the FBI has chosen to keep classified) that revealed the facts to its San Diego office on 5 September 1950: "[Source] advised the San Diego Office that he first met Adamski about three months ago at the café which is named the Palomar Gardens Café, owned and operated by Adamski, at the road junction, five miles East of Rincon, California,

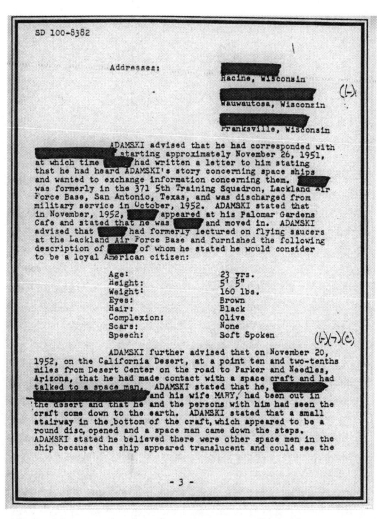

```
SD 100-8382

        Addresses:
                                        ████████████
                                        Racine, Wisconsin
                                                                    (b)
                                        ████████████
                                        Wauwautosa, Wisconsin

                                        ████████████
                                        Franksville, Wisconsin

        ADAMSKI advised that he had corresponded with
████████████  starting approximately November 26, 1951,
at which time ████████ had written a letter to him stating
that he had heard ADAMSKI's story concerning space ships
and wanted to exchange information concerning them. ██████
was formerly in the 371 5th Training Squadron, Lackland Air
Force Base, San Antonio, Texas, and was discharged from
military service in October, 1952. ADAMSKI stated that
in November, 1952, ████████ appeared at his Palomar Gardens
Cafe and stated that he was ██████ and moved in. ADAMSKI
advised that ██████ had formerly lectured on flying saucers
at the Lackland Air Force Base and furnished the following
description of ██████ of whom he stated he would consider
to be a loyal American citizen:

            Age:                    23 yrs.
            Height:                 5' 5"
            Weight:                 160 lbs.
            Eyes:                   Brown
            Hair:                   Black
            Complexion:             Olive
            Scars:                  None
            Speech:                 Soft Spoken
                                                    (b)(7)(c)

        ADAMSKI further advised that on November 20,
1952, on the California Desert, at a point ten and two-tenths
miles from Desert Center on the road to Parker and Needles,
Arizona, that he had made contact with a space craft and had
talked to a space man. ADAMSKI stated that he, ██████████
████████████ and his wife MARY, had been out in
the desert and that he and the persons with him had seen the
craft come down to the earth. ADAMSKI stated that a small
stairway in the bottom of the craft, which appeared to be a
round disc, opened and a space man came down the steps.
ADAMSKI stated he believed there were other space men in the
ship because the ship appeared translucent and could see the

                        - 3 -
```

After proclaiming that his alien visitors were "probably communists" Goerge Adamski became the subject of extensive, official surveillance.

at a point where the highway branches off leading to Mount Palomar Observatory.

"[Source] became involved in a lengthy conversation with Adamski during which Adamski told them at great length of his findings of flying saucers and so forth. He told them of a spaceship which he said he saw between the earth and the moon, which he estimated to be approximately three miles in length, which was flying so fast that he had to take about eighty photographs before he could get three of them to turn out.

"According to [source] Adamski stated that the Federal Communications Commission, under the direction of the 'Military Government' of the United States, has established communication with the people from other worlds, and has learned that they are so much more advanced than the inhabitants of this earth that they have deciphered the languages used here. Adamski stated that in this interplanetary communication, the Federal Communications Commission asked the inhabitants of the other planet concerning the type of government they had there and the reply indicated that it was very different from the democracy of the United States. Adamski stated that his answer was kept secret by the United States Government, but he added, 'If you ask me they probably have a Communist form of government and our American government wouldn't release that kind of thing, naturally. That is a thing of the future—more advanced.'"

Adamski's comments that his alien friends were communists raised eyebrows within the FBI, and led to continued, deep monitoring of his activities. "Adamski, during this conversation, made the prediction that Russia will dominate the world and we will then have an era of peace for 1,000 years. He stated that Russia already has the atom bomb and the hydrogen bomb and that the great earthquake, which was reported behind the Iron Curtain recently, was actually a hydrogen bomb explosion being tried out by the Russians. Adamski states this 'earthquake' broke seismograph machines and he added that no normal earthquake can do that.

"Adamski stated that within the next twelve months, San Diego will be bombed. Adamski stated that it does not make any difference if the United States has more atom bombs than Russia inasmuch as Russia needs only ten atom bombs to cripple the United States by placing these simultaneously on such spots as Chicago and other vital centers of this country. The United States today is in the same state of deterioration as was the Roman Empire prior to its collapse and it will fall just as the Roman Empire did. The Government in this country is a corrupt form of government and capitalists are enslaving the poor."

From thereon the FBI officially considered Adamski to be a "security matter." In January 1953 he was again the subject of FBI interest when the San Diego office began to hear rumors that "Adamski had in his possession a machine which could draw 'flying saucers' and airplanes down from the sky." Despite his the-aliens-are-communists-style statements of 1952, Adamski was concerned that the strange device that supposedly operated on the principle of "cutting magnetic lines of force" could be used against American aircraft. It was Adamski himself who initiated a meeting on 12 January 1953 with the FBI and the Air Force Office of Special Investigations.

From the start of the meeting, Adamski was careful to make it clear that the machine was the creation of another person. Regardless of what the FBI thought it knew or had been told to the contrary, Adamski said he had not yet seen the device—he had only been told of its existence. He did, however, apparently know enough about it and its creator to suggest that production of the device might not be in the best interests of the Government, since the person concerned "was not entirely loyal." On this matter at least, Adamski cooperated fully and provided the Bureau and the Air Force with sufficient information to allow a formal investigation of the machine's "inventor."

Also during the meeting, Adamski took the opportunity to discuss his claimed encounter of 20 November 1952 out in the California desert, as the FBI carefully noted in its write-up of the interview: "At a point ten and two-tenths miles from Desert Center on the road to Parker and Needles, Arizona, [Adamski] made contact with a space craft and had talked to a space man. Adamski stated that he, [deleted] and his wife Mary had been out in the desert and that he and the persons with him had seen the craft come down to the earth. Adamski stated that a small stairway in the bottom of the craft, which appeared to be a round disc, opened and a space man came down the steps. Adamski stated he believed there were other space men in the ship because the ship appeared translucent and he could see the shadows of the space men."

Adamski also revealed that the alien was "over five feet in height, having long hair like a woman's and garbed in a suit similar to the space suits or web suits worn by the U.S. Air Force men." Like George Van Tassel, Adamski related to the FBI and OSI agents that he conversed with the being by means of sign language, but felt that his mind was being "read." As evidence of this, Adamski said that as he was about to take a photograph of the aliens' craft, the humanoid "motioned" him to stop. Adamski told the agents that he took his photograph regardless, but that this was not to the liking of the cosmic visitor, who grabbed the material evidence out of Adamski's hands and soared off into the sky.

Adamski's adventures with the aliens were not over. According to the FBI, "Adamski further advised that he had obtained plaster casts of the footprints of the space man and stated that the casts indicated the footprints had designs on them similar to the signs of the Zodiac. On January 12, 1953, Adamski advised that on December 13, 1952, the space ship returned to the Palomar Gardens and came low enough to drop the [film negative] which the space man had taken from him, Adamski, and had then gone off over the hill. Adamski stated that when he had the negatives developed at a photo shop in Escondido, California, that the negative that the space man had taken from him contained writing which he believed to be the writing of the space men. Adamski furnished the writer with copies of the space writing and photographs of the space ship."

However, from another unnamed source, the FBI was told that, "The photographs were taken by setting the camera lens at infinity, which would sharpen the background of mountains and trees and blurs the saucer, which was probably strung on a thin wire. [Source] advised that if the camera were set at infinity the wire would not show."

An FBI document dated 23 March 1953 focused on the lecture Adamski gave to the California Lions Club two weeks earlier. According to the FBI at San Diego, Adamski had prefaced his talk with a statement that "his material had all been cleared with the Federal Bureau of Investigation and Air Force Intelligence."

FBI and Air Force representatives quickly visited Adamksi and, according to the FBI's records of the visit, "severely admonished" him for even daring to suggest that his strange claims had the support of the FBI and Air Force. Both agencies insisted that Adamksi sign an official document to state that his material did not have official clearance. Adamski kept one copy of this document and additional copies were provided to J. Edgar Hoover's office and to the FBI offices in Dallas, Los Angeles, and Cleveland since "these offices have received previous communications concerning [Adamski]."

Nine months later, Adamski once again found himself in hot water. A representative of the Los Angeles-based Better Business Bureau (BBB) had visited the Los Angeles FBI office and advised the agents that the BBB was investigating Adamski's 1953 book, *Flying Saucers Have Landed*, to determine if it was a fraud.[2]

The BBB said that in an attempt to secure the truth, Adamski had been interviewed by one of its staff during the course of which he—Adamski—had produced a document "having a blue seal in the lower left corner, at the top of which appeared the names of three Government agents." One was from the FBI and two were from the Air Force. Again, there was an implication that Adamski's material had the official clearance of the FBI and the Air Force.

Not surprisingly, the document was unauthentic. Special Agent Willis of the San Diego FBI revealed that the document Adamski had shown to the Better Business Bureau was a doctored copy of the statement he had been obliged to sign for the FBI and the Air Force months earlier. An FBI report of 16 December 1953 from Louis B. Nichols—head of the FBI's public relations department—recorded the somewhat farcical events that surrounded this huge blow to Adamski's credibility: "[Deleted] instructed Willis to call on Adamski at the Palomar Gardens Café, Valley Center, California. (This is located five miles east of Rincon, California, near the Mount Palomar Observatory.) Willis was told to have the San Diego agents, accompanied by representatives of OSI if they care to go along, call on Adamski and read the riot act in no uncertain terms pointing out he has used this document in a fraudulent, improper manner, that this Bureau has not endorsed, approved, or cleared his speeches or book, that he knows it, and the Bureau will simply not tolerate any further foolishness, misrepresentations, and falsity on his part. Willis was told to instruct the Agents to diplomatically retrieve, if possible, the document in [sic] issue from Adamski. Willis said he would do this and send in a report at once."

Although dark threats of prosecution were discussed, the FBI ultimately decided to take no further action against Adamski regarding his proven fakery. Declassified FBI documentation also demonstrated that its interest in Adamski trailed off in the mid-1950s, only to be revived, very briefly, at the end of the decade.

In February 1959 Adamski toured New Zealand and delivered a series of lectures before audiences in Wellington and Auckland. This was of some interest to elements of the American Intelligence community and his talks were monitored—albeit at a sporadic level. As evidence of this, a one-page Foreign Service Dispatch was sent from the American Embassy in New Zealand to the Department of State in Washington, D.C., that provided Adamski's central talking points.

Circulated to the FBI, the CIA, the Air Force, and the Navy, the document was titled *"FLYING SAUCER" EXPERT LECTURING IN NEW ZEALAND*: "Mr. George ADAMSKI, the Californian 'flying saucer expert' and author of the book *The Flying Saucers Have Landed* and others, has been visiting New Zealand for the last two weeks. He has given well-attended public lectures in Auckland and Wellington as well as meetings with smaller groups of 'saucer' enthusiasts. In Wellington his lecture filled the 2,200 seats in the Town Hall. He was not permitted to charge for admission as the meeting was held on a Sunday night, but a 'silver coin' collection was taken up and this would more than recoup his expenses.

"Adamski's lectures appear to cover the usual mass of sighting reports, pseudo-scientific arguments in support of his theories and his previously well-publicized 'contacts' with saucers and men from Venus. He is repeating his contention that men from other planets are living anonymously on the earth and, according to the press, said in Auckland that there may be as many as 40,000,000 of these in total. He is also making references to security restrictions and saying that the U.S. authorities know a lot more than they will tell.

"The report of Adamski's lecture in Wellington in The Dominion was flanked by an article by Dr. I.L. THOMPSON, Director of the Carter Observatory, vigorously refuting Adamski on a number of scientific points. However, the news report of the lecture called it 'the best Sunday night's entertainment Wellington has seen for quite a time.'

"Interest in flying saucers in New Zealand seems to be roughly comparable to that in the United States. There is a small but active organization that enthusiasts have supported for some years. This organization publishes a small paper and receives and circulates stories of sightings. At the Adamski lecture in Wellington, approximately 40 members of the 'Adamski Corresponding Society' wore blue ribbons and sat in reserved seats in the front row. Press reports suggest that Adamski probably is making no new converts to saucer credence in his current tour. His audiences have given forth with a certain amount of 'incredulous murmuring' and are said to be totally unimpressed with his pictures of saucers."

Nearly a year later, Adamski was once again the subject of FBI interest when a member of the American public expressed concern that Adamski was promoting pro-Soviet ideas: "[Censored] said that in recent weeks she and her husband had begun to wonder if Adamski is subtly spreading Russian propaganda. She said that, according to Adamski, the 'space people' are much better people than those on earth; that they have told him the earth is in extreme danger from nuclear tests and that they must be stopped; that they have found peace under a system in which churches, schools, individual governments, money, and private property were abolished in favor of a central governing council, and nationalism and patriotism have been done away with; that the 'space people' want nuclear tests stopped immediately and that never should people on earth fight; if attacked, they should lay down their arms and welcome their attackers.

"[Censored] said the particular thing that first made her and her husband wonder about Adamski was a letter they received from him dated 10/12/59, in which it was hinted that the Russians receive help in their outer space programs from the 'space people,' and that the 'space people' will not help any nation unless such nation has peaceful intent. It occurred to them that the desires and recommendations of the 'space people' whom Adamski quotes are quite similar to Russia's approach, particularly as to the ending of nuclear testing, and it was for this reason she decided to call the FBI."

And thus ended the FBI's surveillance of George Adamski. Until his death on 23 April 1965, Adamski continued to maintain that he had indeed undergone direct contact with alien beings and that he had faithfully recorded all the details. And although the FBI has long forgotten about George Adamski, the controversy surrounding the man continues to circulate.

Declassified FBI records show that other so-called Contactees had attracted the attention of the Bureau, including Truman Bethurum, George Hunt Williamson, and Daniel Fry. Bethurum, for example, stated that he had liaised with humanlike aliens (although of smaller stature and of darker skin) from Clarion, a planet in our solar system hidden from the Earth as a result of its orbit around the Sun. Of all the Contactees, Bethurum was perhaps the most envied among his colleagues since during his alleged experience aboard a UFO he was introduced to its spectacularly attractive female captain named Aura Rhanes.

"Tops in shapeliness and beauty," were the words that the lucky Bethurum used to describe Captain Aura Rhanes in his book *Aboard A Flying Saucer*—a book that comes across like *Baywatch*-meets-*Star*

Trek. Today we may find Bethurum's story to be little more than an amusing aside, but the FBI felt obligated to look into the man's account.

In December 1954 the Palm Springs Republican Club contacted the FBI, as its president had both spoken with Bethurum and read his recently published book. "I am always skeptical and I have been wondering if he could be trying to put over any propaganda," stated the club president in a letter to J. Edgar Hoover.

"Although I would like to be of service," replied Hoover in a letter, "information in FBI files is confidential and available for official use only. I would like to point out also that this Bureau is strictly a fact-finding agency and does not make evaluations or draw conclusions as to the character or integrity of any individual, publication or organization."

Nevertheless, FBI files do reflect knowledge of Bethurum's activities: "In June, 1954, an inquiry was made by the Cincinnati Office concerning Bethurum and his flying disk lectures since that office had received a complaint similar to current correspondents."

To the FBI, Bethurum's activities were of less concern than Van Tassel's. Bethurum was not as outwardly political as Van Tassel, and his dealings with Aura Rhanes bordered on the farcical. On several occasions in the middle of the night, the gorgeous Aura supposedly materialized in Bethurum's bedroom, which did not exactly please his wife who later divorced him—evidently she was unable to compete with a woman of Aura's galactic charms.[3]

George Hunt Williamson had an equally strange tale to tell. Not only did he, too, write a book detailing his encounters—*The Saucers Speak*, co-written with Alfred C. Bailey—he also revealed details to Edward J. Ruppelt, former head of Project Blue Book. Ruppelt recalled in 1955 that, "George Williamson said the story started back in the summer of 1952 when he and a few other people who believed that flying saucers weren't hallucinations got together with a ham radio operator in Arizona. On the night of August 26, they were playing around with the radio receiver when they picked up a strange signal. They listened to the signal and soon found that it was international code coming in at a 'fantastically fast and powerful rate,' from a spaceship hovering off the earth."

Up until February 1953 Williamson's contacts continued imparting a wealth of technological data. He then was advised to go out and "spread the word" to like-minded persons. An FBI document of 2 June 1961 took note of Williamson's activities: "Bufiles indicate that George Hunt Williamson [has] come to the Bureau's attention in the past in connection with allegations that flying disks exist. In 1954, Williamson was connected with a program to be presented in Cincinnati that was entitled 'The Real Flying Saucer Story.'" Williamson retired from the saucer scene in the 1960s.[4]

In 1949, Daniel Fry was employed as an engineer with the Aerojet General Corporation at the White Sands Missile Range, New Mexico. On 4 July of that year Fry claimed that he had made initial contact with an extraterrestrial being named A-lan who "wants everyone in this world to understand the truth about our existence and how we can spiritually profit from the beneficence of extraterrestrial contact."

Six years later Fry was referenced in FBI memoranda following an investigation of the Detroit Flying Saucer Club that intended to have Fry speak at one of its meetings. Since a cousin of Fry's co-directed the club, the FBI was able to glean detailed information about Fry's claimed experiences. One such experience was that Fry flew in a saucer from Sandia Base, New Mexico, to New York City in only thirty minutes. An FBI memorandum states: "FRY CLAIMS SAUCER CLUBS HAVE ACTUALLY RECEIVED MESSAGES FROM OUTER SPACE AND ALTHOUGH [HE] SAYS HE DOES NOT KNOW, HE FEELS THEY DO EXIST; HAVE BEEN SEEN BY MANY PEOPLE AND CLAIMS HE HAS SEEN THEM HIMSELF. HE FEELS THE PURPOSE OF CONTACTS WITH EARTH IS LIMITED AT THIS TIME TO PREPARING PEOPLE TO RECEIVE LANDINGS FROM OUTER SPACE. HE SAID THE SAUCERS ARE FRIENDLY TO US HE SAID MESSAGES

RECEIVED INDICATE ALL PLANETS BUT EARTH HAVE CONQUERED OUTER SPACE. OUTER SPACE PEOPLE CONSIDER THOSE ON EARTH THE LOWEST FORM OF UNIVERSAL EXISTENCE."[5]

Other people involved in the Contactee mystery were the subject of FBI files, too. Heavily censored August 1954 memoranda refer to an unnamed woman who claimed repeated contact with non-human entities in the mid-1950s: "According to [censored] stated that there were two spaceships from which she had been receiving messages. They were described as 150 miles wide, 200 miles in length, and 100 miles in depth…these ships are designated M-4 and L-11 and they also contain mother ships which measure approximately 150 to 200 feet in length….there were approximately 5,000 of these mother ships… 'Affa' is the Manager or the Commander of the ship M-4 which is from the planet Uranus and 'Ponnar' is the Manager or the Commander of the ship L-11 which is from the planet Hatann… These contacts with 'Affa' and 'Ponnar' were for the purpose of protecting our own earth from destruction caused by the explosion of the atom bomb, hydrogen bomb, and wars of various kinds which they, 'Affa' and 'Ponnar,' say disrupt the magnetic field of force which surrounds the earth… 'Affa' and 'Ponnar' are presently working the area of the Pacific Ocean repairing 'fault lines' which are in danger of breaking…."

There are several reasons that may have led the FBI to closely monitor the activities of certain Contactees: (a) their links with ultra-right-wing groups and personalities; (b) the fact that some of them moved in influential circles; (c) the intriguing possibility that some Contactees were official "plants" whose ridiculous stories were created out of the fertile imagination of another Government body—possibly the CIA—whose intent was to play down the seriousness of the UFO presence in the 1950s in the United States; and (d) the fact that many of the Contactees had a fanatical, cult-style following.

With respect to reason (a), in the early 1930s, William Dudley Pelley was the leader of an American Nazi association known as the Silver Shirts. This group, in turn, was linked closely with a similar organization: Guy Ballard's I AM movement. Following the end of the Second World War—during which he was interned for sedition—Pelley formed an occult-based group known as Soulcraft. It so happens that direct ties can be found between the Contactees investigated by the FBI in the 1950s and personalities affiliated with I AM, the Silver Shirts, and Soulcraft.

Investigator Jacques Vallee learned that George Adamski had pre-war connections with Pelley, as did George Hunt Williamson in 1950, when Williamson began working for Soulcraft's office in Noblesville, Indiana. Two years later, Williamson allegedly witnessed Adamski meeting an extraterrestrial in the California desert. Moreover, George Van Tassel's Integratron was adorned with prominent I AM designs which had been commissioned by the aforementioned Guy Ballard, who was well known to William Dudley Pelley.[6]

With respect to point (b), Van Tassel had other intriguing contacts. Although the FBI of the 1950s was hardly enamoured of Van Tassel's activities, in previous years the man had what could be termed quasi-official links to the FBI that were not frowned upon. An FBI document of 16 November 1954, for example, references Van Tassel as having been "acquainted" with FBI Special Agent Walter Bott (who had then recently died), and that, furthermore, Van Tassel had "helped [Bott] on many cases at Lockheed," where Van Tassel had previously been employed.

In addition to that startling revelation, and on the issue of point (c), it will be recalled that while employed with Hughes Aircraft, Van Tassel had acted as an assistant to Howard Hughes himself. In 1977, a book titled *The Hughes Papers*—written by Elaine Davenport, Paul Eddy, and Mark Hurwitz—disclosed a wealth of unknown material pertaining to Hughes, including his connections to the CIA. This does not link Van Tassel with the CIA in any capacity; however, as will shortly become apparent, other people had suggested links between the CIA and the Contactees.[7]

On the issue of Howard Hughes, it may not be entirely coincidental that his name crops up in another FBI document relating to UFOs. Dated 31 July 1950, and captioned "Flying Discs," the "Air Mail, Special Delivery" memo for J. Edgar Hoover's attention had come from the Bureau's Chicago office and dealt with the following letter, a copy of which the FBI had obtained from a Chicago-based newspaper, its original recipient. The letter read thus:

"Since we are on the brink of a third world conflict, the world is more air conscious than ever. Aviation in some phase is yet in its pioneering days. Much talk goes on about the flying saucers or discs. The saucer we speak about is not a military secret, and is not yet owned by any government. The flying saucer which was seen over south Chicago last April is a large fuel tank with crystal glass wings. It has two large jet engines on both sides. It is radio controlled. It resembles a saucer very much when in flight. The wings cannot be seen on a clear day. This is so it is a most difficult target for anti aircraft gunners. The reason for the large flat gas or fuel tank is to give the ship a long range for atomic bombing. The ship was financed by HOWARD HUGHES, the millionaire aviation enthusiast. It is now being tested by the Glen F. Martin Aircraft Co., makers of the Martin Marauder. The craft is only made for one-way trips. It has a range of 4,000 miles, ceiling of 25,000 feet, and a speed of 750 miles per hour. So far only a few of these craft have been made, and they usually are pitched in the lake or ocean as they cannot be landed. They are merely to carry a bomb of high destruction to an enemy country. They have no wheels, but small steel rails on the bottom from which they take off. All other mechanism can be explained in detail. The man who welded the ship says it is by far the best long rage bombing instrument he has ever seen. The name of the ship is the 'Danse Macabre.'"

FBI files reveal that the newspaper did not wish to publish the letter since it felt that "the Army desired that the matter be kept confidential." The FBI took little action beyond filing the letter for future reference purposes. However, this would not be the only occasion upon which the Contactees and people associated with the

CIA would cross paths. As researcher George C. Andrews noted: "People who travelled with Adamski noticed that he had been issued a special passport, such as is usually reserved for diplomats and high government officials. It is entirely possible that he may have been a CIA disinformation agent, who successfully fulfilled the mission of making the subject of UFOs seem so absurd that no independent in-depth investigation would be made by qualified academics."[8] And matters do not end there.

In 1954 a group of West Coast Contactees, including both Truman Bethurum and George Hunt Williamson, gave a series of lectures at the Hotel Gibson in Cincinnati. As this was also the hometown of the well-known UFO researcher and author Leonard Stringfield, paths inevitably crossed. Hoping to get Stringfield to endorse their lectures, Bethurum, Williamson, and their flock called at his home and introduced themselves.

Stringfield flatly refused to lend his support to their cause, but had an interesting experience that he recorded which is worth noting. "After their departure I began to wonder about their causes. At one point during the evening's many tête-à-têtes, I chanced to overhear two 'members' discussing the FBI. Pretending aloofness, I tried to overhear more. It seemed that one person was puzzling over the presence of an 'agent' in the group. When I was caught standing too close, the FBI talk stopped. Whether or not I had reason to be suspicious, it was not difficult for me to believe that some of the Contactees behind all this costly showmanship were official 'plants.'"[9]

Similarly, commenting on the alleged experiences of Contactee Howard Menger (a well-known figure much in the spotlight in the 1950s and 1960s and the author of the book *From Outer Space To You*, a book that dealt with Menger's contacts with supposed humanlike aliens), investigative writer John Keel said, "…in letters to [the researchers] Gray Barker and *Saucer News* editor Jim Moseley, Menger termed his book 'fiction-fact' and implied that the Pentagon had asked him to participate in an experiment to test the public's reaction to extra-terrestrial contact."[10]

On the final point—(d)—it is worth noting that the FBI was very carefully monitoring cult-style activity on the West Coast throughout the 1950s. An FBI document of 13 November 1954 makes that point very clear: "As the Bureau is aware, there are numerous individuals operating in Southern California under the guise of religion or religious cults with a prophet or director who have a certain emotional appeal."

It is not totally inconceivable that the FBI's surveillance of George Van Tassel and George Adamski was solely the result of the men's claimed alien encounters. However, Adamski's statements that "Russia will dominate the world" and that his alien friends were Communists, Van Tassel's observations and comments concerning nuclear weapons, and the many links between the Contactees and ultra-right-wing political groups (not to mention the fact that some of the Contactees may have been CIA assets whose job was to discredit the UFO subject), really leads to only one, inevitable conclusion. In the 1950s era of the Cold War and McCarthyism, the FBI's deep surveillance of those loudly proclaiming alien contact was the result of the extreme political nature of their statements and connections and nothing more.

4

HERE COME THE MEN IN BLACK

Since the early 1950s, the mysterious Men in Black (MIB) have been a persistent part of UFO lore, as have their attempts to silence UFO witnesses. Precisely who they are and what lies behind their sinister activities provokes controversy to this day. Time after time the Men in Black are described as being dressed in black suits, black hats, black ties, and white shirts. They are often short in stature, extremely thin, with slightly Asian features. They also seem to have a tenuous grasp of the English language, with some even exhibiting a monotone-style of speaking, and they are glaringly unaware of our most basic customs and conventions – particularly with regard to such everyday activities as eating and drinking.

One of the most learned Men in Black scholars is John Keel. The author of numerous books on unexplained phenomena—including the celebrated title that became a hit movie starring Richard Gere, *The Mothman Prophecies*—Keel has spent decades chronicling the accounts of Men in Black activity and presents a strong case for the reality of the mystery. Keel, too, had his run-ins with one particular type of MIB that he termed "the cadavers."

"These are people who look like they've been dead a long time," said Keel. "Their clothes hang on them; their flesh is pasty white and they look like maybe somebody's dug them up from a cemetery. This cadaverous type has turned up in strange places: England, Sweden. [The writer and investigator] Brad Steiger saw one. I saw one in the early '60's. They're very elusive when you approach them, and hurry away [and] they do have a habit of turning up in UFO areas and following UFO investigators around."[1]

The Men in Black mystery really began in earnest back in 1952. That year, Albert K. Bender, a resident of Bridgeport, Connecticut, established a UFO investigative society known as the International Flying Saucer Bureau (IFSB). Bender's group was warmly received by UFO researchers both in the United States and abroad and soon blossomed into an impressive network of investigators. A year later, without warning, Bender disbanded the IFSB, alluding to an unusual experience in which three men dressed in black suits had visited him to discuss his UFO research. Supposedly, Bender had discovered the truth of the UFO mystery and the Men in Black wished him to remain silent, which he did for a number of years. To ensure that silence, Bender was given the full, unexpurgated facts pertaining to an alleged alien mission on Earth.

According to Bender, he had been overcome with a sensation of dizziness and retired to his bedroom when suddenly he became aware of "…three shadowy figures in the room. The figures became clearer. All of them were dressed in black clothes. They looked like clergymen, but wore hats similar to Homburg style. The faces were not clearly discernible, for the hats partly hid and shaded them. Feelings of fear left me. The eyes of all three figures suddenly lit up like flashlight bulbs, and all these were focused upon me. They seemed to burn into my very soul as the pains [sic] above my eyes became almost unbearable. It was then I sensed that they were conveying a message to me by telepathy."

The three men did indeed convey a message, but Bender stayed silent for years, conveying only the basic facts of the visit to a few trusted colleagues. One was Gray Barker, who went on to write the definitive history of the Men in Black in 1956, *They Knew Too Much About Flying Saucers.*[2]

A full decade after he retired from the UFO scene, Bender's uncensored story surfaced in the form of *Flying Saucers and the Three Men*, an extremely bizarre book that was privately published by Gray Barker. It contained all manner of weirdness pertaining to Albert

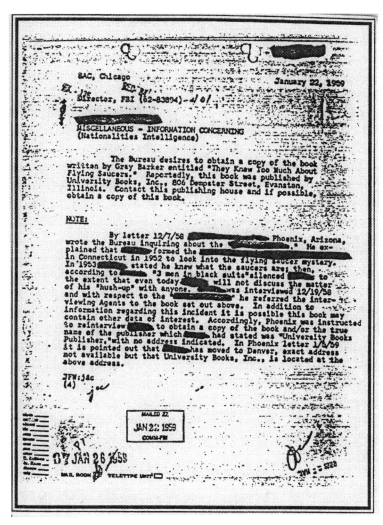

SAC, Chicago   January 22, 1959

Director, FBI (62-83894)-4/01

MISCELLANEOUS - INFORMATION CONCERNING
(Nationalities Intelligence)

The Bureau desires to obtain a copy of the book
written by Gray Barker entitled "They Knew Too Much About
Flying Saucers." Reportedly, this book was published by
University Books, Inc., 806 Dempster Street, Evanston,
Illinois. Contact this publishing house and if possible,
obtain a copy of this book.

NOTE:

By letter 12/7/58 ██████████████ Phoenix, Arizona,
wrote the Bureau inquiring about the ████████████. He explained that ████ formed the ████████████████████████
in Connecticut in 1952 to look into the flying saucer mystery.
In 1953 ████ stated he knew what the saucers are, then,
according to ██████ "3 men in black suits" silenced ████ to
the extent that even today ████ will not discuss the matter
of his "hush-up" with anyone. ████ was interviewed 12/19/58
and with respect to the ██████████████ he referred the interviewing Agents to the book set out above. In addition to
information regarding this incident it is possible this book may
contain other data of interest. Accordingly, Phoenix was instructed
to reinterview ████ to obtain a copy of the book and/or the true
name of the publisher which ████ had stated was "University Books
Publisher," with no address indicated. In Phoenix letter 1/8/59
it is pointed out that ████ has moved to Denver, exact address
not available but that University Books, Inc., is located at the
above address.

JFW:jac
(4)

MAILED 27
JAN 22 1959
COMM-FBI

07 JAN 26 1959

MAIL ROOM   TELETYPE UNIT

In 1959, elements of the U.S. Government took a deep interest in the "Men in Black" research of author Gray Barker and investigator Albert Bender.

Bender's alleged experiences, including information on a "secret UFO base" in Antarctica, along with demonology, the occult, spiritualism, and black magic. It claimed that the mission of the Men in Black was to obtain a unique element from the Earth's oceans. Put off by this material, many of the seminal UFO researchers in the United States largely ignored *Flying Saucers and the Three Men* when it was first published.[3]

If Bender's account was isolated and a one-of-a-kind, there would be acceptable grounds for believing that his claims were simply the product of a disturbed mind. But quite literally dozens of similar stories have surfaced since then. Indeed, there is official FBI documentation at our disposal that has a bearing on the Bender affair and demonstrates that official surveillance of those implicated in the Men in Black mystery was well underway by the early-to-mid-1950s.

On 28 August 1953, an FBI agent visited Gray Barker and asked him a number of questions concerning Albert Bender's International Flying Saucer Bureau. It turns out that Bender had forwarded to Barker a number of business cards that he had printed identifying Barker as "Chief Investigator" for the IFSB. In *They Knew Too Much About Flying Saucers*, Barker admitted having given "four or five [of the cards] to close friends, who still had them when I checked with them one week later." It was therefore something of a surprise when the agent turned up on Barker's doorstep with one of the aforementioned business cards. "I have always been puzzled about how the Federal Bureau of Investigation got hold of one of them," Barker later said.

"What's this all about?" asked the agent. Somewhat nervously, Barker explained that the IFSB was simply an organization formed to investigate "flying saucer phenomena" and that the business cards were a means by which IFSB investigators could be identified.

The FBI man then proceeded to ask Barker if he knew a certain individual (whose name Barker could not later recall) who lived in Florida. Barker replied that he did not. This prompted the agent to advise Barker that the man had suffered an epileptic fit and had been taken to the nearby St. Mary's Hospital. With his belongings was one of Barker's cards. Satisfied that Barker was not acquainted with the man, the FBI agent thanked him and departed. "Then it struck me," recalled Barker, who was based in West Virginia, "How in the world had anyone from Florida come into possession of one of my business cards?"

Barker began to wonder if there really had been an epileptic man, or if this had simply been a ruse to allow the FBI to covertly check out Barker, Bender, and the IFSB. Barker voiced these concerns in a report to Bender, who wrote back, "I cannot for the life of me see why [the FBI] would be checking up. It certainly proves one thing— the government is more interested in the Saucers than we realize."[4]

Five years later, Barker and Bender were once again the subjects of FBI interest. On 22 November 1958, an enquiring citizen of Oklahoma City contacted J. Edgar Hoover about the FBI's treatment of UFO investigators: "Recently many rumors have been printed in UFO periodicals, concerning reports that Special Agents of the Federal Bureau of Investigation have discouraged certain saucer investigators, particularly Mr. Albert Bender of Bridgeport, Connecticut, from further research into the secret of these elusive discs. Since you are the Director of the FBI, I would like to know whether or not these reports are factual or whether they are just rumors."

Hoover's response was swift: "I am instructing a Special Agent of our Oklahoma City Office to contact you concerning the matter you mentioned." A note from Hoover to the Special-Agent-in-Charge at Oklahoma City added, "An agent of your office should contact [the letter writer] immediately and secure copies of or information concerning the periodicals described."

In a memorandum to Hoover on 9 December 1958, the Oklahoma office reported that the periodical in question was the *Saucerian Bulletin* published by Gray Barker. It stated that the three men responsible for silencing Albert Bender were from "the FBI, Air Force Intelligence, and the Central Intelligence Agency." An FBI report of 12 December reads as follows: "Bender formed the International Flying Saucer Bureau in Bridgeport, Connecticut, in

1952 to look into the flying saucer mystery. In 1953 Bender allegedly stated that he knew what the saucers are. Then 'three men in black suits' silenced Bender to the extent that even today Bender will not discuss the matter of his 'hush-up' with anyone."

A month later on 22 January 1959, Hoover was still hot on the trail of Barker and Bender. "The Bureau desires to obtain a copy of the book written by Gray Barker entitled *They Knew Too Much About Flying Saucers.* Reportedly, the book was published by University Books, Inc., Illinois. Contact this publishing house and if possible, obtain a copy of this book." Three weeks later a copy of Barker's book was in Hoover's hands, as were copies of Bender's *Space Review* magazine. The FBI subsequently noted that its files contained "no information pertaining to the hush-up of Bender." On the subject of his *Space Review* journal they noted, "This magazine contains numerous articles and squibs concerning the sighting of flying saucers throughout the world. It does not appear to have any security significance."

This would seem to imply that whoever Bender's mysterious visitors were, they were not FBI agents. It is curious that nowhere in the released papers is there any mention of the FBI's 1953 interview with Gray Barker. Was this simply an off-the-record interview, or does the FBI have its reasons for not releasing its files on the matter? Thus far, that is a question that remains unanswered.

Many people with an interest in the UFO mystery will have heard of the so-called "Flying Triangle" puzzle. For more than two decades, sightings of large triangular-shaped UFOs, often black in color with rounded corners and that make a low humming noise have been reported throughout the world. These reports are in stark contrast to the classic saucer-shaped UFOs and have led some commentators to suspect that the triangles are military aircraft developed relatively recently, and perhaps are along the lines of a next-generation Stealth-type vehicle. Some probably are; yet, it can now be demonstrated that sightings of practically identical vehicles date back at least forty years—and can be documented at an official level.

While digging through a whole host of formerly classified UFO files at the National Archive at Kew, England, I came across a one-page report dated 28 March 1965 that, I confess, I almost overlooked. On closer inspection, however, I realized that it was potentially one of the most important UFO-related documents that I had ever come across.

According to the Ministry of Defense (MoD) paperwork, on the night in question at approximately 9:30 p.m. over moorland near Richmond, North Yorkshire, a man saw "Nine or ten objects—in close triangular formation each about 100ft long—orange illumination below—each triangular in shape with rounded corners, making low humming noise." Interestingly, the "rounded corners" and "low humming noise" are, as I said above, precisely what many witnesses to Flying Triangle-style UFO encounters are reporting today—in a worldwide capacity, no less. Recognizing the significance of this, I made a photocopy of the document and set about locating the witness.

When I found the witness, I introduced myself and explained that I had located at the National Archive a copy of the original report that dealt with his sighting all those years ago. It is fair to say that he was shocked, to say the least, to find that details of his long-gone encounter had been kept on file by the Ministry of Defense for decades.

"Yes, I did send in a report all those years ago, but I didn't think they would have kept it all this time," he told me, with astonishment in his voice. As he explained, on 28 March 1965 at approximately 9:30 p.m., he had been driving through the North Yorkshire moors of England, when, on approaching the village of Skeeby, near Richmond, the engine of his car began to splutter and die.

"It was a 1951 Ford," he stated, adding with some humor, "and it was a good car but a bit unpredictable at times. I didn't want to break down on the moor because it was icy cold. I got out of the car to have a look at the engine and that's when I saw this light."

He continued, "At first, because it was so dark, I wondered if it might be a weather balloon. But then I had a good look at it over the hedge and realized how big it was and how low down it was. It was about one hundred feet from end-to-end, about one hundred feet above the moors and shaped like a huge triangle and white, milky-white in color. It kept coming towards me and then stopped about two hundred yards from me over the moors. It hovered for a while—nothing came out of it, but there was a light below it that just pulsated like a light bulb. There could have been quite a few lights on it but from a distance the light just looked like a glow. Then without a warning, it just took off at a speed that isn't recognized. Good gracious, I thought, it must be a UFO.

"As it shot up, not vertically but at an angle, it joined a group of others that were identical and that were in a triangular or V-formation. The others were very, very high; a whole fleet of them. They all then headed south, I think, at a tremendous speed and disappeared over the horizon. I saw the main one for no more than a couple of minutes, but after they had gone I was still stood by the moor watching this fleet disappear. I waited in case something else exciting happened, but of course it didn't."

Shortly after the encounter and after reporting the incident to the Ministry of Defense at Whitehall, the man began to notice, "awful red marks on my skin which were like a stretch mark, but they were like a deep salmon red and they kept coming and going. But I didn't have them before."

The most bizarre angle of the entire episode was still to come as the man graphically illustrated: "For about eighteen months after the sighting, I would get strange telephone calls from people. These would be every two or three months. They just phoned out of the blue but didn't introduce themselves. They just said they were from some bureau or other. They didn't mention the name of the bureau but kept mentioning 'sightings' and asked whether I had seen anything else strange. Had any men come to interview me?"

The man was never visited by anyone with regard to his Flying Triangle encounter, nor did the MoD ever offer an explanation as to what it was that he saw on that fateful night in March 1965. To this day, that series of strange and unnerving telephone calls continues to mystify him, primarily because aside from informing the MoD of what had occurred, he made no other report to anyone—either official or unofficial as he is at pains to point out: "The only report I ever made was the one I sent to the MoD. It was so exciting that I had to tell someone."

His important testimony raises a number of vital questions: Why was someone so determined to find out if he had received any strange visits with regard to his encounter? Why the interest in knowing if he had had any other unusual encounters of a UFO nature? Who were his mysterious callers? Was he subjected to such lengthy questioning because he inadvertently caught sight of a classified military project that the authorities wanted to keep under wraps? Or perhaps he had viewed something that was truly out of this world? To this day, he remains mystified by his extraordinary encounter over the Yorkshire moors in 1965. Of one thing we can now be certain: the Flying Triangles are not a new phenomenon. It is truly ironic that confirmation of this fact should come via the previously withheld files of the British Ministry of Defense.[5]

In the 1960s when interest in MIB was at its height, even the U.S. Air Force was plunged into the controversy, as a widely circulated memo of 1 March 1967 prepared by the Assistant Vice Chief of Staff shows:

"Information, not verifiable, has reached HQ USAF that persons claiming to represent the Air Force and other Defense establishments have contacted citizens who have sighted unidentified flying objects. In one reported case an individual in civilian clothes, who represented himself as a member of NORAD, demanded and received photos belonging to a private citizen. In another, a person in an Air Force uniform approached local police and other citizens who had sighted a UFO, assembled them in a school room and told them that they did not see what they thought they saw and that they should not talk to anyone about the sighting. All military and civilian personnel and particularly Information Officers and UFO investigating Officers who hear of such reports should immediately notify their local OSI offices."

On 14 May 1969, the FBI was in receipt of yet another letter from a member of the public who had latched onto the stories surrounding the Men in Black. "There currently are rumors over [sic] the grapevine and in print that suggest men with oriental features wearing dark clothes go around terrorizing people who have had close-up views of UFOs. It is also rumored these creatures have impersonated armed forces officers and FBI investigators. They are supposed to ride around in black or dark automobiles that either have old license tags or none at all. Several are reported to have attempted to run down witnesses of UFO sightings, made disturbing almost macabre phone calls, silenced several investigators who were supposed to have learned some dark secret about extra-terrestrial craft or mission plans and opened mail, tapped telephones and even taken pictures of several homes where UFO witnesses lived. Can you give me any information on such rumors?"

In light of the fact that both Albert Bender and Gray Barker were well known to the FBI, and that J. Edgar Hoover himself possessed a copy of Barker's book on the Men in Black, it is somewhat amusing to note that the FBI responded by assuring the letter writer that it was completely ignorant of the Men in Black mystery, and therefore had no information in its possession that related to rumors of their bizarre activity. Nevertheless, this odd affair is prime evidence of official interest in monitoring the activities of those researchers implicated in the Men in Black mystery.

Patricia Hyde is a former FBI employee who, in July 1972, had an experience that brought her into direct contact with one of our mystery men. At around nine o'clock on a summer's evening, Hyde witnessed a strange object, described as "bat-like," flying over Arcadia, Florida. As is often the case following UFO encounters, Hyde naturally wished to find out more about what she had seen and dug deep into the UFO mystery.

Shortly after, while still employed by the FBI, she was confronted at her apartment by an unusual-looking "Oriental man" dressed in dark clothing, and who had "deeply slanting eyes." "Miss Hyde," he said, "you will stop investigating flying saucers." Additional veiled threats were made and Patricia Hyde eventually resigned from the FBI. Such is the effect that encounters with the Men in Black can have on a person.[6]

I am also conversant with the facts surrounding a doctor's experience with the Men in Black in the late 1970s in U.S. Midwest. In this instance the doctor was asked to conduct an examination of a young boy's arm that was marked with an unusual abrasion. The doctor stated: "I asked him how he got the strange marks and what created them. He replied: 'The space doctors.'" As the doctor listened, the boy related seeing a "low flying plane" enter a secluded area of woodland near his home. Curious as to what was going on, the boy ventured into the woods and came across a group of strange-looking people who, said the doctor, captured the boy, transferred him to some form of craft, and subjected him to countless medical and intelligence tests.

All of this could be considered nothing more than the result of an overactive imagination on the part of the boy. However, five years later, the doctor was at home watching television when there was a knock at the door. There before him were two men dressed in "black jumpsuits, black shoes, and black gloves and even sunglasses." Only one spoke, and inquired as to whether or not the doctor had "known of the boy." The doctor asked why the man wanted to know, and the response was that he was simply "curious." Naturally suspicious, the doctor related only part of the story, after which one of the MIB "managed a slight emotionless smile," before leaving.

From UFO author and researcher Jenny Randles comes an intriguing account that implicates the MIB in the 1980 UFO event at Rendlesham Forest, Suffolk, England. This event involved a number of military personnel from the twin military bases of RAF Bentwaters and Woodbridge, who may possibly have been witnesses to the landing of a vehicle from another world. What perhaps sets this case apart from many others is the quite stunning amount of evidence that supports the notion that something truly other-worldly had occurred, including on-the-record testimony from

U.S. Military personnel who attested to seeing a triangular-shaped UFO and strange-looking creatures in the forest.

As well as official documentation and witness accounts, there is another piece of remarkable evidence: an 18-minute audiotape made in the forest on the night of one of the encounters. As Randles stated, "A number of sources on base told us that a taped record of some of the activity had been made. We were given a description and knew by early 1983 that it was recorded in the forest during the second night of encounters, featuring officers and men who were seeing various UFOs."

Ultimately, this unique piece of evidence did surface into the public domain and did confirm much of the testimony of the first-hand military participants. There is an interesting and little-known sequel to this matter that echoes much of what has been discussed in this chapter. It was late 1988 when Randles had a notable encounter with a man who may very well have been one of our mysterious MIB. The subject of that strange encounter was the U.S. Air Force audiotape that chronicled the UFO events at Suffolk in 1980.

Randles was approached by a journalist working on a UFO documentary with the BBC that was to be aired in December 1988. Would she consent to an interview?

"I agreed," said Randles, "and he arrived with very professional equipment which I recognized as that used by BBC staff, having spent six months making a series of radio documentaries with them myself during 1986."

The documentary, she was advised, would focus on the Rendlesham Forest case and all questions put to her would be about her opinions and findings regarding the incident. During the course of the interview, the man (who used the name Tom Adams) turned his attention to the audiotape made by the airmen and insisted that Randles hand it over for use in the BBC's project.

"Immediately I said no," she recalled. Advising Adams that he could certainly have a copy of the tape, Randles informed him that under no circumstances could she give out the original. Adams, however, could not be budged. He needed the original.

"I pointed out that my original was not the original," said Randles. "It was obviously copied by the military source that sent it to me, so adding one more generation to the list was not going to make much difference." Despite repeated demands on Adams's part for the tape, she eventually relented and said that she would grant him access to the original. What Adams did not know, however, was that Randles merely gave him a third-generation copy and not her (second-generation) copy. Needless to say, Adams was more than satisfied and left with the evidence.

After several weeks had passed, Randles checked in with the BBC to see when the program was scheduled for broadcast. "What program?" the BBC replied. No one at the BBC knew anything about a proposed UFO documentary and no one there knew a Tom Adams. "I do find it odd that he should be particularly insistent about needing the original tape," says Randles. "This rather infers some ulterior motive."

Perhaps inevitably, Adams did not resurface. And, had Randles not had the foresight to merely supply Adams with a copy of the audiotape, he would have disappeared with what is certainly one of the most important pieces of UFO evidence at our disposal.[7]

From a woman who had a truly bizarre experience with one of the Men in Black in late 1993 comes the following: "The door banged really slowly but hard, like someone was hitting it with their fist instead of knocking, [and] when I opened it there was this horrible little man about five feet tall. He was dressed in a black suit and tie and had a funny little black hat on. His face was really strange: he looked like someone with anorexia, you know? His cheeks were all gaunt; his eyes were dark and his skin was almost white.

"I didn't know what to do and just stared; it was really frightening. Then he suddenly gave me this horrible grin, and I could tell his lips had been colored, like with make-up or something. He took off his hat and had this really bad wig on. You know, he looked about sixty but the wig was jet black.

"All he said was: 'We would ask you cease your studies.' I said: 'What?' Then he repeated it, exactly the same and I had to ask what he meant. 'The sky lights; always the sky lights,' he said. Then it dawned on me. I'd seen a UFO late at night about a week before when me and my husband had been driving home and we both had a really weird dream after about some little men standing around our car on the edge of the woods.

"Then he said something like: 'Cease and dream easy.' I think that was it, and he gave me a really long stare like he was going to attack me, or something. But he just walked away down the drive. I started to feel dizzy and slammed the door. I just crawled to the bed, and fell asleep for about three hours. But when I woke up there was this horrible smell like burning rubber all through the house. We had to have the windows wide open for days and get the carpets and furniture cleaned to get rid of [the smell]. It really shook me up, and apart from telling you I haven't really talked to anyone—and I don't really want to."[8]

So who are the Men in Black? During the course of my research I spoke with Nick Pope of the British Ministry of Defense. A firm believer in the theory that some UFOs are alien spacecraft, Pope told me:

"Men in Black stories? From what I understand, [at] some of these UFO conferences, the front rows are taken up by Walter Mitty-type characters who dress in black with sunglasses and take notes on everything. If there was one thing that anyone who was trying to be unobtrusive would not do, it would be that. I think that any allegations about people turning up and wanting to know about sightings, what you're dealing with is either people who are lying, and saying it happened when it didn't. Or, perhaps, more likely, people who have genuinely been visited by someone, but where that someone is some Walter Mitty-type character who likes to think he's some sort of James Bond secret agent. If anyone's going around saying: 'You must keep quiet about that,' it's the opposite of what we do. So it's nothing to do with us."[9]

The researcher Bill Moore has a very different view and states that the MIB are "really government people in disguise," who originate with a "rather bizarre unit of Air Force Intelligence known currently as the Air Force Special Activities Center." Moore relates that the history of the AFSAC can be traced back to the 1127th Field Activities Group—"an oddball unit, a composite of special intelligence groups. The men of the 1127th were con artists. Their job was to get people to talk." Recruited into the group, Moore elaborates, were "safe-crackers, cat-burglars, lock-pickers, impersonators, assorted masters of deception and useful flakes of all types."[10]

Whoever the MIB really are—and perhaps, as we have seen, they may have multiple origins—it seems that where UFO researchers and witnesses can be found, the Men in Black are never far behind.

5

WATCHING THE WATCHERS

What is without doubt one of the strangest (but notably documented) alleged crashed UFO incidents occurred in the New Mexico desert in early 1952. The case is a puzzling one in the sense that there are but two possibilities: the first is that the event occurred precisely as the witness claimed, and the second is that it was merely the product of a deluded mind. Interestingly, official records not only chronicle the event, but also reveal that U.S. authorities took steps to secretly speak personally with the alleged witness—particularly when it became apparent that he claimed to have been covertly visited by a mysterious representative of the Russian Government.

In a 13 November 1952 document titled "Unconventional Flying Objects Sighted; And Portions Recovered By [First Name Deleted] McLean, Friona, Texas," prepared by the Air Force Office of Special Investigations at Tinker Air Force Base, Oklahoma City, Oklahoma, and marked for the attention of the Director of Investigations at Washington, D.C., the following was disclosed: "Special Agent in Charge, Dallas, Texas, Texas Field Division, FBI, advised this district that [First Name Deleted] McLean of Friona, Texas, had reported seeing flying saucers at an unnamed point in New Mexico; had recovered three fragments which landed close to him; and had notified the Pentagon but hearing nothing had sold a portion of one object to a Russian scientist from the USSR Embassy.

"FBI received information to the effect that McLean had written a letter to an unnamed friend in Amarillo, Texas, and it read in part as follows: 'To get back to flying saucers that are real, recently I was camped on a mountain in New Mexico and saw a dim light at first circling around up high. It circled in a mile across circle but kept descending. First the light was white but as it got lower it turned green and exploded showering light objects in all directions. Several of those fiery objects landed close to me, most of them were buried in the ground, but I gathered up three that were only partly buried and brought them home with me.

"'I notified the Pentagon in Washington what I had saw fall. I heard nothing from them but a Russian scientist from the USSR Embassy did come and buy one half of one of those objects. It was so hard we had to use a sledgehammer to break into [sic]. In the center was a round hole or vacuum filled with fine powder. This scientist scraped every bit of the dust up and put it in a bottle. He claims the object was uranium and other unknown minerals.'"

The document continues, "Mr. and Mrs. McLean, Friona, Texas, were interviewed and Mr. McLean advised that he was a retired farmer. He stated that he had always been interested in meteors ever since he took a correspondence course concerning meteors some 50 years ago. McLean stated that in the spring of 1952 he was traveling in the eastern part of San Miguel County, New Mexico, with his wife, when he found a large deposit of a metal unknown to him. He stated that he picked up a piece of this metal and brought it back to Friona, Texas, with him. Mrs. McLean verified this statement inasmuch as she stated that she was with him at the time he picked up the metal.

"McLean was questioned concerning his statement in the above letter that he saw the material fall but stated that he did not remember writing any such information in the letter and emphatically stated that he did not see the material fall to earth. McLean stated that after he found this material and returned to Friona, Texas, he wrote letters to Senator LYNDON B. JOHNSON of Texas and Senator CLINTON ANDERSON of New Mexico concerning the material. He stated that both senators replied requesting that he ship samples of this material to a Government Laboratory in Tucson, Arizona. McLean stated that he sent samples of this material to the Government Laboratory in Tucson, Arizona, and stated that they replied advising him that the material was part of a meteor. McLean was asked if he were still in possession of all this correspondence but stated that he had destroyed it all.

"McLean advised that shortly after he wrote to the two senators about this material he was visited by an unknown individual who, according to McLean, displayed the credentials of the Soviet Embassy. McLean was asked to describe the credentials of this person and stated that they were very similar to the credentials of the writer but that the writing was in Russian. McLean was then asked if he could read the writer's credentials, and he stated that he could not read very well but he felt sure that they were in English. McLean could not place the time of this visit and could furnish no other information concerning this alleged individual with the exception of the fact that he stated that he thought this individual came from the Russian Consulate in Amarillo, Texas.

"McLean stated he was no longer in possession of any of the unknown material inasmuch as he had recently given the remainder of the material to his wife's nephew, Mr. [Deleted] of Lawrenceville, Illinois. It was also pointed out that in the letter set out above McLean advised that he sold half of the material to the representative of the Russian Embassy. At the time of the interview he emphatically denied selling any of the material to the representative of the Russian Embassy and stated that he could not remember having made such a statement in the letter to the individual in Amarillo, Texas.

"Deputy Sheriff C.M. JONES, Friona, advised that he had known the subject for many years and advised that the subject is an elderly man approximately 71 years of age. JONES advised that the subject has nothing whatsoever to do and is somewhat of a dreamer. JONES explained that McLean dreams of various things and then thinks about them to the extent that he actually believes what he dreamed. JONES stated that the subject will then come to the downtown section of the little town of Friona and attempt to convince people that his dreams are actually the truth. JONES stated

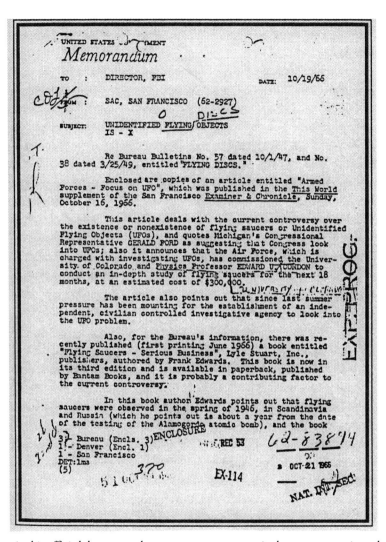

UNITED STATES ~~JVERNMENT~~

Memorandum

TO : DIRECTOR, FBI   DATE: 10/19/66

FROM : SAC, SAN FRANCISCO (62-2927)

            0   DISCS

SUBJECT: UNIDENTIFIED FLYING OBJECTS
IS - X

       Re Bureau Bulletins No. 57 dated 10/1/47, and No.
38 dated 3/25/49, entitled "FLYING DISCS."

       Enclosed are copies of an article entitled "Armed
Forces - Focus on UFO", which was published in the This World
supplement of the San Francisco Examiner & Chronicle, Sunday,
October 16, 1966.

       This article deals with the current controversy over
the existence or nonexistence of flying saucers or Unidentified
Flying Objects (UFOs), and quotes Michigan's Congressional
Representative GERALD FORD as suggesting that Congress look
into UFOs; also it announces that the Air Force, which is
charged with investigating UFOs, has commissioned the University of Colorado and Physics Professor EDWARD U. CONDON to
conduct an in-depth study of flying saucers for the next 18
months, at an estimated cost of $300,000.

       The article also points out that since last summer
pressure has been mounting for the establishment of an independent, civilian controlled investigative agency to look into
the UFO problem.

       Also, for the Bureau's information, there was re-
cently published (first printing June 1966) a book entitled
"Flying Saucers - Serious Business", Lyle Stuart, Inc.,
publishers, authored by Frank Edwards. This book is now in
its third edition and is available in paperback, published
by Bantam Books, and it is probably a contributing factor to
the current controversy.

       In this book author Edwards points out that flying
saucers were observed in the spring of 1946, in Scandinavia
and Russia (which he points out is about a year from the date
of the testing of the Alamogordo atomic bomb), and the book

3 - Bureau (Encls. 3) ENCLOSURE
1 - Denver (Encl. 1)   REC 53   62-83874
1 - San Francisco
DET:lms
(5)

EX-114   OCT 21 1966

NAT. INT. SEC.

As this official document shows, government agencies have even monitored published books on the UFO controversy.

that the people of Friona, Texas, very seldom believe or put any faith in any matters discussed by the subject due to his mental condition. JONES stated that the subject is entirely loyal to the United States but has merely reached that age in life where his mind has begun to deteriorate."

An examination of the relevant documentation and the case as a whole would suggest at first glance that the entire controversy was purely the creation of an elderly, confused, and fading mind. And perhaps it was. It should not be forgotten, however, that the discovery of the "large deposit" of a "metal unknown" at San Miguel County, New Mexico, was confirmed to the Air Force by McLean's wife—who was apparently of sound mind. Therefore, that something was indeed recovered by McLean does seem likely. In addition, the reference to the alleged and slightly mysterious "Russian scientist from the USSR Embassy" that purportedly visited McLean and subsequently departed with some of the recovered material has an air of the Men in Black mystery to it, as well. More than half a century on and with the key player in this case long departed, this event remains intriguingly unresolved.[1]

U niversally acknowledged as the premier collector of data on alleged crashed UFO reports, the late Leonard Stringfield was a high-profile figure within the American UFO research community from the mid-1950s right up until his death forty years later. The author of two books on UFO encounters, as well as numerous "Status Reports" on crashed UFO data, Stringfield first attracted official attention in 1954—from the FBI, no less—whose now-declassified documentation on Stringfield makes it very clear that the man himself suspected more than fifty years ago that his UFO activities were the subject of an official monitoring operation.

According to the FBI, "A source of unknown reliability, an acquaintance of Leonard H. Stringfield, who is the Director of the captioned organization Civilian Research Interplanetary Flying Objects, in October 1954 advised that Stringfield is the Director of the organization and is assisted by his wife, and that Stringfield writes and publishes monthly the multi-lithographed 'Newsletter' of the organization. He uses the 'Newsletter' to report news pertaining to the sightings of flying saucers and he claims the 'Newsletter' now has a worldwide circulation of about 4,000 copies.

"The same source furnished a copy of the 'Newsletter' [that] reports that Stringfield had a private talk with Lieutenant Colonel John O'Mara, Deputy Commander, Intelligence, United States Air Force, on September 21, 1954, and that in essence Colonel O'Mara told Stringfield that flying saucers do exist and that past contradictions were unfortunate. Stringfield has stated that he believes his home telephone is being monitored, presumably by the Air Force, and that he therefore makes his phone calls to Lieutenant O'Mara at Wright-Patterson Air Force Base from his office. Stringfield, in talking about the possibility that the U.S. Air Force might stop his operations, made a statement to the effect, 'The Air Force can't do anything to me. I'm claiming saucers are interplanetary.'"

As far as official surveillance of Stringfield in later years was concerned, Bill Moore—a researcher who had widely acknowledged links with the U.S. Intelligence community in the 1980s and who co-authored with Charles Berlitz the first book on the Roswell "crashed UFO" controversy of 1947, *The Roswell Incident*—stated in 1989: "Drawing from my own knowledge and experience, I can summarize the individuals who were the subject of intelligence community interest between 1980 and 1984. It is important to remember here that in some cases, I was not personally involved, but rather only aware of these goings-on through conversations with others..."

Moore continued, "Stringfield remained the subject of some interest through 1983, after which I heard very little about him. The [counterintelligence] people seemed to know a lot about Len and his sources. The impression I got was that someone else much closer to him than I, was keeping tabs on his activities, but of course, I never knew for certain."[2]

In 1991 Stringfield wrote, "I have other sources today who seem to know that I am currently a subject of interest to the intelligence community. If I could draw any conclusions from the travails of my past experiences, then I am also being subjected to both good information and disinformation…"[3]

Leonard Stringfield died in December 1994, never really knowing if the data provided by his whistleblower sources on crashed UFOs was genuine or carefully orchestrated disinformation.

I n 1955 two elderly sisters in Chicago, Mildred and Marie Maier, reported in the *Journal of Space Flight* their experiences with UFOs, including the recording of a radio program in which an unidentified code was allegedly heard. The sisters taped the program and other ham radio operators also claimed to have heard the "space message." The CIA's Office of Scientific Intelligence (OSI) duly became interested and asked its Scientific Contact Branch to obtain a copy of the recording.

Field officers from the Contact Division, one of whom was a man named Dewelt Walker, made contact with the Maier sisters, who were "thrilled that the government was interested" and set up a time to meet with them. In trying to secure the tape recording, the agency officers reported that they had stumbled upon a scene from *Arsenic and Old Lace.* "The only thing lacking was the elderberry wine," Walker wryly cabled headquarters.

After reviewing the sisters' scrapbook of clippings from their days as entertainers on the stage, the bemused and amused officers secured a copy of the recording. OSI analyzed the tape and found it was nothing more than Morse code from a U.S. radio station. The matter rested there until UFO researcher Leon Davidson talked with the Maier sisters in 1957. The sisters told Davidson that they remembered they had talked with a Mr. Dewelt Walker who said he was from the Air Force.

Davidson then wrote to Mr. Walker, believing him to be an Air Force Intelligence Officer from Wright-Patterson, to ask if the tape had been analyzed at the Air Technical Intelligence Center. Walker replied to Davidson that the tape had been forwarded to proper authorities for evaluation, and no information was available concerning the results.

Not satisfied and very perceptively suspecting that Walker was really a CIA officer, Davidson next wrote to none other than Allen Dulles, the Director of Central Intelligence, and demanded to learn what the coded message revealed and who Mr. Walker really was. The agency, wanting to keep Walker's identity as a CIA employee secret, replied that another agency of the Government had analyzed the tape in question and that Davidson would be hearing from the Air Force.

On 5 August the Air Force wrote Davidson saying that Walker "was and is an Air Force Officer" and that the tape "was analyzed by another government organization." The Air Force letter confirmed that the recording contained only identifiable Morse code that came from a known licensed radio station. Davidson wrote Dulles again. This time he wanted to know the identity of the Morse code operator and of the agency that had conducted the analysis. Both the CIA and the Air Force were now in a quandary—and all as a result of their interest in the activities of two little old ladies.

The agency had previously denied that it had actually analyzed the tape. The Air Force had also denied analyzing the tape and claimed that Walker was an Air Force officer. Undercover CIA officers contacted Davidson in Chicago and promised to get the code translation and the identification of the transmitter, if possible. In another attempt to pacify Davidson, a CIA officer, again under cover and wearing his Air Force uniform, contacted Davidson in New York City.

The CIA officer explained that there was no "super agency" involved and that Air Force policy was not to disclose who was doing what. While seeming to accept this argument, Davidson nevertheless pressed for disclosure of both the recording and the source. The officer agreed to see what he could do. After checking with headquarters, the CIA officer phoned Davidson to report that a thorough check had been made and, because the signal was known to be of American origin, the tape and the notes made at the time had been destroyed to conserve file space.

Incensed over what he perceived was a runaround, Davidson told the CIA officer that "he and his agency, whichever it was, were acting like Jimmy Hoffa and the Teamsters Union in destroying records which might indict them." Believing that any more contact with Davidson would only encourage more speculation, the Contact Division washed its hands of the issue by reporting to the Director of Central Intelligence and to the Air Force's Air Technical Intelligence Center that it would not respond or try to contact Davidson again. Thus a minor incident, handled poorly by the CIA and the Air Force, turned into a major flap that added fuel to the growing mystery surrounding UFOs and the CIA's surveillance of UFO "witnesses" such as the Maier sisters and researcher Leon Davidson.[4]

As humorous as this *Keystone Cops*-meets-*The X-Files* fiasco certainly was, the episode offers us more clues into the workings of the CIA and its relationship to the UFO mystery. First, the fact that the CIA would take an interest in a relatively obscure case such as this demonstrates that all avenues were being pursued in monitoring breaking stories on the subject. Second, the strange saga shows that the CIA was not above passing its agents off as employees of other agencies as it attempted to gain possession of UFO data and to determine what the Maier sisters had come across. That the two elderly sisters had stumbled onto nothing more sinister than a Morse code transmission is irrelevant. The clear fact is that CIA personnel sought to obtain under covert and misleading circumstances what was perceived initially to be UFO-related evidence. Indeed, this case has Men-in-Black-style overtones to it.

How often have we heard of alleged Government officials apparently keeping watch on UFO witnesses and researchers, turning up on people's doorsteps, demanding evidence of UFO activity in the form of photographs, etc., only to have the relevant Government agency that the men allegedly work for assert that it has no record of them?

Another perfect example of such a situation comes from Colin Stanton, a former British Royal Air Force employee, who claims that in 1955 he photographed a "golden UFO hovering near the edge" of RAF West Freugh, Scotland. According to Stanton, the object was in view for only a few seconds, as it "seemed to respond to my presence and shot off like a rocket." The picture, he states, was very clear and displayed a classic saucer-shaped object. Although he mentioned the existence of the photograph to friends and family only, Stanton asserts that after he left the RAF in 1957 he was visited by "a fellow from the Air Ministry who asked for the picture and told me I should not be speaking about such things."

Stanton added: "I told him he was 'talking rot' and if he needed the picture then I wanted something in writing. He didn't [have anything in writing] and he left. I was quite the angry young man in those days and made a complaint to the Ministry. Of course, no one knew anything about it."

For their part, the Maier sisters may not have made contact with aliens; however, the fact that their research had led to official interest on the part of none other than the CIA is a prime example of the way in which the agency keeps a close watch on those of us who are, in turn, keeping a close watch on the skies above.

I n 1959 Stan Seers, who was then the President of the Queensland Flying Saucer Research Bureau (QFSRB) of Australia, received a somewhat enigmatic telephone call from a man who wished to meet with him in a large car park in Brisbane to discuss the subject of UFOs. Suspecting a potential hoax, Seers waited a while and, after several follow-up calls from the man, finally relented and agreed to a meeting.

Sure enough, at the appointed time and location the man showed up. More intriguing, however, was the fact that he identified himself as working for the Australian Security and Intelligence Organization—ASIO. According to Seers, the man—who he dubbed "Mr. D"—knew all about his background and that of several of his colleagues, and "dangled the Communist bogey, this being very much in the forefront in those days."

And although Mr. D claimed that he wished to make an offer to Seers that would lead to cooperation between his research group and ASIO on the UFO issue, the resultant effect was one that led to intense surveillance of the QFSRB, its members, and their motives, as Colin Phillips, a committee member of the group, revealed: "… it must be remembered that the Australian Government in 1950–1960 was very sensitive about Communists, and people with new and different ideas who talked about peace, etc., were suspect. It was therefore quite natural that ASIO should send someone along to our meetings to keep an eye on us—I would not be very impressed with the operation of ASIO if they had not." Phillips is likely correct. So it seems that, several years after the CIA had recommended that UFO groups be subjected to official surveillance, Australian authorities had begun to follow an identical path.[5]

One of the more unusual UFO cases brought to the FBI's attention—that led them to open a secret case file on the witness and his claimed experience—was that involving Joseph Perry of Grand Blanc, Michigan, who was interviewed by Detroit FBI on 5 March 1960. Perry became the subject of the following memorandum of 9 March: "Mr. Perry advised that he operates a Pizza House at 3075 Edwards Street, Grand Blanc, and that he has been a professional photographer for thirty years. He explained that he has a hobby of taking photographs of the moon through a homemade telescope. At about 1:00 a.m. on February 21, 1960, he took some photographs of the moon and after developing same, he put them in his viewer and in one photograph he observed what appears to be a flying object somewhere between the end of his telescope and the surface of the moon. He said that when blown up, this object is flat on the bottom, is oval shaped, and appears to have a fluorescent glow around the entire object, and that it is apparently moving as it has a vapor trail running behind it. He has taken over one thousand pictures of the moon and has never seen anything resembling this object."

Certain that he had photographed something truly anomalous, Perry furnished the FBI with the relevant photograph for expert analysis. As a Teletype message of 9 March 1960 showed, the FBI in turn contacted the Air Force Office of Special Investigations at Selfridge Air Force Base, who assumed custody of Perry's picture. However, the FBI continued to monitor aspects of the case and Perry himself, particularly in light of the fact that Perry's photograph had caught the attention of the media. An FBI Airtel of 28 March 1960 to Hoover reveals:

"An article appeared in the 'Flint Journal,' Flint, Michigan, dated 3/27/60 by Reporter ALLAN R. WILHELM. This article appeared on Page 13. The article reflects an interview with PERRY and in part states that PERRY had received at least 50 letters and calls in regard to the photograph he had taken. One letter was from [the] National Investigation Committee on Aerial Phenomenon. The article contains the following quote from this letter, 'From past experience with photographic evidence we consider it unlikely that you will ever see your picture again.' PERRY had advised the newspaper that all he knew was that the picture was in Air Force hands. The FBI only says that it is in 'proper hands,' according to PERRY. The article continued, 'So last week PERRY wrote to the President telling him he can't find out where his slide is and asking assurance that he will get it back.' PERRY was quoted as saying, 'The only way I will be satisfied if I don't get it back is if the Government tells me it is top secret.'"

In the weeks and months that followed, a considerable file was built up by the FBI with respect to both Perry and his photograph, much of which dealt with his concerns about retrieving his property from the Air Force. "PERRY by letter dated 3-21-60 wrote to President Eisenhower pointing out he did not know where his photographs were but he would like assurance that they would be returned to him," it was recorded in an FBI memo of 21 April 1960. "He pointed out that 'thousands are looking forward' to viewing the photographs."

Matters were resolved—at least to the satisfaction of the FBI and the Air Force—when, according to official records, Perry was advised by the Air Force that "what appeared to be a flying object in this slide is actually a part of the negative which was not properly developed." Naturally this did little to satisfy those who insisted that the photograph genuinely showed some form of structured device, as the FBI noted: "[An acquaintance of Perry] reportedly told the 'Detroit Times' that he does not believe this story as he knows that Joe Perry is very meticulous when he develops pictures; therefore he feels the slide actually does contain a picture of a flying object."

Possibly recognizing that the controversy surrounding this particular case was likely to run and run, the FBI insisted to all inquirers that this was a matter strictly for the Air Force, and steered all letters in the Air Force's direction. Indeed, such was the interest in the Perry case that six years later the FBI was still receiving correspondence from interested members of the public. "Inasmuch as your communication is of interest to another governmental agency, I am referring a copy of it to the Office of Special Investigations, Department of the Air Force," wrote FBI Director Hoover on 15 April 1966 to an inquirer asking about the status of the FBI's investigation of Perry and his photograph.

Interestingly, Hoover's final comment on the case refers to a local newspaper (possibly the aforementioned *Flint Journal*, although this is not made explicitly clear from the now-declassified documentation) that reported that the FBI was involved in the Perry affair. As Hoover ominously stated, "It was necessary for this Bureau to straighten the record with that newspaper…"

Joe Perry's photograph may have shown a UFO. Or it may have displayed something far more innocuous, as the Air Force asserted. However, what is most important of all is the fact that the Perry case perfectly demonstrates the way in which those who believe they may have seen a UFO—and who subsequently report it to Government and Military agencies—can find themselves the subject of official files that find their way to the desk of the Director of the FBI, no less.

When in 1964 Larry Bryant, a UFO researcher and U.S. Army employee, wrote an article titled "Let's Challenge the UFO Censors" that addressed his UFO-related dealings with elements of the American Military, the FBI was quickly apprised of the nature of the article. A report dated 25 May 1964 to Cartha DeLoach, the former assistant director of the FBI, stated: "On 5-21-64 the Department of Defense delivered at the Bureau a manuscript by Larry Bryant entitled Let's Challenge the UFO (Unidentified Flying Objects) Censors. The Department of the Army, according to the transmittal form from the Department of Defense, has no objection to the publication of the article. The FBI's attention was directed to page 6. Also included with the manuscript was a copy of the author's transmittal letter to the Department of the Army stating he would like to know the name, rank/grade, title and office of each person who actually conducts the review of Bryant's article. A review of the article revealed it is a criticism of the Department of Defense's policy with regard to issuing clearances of articles relative to Unidentified Flying Objects (UFOs), particularly when the author is employed by the U.S. Army as in the case of Bryant. The article is in essence a history of Bryant's problems in getting articles published on UFO [sic].

"References to the FBI are as follows: On page 2, Bryant indicates he will reveal the role played by the FBI in monitoring UFO research activities of Army civilian employees. On page 6, Bryant refers to his being interviewed on 9-17-63 by Special Agent [deleted] of our Norfolk Office. Bryant states [the] Special Agent contacted him in response to Bryant's letter of 7-23-63 to the Sheriff of Sussex County, Virginia, requesting UFO sighting data.

"Bryant claims he asked SA [deleted] if it was customary for the FBI to question people who expressed an interest in UFO. SA [deleted] replied in the negative and added that: 'Since his office was queried...he was just seeking information on which he could write a memorandum for the files.' Bryant also states that SA [deleted] volunteered the following: 'If the FBI has any such data (on UFO sightings), it is probably of an intelligence nature and thus would be unavailable to the public and to private individuals.'"

It transpired that the FBI office had been brought into the picture because "Bryant has directed a voluminous amount of correspondence to military officials in the area and as Bryant was employed by the Department of the Army, Fort Eustis, Virginia, the G-2 Section of the Second Army, Fort Meade, Maryland, was conducting a background check on Bryant. Bryant was interviewed on 9/7/63 by SA [deleted] in order to obtain background information concerning him in order to reply to the correspondence from the [agency name deleted] and the U.S. Naval Base, Norfolk, Virginia."

The FBI added, "The reference to the FBI on page 6 of Bryant's manuscript is not completely true. [sic] However, it has the effect of leaving the wrong impression; the FBI was not investigating Bryant but was merely interviewing him in order to respond to inquiries directed to us from other agencies."

Here we see undeniable proof that as a result of Bryant's "voluminous amount of correspondence to military officials" on the subject of UFOs, the authorities responded by having him interviewed by the FBI. And official interest in Bryant's activities did not end there, as Bryant himself noted in 1990:

"Back in the winter of 1971–72, when I was employed by the Industrial College of the Armed Forces in Washington, D.C., two of my superiors there, USAF Col. Samuel B. Adams and Army Col. Patrick J. Kenney, called me into their office to discuss their role in the College's decision not to process my immediate supervisor's recommendation that I be granted a Top Secret security clearance. They explained to me that the College's secretary, Army Col. John S. Sullivan, had expressed resistance to process the recommendation because of the vigor and determination by which I had been pursuing UFO research during the past dozen years or so."[6]

Bryant continues his UFO research to this day.

The idea that some of humankind's most impressive constructions, such as the Pyramids of Egypt and the standing stones of Easter Island and Stonehenge, were built with the assistance of extraterrestrials—so-called "Ancient Astronauts"—is not a new one, as the books of Erich von Daniken, Robert Charroux, and Morris Jessup make clear. Conversely, the works of those within the skeptical camp, such as Ronald Story, convincingly argue that much of the data in favor of the existence of the Ancient Astronauts is dubious at best.

One person who has stuck firmly to his guns when it comes to the issue of extraterrestrial intervention in our civilization millennia ago is Captain Bruce Cathie, formerly a New Zealand-based airline pilot. He put forward an intriguing theory that there exists around the Earth a "power grid" that UFOs utilize as a form of energy source to enable them to soar around our skies. Cathie also postulated that this same power grid had been utilized by extraterrestrials to construct the giant Pyramids of ancient Egypt. According to Cathie, "It is inconceivable that the thousands of stone blocks, each weighing many tons, that were used in the construction of the Great Pyramid were dragged hundreds of miles by slaves, then fitted together with such precision that a visiting card cannot be pushed between them… These massive blocks were moved by the utilization of the power grid…"

Notably, Cathie claimed that ancient lore supported such a notion: "The Arabs have an interesting legend that when the Pyramid was built, the great stones were brought long distances from the quarries. They were laid on pieces of papyrus inscribed with suitable symbols. They were then struck by a rod, whereupon they would move through the air the distance of one bow shot…there is only one answer to the riddle of such construction methods: anti-gravity. Only by this means could the large blocks be moved over great distances and placed so accurately."

During the 1960s when Cathie's research was taking shape, he contacted U.S. defense personnel at Wellington, New Zealand, in an effort to get his views heard, and in the hope that this would help provide answers to his quest. Having put forward his views on the "power grid," "ancient civilizations," "anti-matter," and much more, Cathie was engaged in correspondence with officials who, in an internal memorandum described him as: "a lean, wiry New Zealander with an apparently above average knowledge of mathematics."

A formerly classified Defense Intelligence Agency report on Cathie's work stated: "Captain Cathie is still employed as an aircraft pilot by National Airways Corporation. His superiors know of his interest and activity in UFOs and his forthcoming book, Harmonic 33. He has been checked for security reasons and no adverse reports are known. He has received considerable publicity in newspapers and on television. He admits that many people consider him 'some kind of a nut' but he persists in his theory."

Notably, a Department of Defense (DoD) report of May 1968 references complaints received from Cathie that "U.S. personnel" were "tailing him." As the official DoD report went on to state: "[Cathie] went on to say that he thought he was being followed by some persons but was not certain until 3 weeks ago when he was accosted by 3 Americans in the Grand Hotel in Invercargill. He said these persons asked him to accompany them which he refused to do. He could (or would) not identify them other than to say he believed they were from a U.S. Navy vessel in the area. NOTE: The only U.S. vessel known to be south of Auckland is the USS Eltanin, a submarine assigned to the U.S. Antarctic program, and which was in Antarctic waters at the time. Captain Cathie said that he had been cleared by the NZ Government to pursue his research and that he had a letter to this effect signed by the Prime Minister. He stated that the Member of Parliament from his area, Dr. Findley, had interceded for him and obtained government approval for his work. He then asked the DOD to 'call your agents off. I have official approval to continue my work. I don't want them tailing me.'"

UFO propulsion systems, long-lost anti-gravity-style technology in the hands of the Pharaohs, once classified U.S. Defense Department files, and an apparent covert surveillance operation were all key parts in the research and life of Captain Bruce Cathie. It is perhaps apposite to close with the words of the man himself, who wrote in 1977, "Ten years ago I lived in a well-ordered world, but since that time as I have learned what is quietly and unobtrusively going on around me, this orderliness has well and truly been shattered."[7]

During the early hours of 6 January 1966, in the Cheshire, England, town of Wilmslow, an extraordinary UFO event occurred that led an elite division of the British Ministry of Defense to personally—and secretly—interview the witness and undertake a careful, on-site examination of the location of the encounter. Police Constable (PC) Colin Perks had begun his night-shift at 10:00 p.m. and had no idea that he would shortly thereafter find himself implicated in a face-to-face encounter with what might very well have been visitors from another galaxy. In a graphic two-page report filed with his superior officer in the immediate aftermath of the incident, Constable Perks stated:

"Sir, I have to report that I have been in the Police Force for almost four years. I am 28 years of age, a married man, and I reside with my wife and child in [witness's address]. I am in excellent health and I have no worries of any description. On the night of Thursday/Friday the 6th to 7th January 1966, which was a cold clear night and started [sic] with a full moon which made visibility good. I commenced duty at 10pm on the 6th and due to finish duty at 6am on the 7th. At 1.15am on the 7th I had my refreshments at Wilmslow Police Station where I resumed normal patrol at 2am on this date where I commenced walking around the village. I was alone on this occasion.

"About 4am on the 7th I was checking property at the rear of a large block of shops which are situated off the main A34 road (Alderley Road) Wilmslow. At 4.10am I was still checking property and facing the back of the shops when I heard a high pitched whine, for a moment I couldn't place the noise as it was most unfamiliar to the normal surroundings. I turned around and saw a Greenish/Grey glow in the sky about 100 yards from me and about 35 feet up in the air. I stopped in my tracks and was unable to believe what I could see. However I gathered myself together after a couple of seconds and made the following observations. The object was about the length of a bus (30 feet) and estimated at being 20 feet wide. It was elliptic in shape and emanated a greenish gray glow which I can only describe as an eerie greeny [sic] color. It appeared to be motionless of itself, that is there was no impression of rotation. The object was about 15 feet in height. The object had a flat bottom.

"At this time it was very bright and there was an East wind. Although it was cold there was no frost. No cloud formation was anywhere near ground level. The object remained stationary for about five seconds then without any change in the whine it started moving at a very fast rate in an East-South-East direction. It disappeared from view very quickly. When it started moving it did not appear to rotate but moved off sideways with the 30-foot length to the front and rear. It is possible the short side given as 20-feet may in fact be longer as I was looking underneath the object and may have been deceived.

"About 500 yards away from where I was standing there is an electric railway line but the noise I heard was nothing to do with either electric or diesel trains. About 50 yards from where I was standing is a transformer belonging to the Electric Company. This is a sub-station and the noise I heard is of no comparison to the hum from this.

"There is no doubt that the object I saw was of a sharp, distinctive, definite shape and of a solid substance. However I did not notice any vents, portholes or other places of access. The glow was coming from the exterior of the object and this was the only light which was visible. I checked with Jodrell Bank and Manchester Airport shortly after the incident but they could not help or in any way account for what I had seen."

After having received Police Constable Colin Perks's report, his Deputy Chief Constable contacted the Ministry of Aviation, and, from there, the report was forwarded to the Ministry of Defense at Whitehall, London, and specifically to a covert division of the MoD's elite Defense Intelligence Staff known as DI61e(AIR). Perhaps aware that this was no run-of-the-mill report, DI61e(AIR) secretly dispatched agents to Wilmslow to interview Constable Perks and to investigate the area where the UFO was seen. "Constable Perks was interviewed by DI 61e(AIR) on 1st February 1966," reported Flight Lieutenant M.J.P.H. Mercer in a restricted memorandum drawn up in response to the DI61e(AIR) investigation. "He was questioned on a number of points arising from the statement he made on the 8th January."

"What sort of noise did the UFO make?" "What was its speed when it began to move?" "What was its altitude?" asked the DI61e(AIR) agents. Impressed by Perks's conviction, the secret intelligence team headed for their next destination: the actual site of the UFO encounter. Upon arriving at the location where PC Perks had seen the UFO, DI61e(AIR) noted that on the morning following the incident "some glass like substance" was found on the ground below where the UFO had been seen. While DI61e(AIR) felt that there was not enough firm evidence in hand to make a definite connection between the "substance" and the UFO encounter, it is worth noting that their investigation was extremely meticulous.

After interviewing the Police Constable at length, scrutinizing his report, and visiting the area of the sighting, DI61e(AIR) stated in their final analysis of the case that although it was not "possible to arrive at any concrete conclusion, there is no reason to doubt the fact that this constable saw something completely foreign to his previous experience." Two weeks after these remarkable events occurred, Police Constable Perks was granted permission to relate the details of his encounter to the media. Until the files were declassified, no indication surfaced to the effect that Perks had been visited secretly by MoD officials. We can speculate that perhaps he been advised by his superiors or the Ministry of Defense to omit this specific part of the experience when speaking with the press.[8]

On 6 February 1966 a group of soldiers at an ammunition dump in Aluche, Spain, allegedly observed the flight of a white-colored flying saucer that had a strange symbol on its undersurface: a closed parenthesis connected by a crossed bar to an open parenthesis. A similar craft—displaying the same symbol—was supposedly seen on 1 June 1967 in a suburb of Madrid and photographed. However, the five photographs were later proven to be fakes. Nevertheless the story did not die. In fact, it flourished for years. And thus was born the cult of UMMO – named after the planet from which the UFOs and their occupants reportedly originated.

According to the late researcher Jim Keith, "The UMMO case was created through a large number of contacts—UFO sightings, personal contacts, messages through the mail and telephone—alleged to be from space brothers from the planet UMMO...located 14.6 light years from our solar system." Concerning the "messages through the mail," Keith stated, "They are a large collection of six-to-ten page letters containing diagrams and equations, delineating UMMO science and philosophy. Differing from most channeled and beamed by space beings, they were scientifically savvy, although according to Jacques Vallee, smacked more of Euro sci-fi than superior extraterrestrial knowledge."[9]

But was the UMMO saga really evidence that extraterrestrials were among us? According to Keith, no. "Spanish journalist Manuel Carballal wrote that researchers Cales Berche, Jose J. Montejo and Javier Sierra had named well-known Spanish parapsychologist Jose Luis Jordan Pena as being the originator...and is later reported to have admitted his creation of the complex hoax, stating that it had been a 'scientific experiment' aimed at testing the gullibility factor amongst Spanish UFO researchers."[10]

Notably, there were those who postulated that the original UMMO hoax had been seized upon by certain official intelligence services who then began exploiting the original hoax as a cover for the dissemination of psychological warfare within the public UFO research community, as well as a means of secretly infiltrating that same community to gather information.

Jacques Vallee, who has dug deep into the UMMO affair, revealed that some researchers "...thought that the cult had been used or was manipulated by the KGB...some of the data that was supposedly channeled from the UMMO organization in the sky—was very advanced cosmology...It came straight out of the notes of Andre Sakharov, including some of the unpublished notes of Sakharov...And so some people—and I don't know who's right—felt that somebody had to have access to those notes, to inspire those messages, perhaps the KGB. It wasn't just ordinary science fiction; it was somebody who knew what some of the more advanced cosmologists were thinking."

Sakharov—who died in 1989—was a Soviet physicist who became, in the words of the Nobel Peace Committee, a spokesman for the conscience of mankind. He was fascinated by fundamental physics and cosmology, but had to spend two decades designing nuclear weapons. The acknowledged father of the Soviet hydrogen bomb, he contributed perhaps more than anyone else to the military might of the USSR. But it was his top secret experience as a leading nuclear expert that was instrumental in making Sakharov one of the most courageous critics of the Soviet regime, a human rights activist, and the first Russian to win the Nobel Peace Prize.

When asked why would the KGB initiate such an elaborate hoax, Vallee replied: "About fifteen years ago there was a group that suddenly appeared in San Francisco. They had a big party downtown. And they invited everybody who was anybody in parapsychology. And they made a little speech saying, '...Give us your best ideas; we will send it to a panel who will review it, and we will fund the best research.' After the party, a lot of people rushed home to their computers and typed in all their best ideas, sent it on—but the organization never existed, was never heard from again. Somebody was fishing. So having a cover as a group sometimes, a completely weird group, can be a convenient way of getting technical intelligence."[11]

Although not widely known, the FBI has on various occasions taken more than a passing interest in monitoring publications on the UFO subject. To illustrate this, June 1966 saw the first printing by Lyle Stuart Publishers of Frank Edwards's book, *Flying Saucers—Serious Business*.[12]

By October of that year, Edwards's book was in its third printing. On 16 October *The Examiner & Chronicle*, a San Francisco-based newspaper, announced that Gerald Ford, the Congressional Representative of Michigan (and later U.S. President), was pressing for Congress to look into the UFO matter. It was also announced that the U.S. Air Force had commissioned a University of Colorado physics professor named Edward U. Condon to head up an in-depth study of unidentified flying objects.

An FBI memo of 19 October 1966 stated: "...The [This World] article also points out that since last summer pressure has been mounting for the establishment of an independent, civilian controlled investigative agency to look into the UFO problem...[Edwards' book] is probably a contributing factor to the current controversy."

That both Edwards and his book were of interest to the FBI is something spelled out further in the three-page Bureau document of 19 October: "In [Flying Saucers—Serious Business] Edwards points out that flying saucers were observed in the spring of 1946, in Scandinavia and Russia (which he points out is about a year from the date of the testing of the Alamogordo atomic bomb), and the book documents many reports throughout the world of UFOs since that date, and claims that 1965 was the year of the greatest number of UFO sightings and that these were observed by multiple witnesses. It is author Edwards' contention that UFOs are space vehicles sent to observe activities on earth and the Air Force, which is charged with the responsibility of investigating UFOs, has deliberately withheld information and given misleading explanations because it fears a mass panic by the public if the public were told the truth.

"The book describes UFOs as polished metal objects, radiating heat and light (sufficient to have burned witnesses who were too near), and emitting some force field that interferes with electromagnetic instruments and power sources. Colors range from brilliant white to dull reds and brilliant orange. Some objects have carried blinking lights. There are three basic shapes: 1) Zeppelin-shaped ships up to 300 feet long; 2) disk-shaped objects ranging from a few feet in diameter to 100 feet, with many reported at about 30 feet diameter; and 3) egg-shaped objects, which according to the author are the ones most recently sighted.

"According to the book, the objects move silently and attain fantastic speeds, yet can hover motionless in mid-air; they have been reported to land and take off with great speed, usually with a burst of light from the underside, which in some cases has left the ground beneath them scorched.

"Many of the persons named in the book who have reported them are reliable individuals, including law enforcement officers, military personnel on official duty, military pilots, commercial airline pilots, civilian defense officials, etc. A number of photographs of the objects have been reproduced in the book, some reportedly taken by reputable persons. Many reported sightings are from atomic and missile research areas. Wreckage of crashed saucers has been reportedly recovered on at least three occasions, in one case described as a magnesium alloy, in another as pure magnesium, and in a third case, attributed to an official of the Canadian government, the material was described as an exceptionally hard unknown metal, which contained thousands of 15-micron spheres throughout, and showing evidence of micro-meteorites on its surface.

"A few witnesses have reported seeing crewmen who have landed from the objects, who are described as three and a half to four feet tall, wearing what appear to be space suits and helmets.

"Author Edwards concludes this book with a prediction that in the near future UFOs will make an 'overt landing' or deliberate contact with earth. A copy of this letter is being directed to Denver, in view of the contract to Dr. Edward U. Condon. The above is being called to the Bureau's attention in view of the press report of mounting pressure for a civilian controlled investigative agency to handle UFO matters."

Having discussed the issue of UFOs with a number of journalists in the mainstream media, I know that many dismiss the hypothesis that Government and intelligence agencies are taking an interest in the activities of civilian UFO researchers as little more than paranoia. Yet, as the remarkably detailed document cited above makes clear, those who enter the field of UFO research and begin publishing the details of their discoveries can expect to attract the close attention of such officials.

It is not just witnesses, authors, researchers, and lecturers that Government agencies routinely monitor with regard to the UFO puzzle. Agencies also spy upon each other when it comes to this emotive and controversial topic. A classic example can be found within the now-declassified files of the U.S. Defense Intelligence Agency (DIA). In 1967, the DIA was secretly spying on British and Russian authorities, after they learned the startling fact that the British were seeking to cooperate "with the Russians in observation teams for UFOs." That this attempt to covertly initiate a joint UK-USSR UFO project at the height of the Cold War—and at a time when the Western Alliance and the Soviet Union were certainly not on good terms—is extraordinary; but it is hardly surprising that the Americans would want to ensure they were in possession of the full facts. According to the DIA documentation at issue:

"SUMMARY:
Report includes information on Russia commission set up to study Unidentified Flying Objects. Of particular interest is the fact that at first the Russians publicized the commission, but now claim the commission has been disbanded.
REPORT:

1. In early November 1967 (exact date believed to be 10 Nov) Moscow TV presented a program on Unidentified Flying Objects. On 12 Nov 67 a Reuters release in the U.K. press (believe article was in *Daily Telegraph*) reported the TV program.

2. The essence of the TV program, and the Reuters report based on the TV program, was that the Russians had recently set up a commission to study UFOs. The Chairman of the commission is retired SAF [Soviet Air Force] Major General A.F. Stolyarov, a former Technical Services Officer. The group consisted of 18 astronomers and SAF officers plus 200 observers.

3. A day or two after the TV program, the Reuters correspondent went to see General Stolyarov. The General was very polite, confirmed the information about the commission, the 18 astronomers and SAF officers and the 200 observers. In addition, he said five positive sightings had been made.

4. Approximately a week later the Reuters correspondent went back to see General Stolyarov. However, this time the correspondent couldn't get past the General's secretary, who politely but firmly told the General was no longer available for interview.

5. On 12 December 1967, the British Embassy was directed by London to further investigate the subject with a view to cooperating with the Russians in observation teams for UFOs.

6. The Scientific Counselor of the British Embassy went to the State Committee for Science and Technology and inquired about the UFO Commission and the possibility of British-Russian cooperation in observation of UFOs. The British Counselor was politely received and the Commission was freely discussed. The British were told they would receive a reply to their request about cooperation.

7. The British did not receive an answer and did not pursue the subject. However, on 6 January 1968 while on a routine visit to the Soviet State Committee for Science and Technology, the British Scientific Counselor was told the following: The Commission for investigating UFOs had been set up in response to a popular demand. The Commission had met twice, but since there was insufficient information to sustain it the Commission would be disbanding after the next meeting.

8. The British Scientific Counselor believes that the original announcement of the work of the Commission on TV was an oversight on the part of the censors because the Commission has not been reported or referred to anywhere else. Mr. [Deleted] believes the Commission has not been disbanded, but will continue under cover. This information was sent to London.

COMMENT:

1. The preceding information was given to RO by source. RO also read confidential British files on this subject. RO did not

approach Reuters correspondent because of delicate position of source. RO was unable to find anyone in Moscow who saw TV program or read article in the UK press.

2. On 10 or 11 November 1967 the U.S. Science Attaché received a telephone call from the Reuters correspondent and was asked if he had seen the TV program. When the Science Attaché replied that he had not seen the program, the correspondent described it and asked the Science Attaché if he thought the information was worth reporting. The Science Attaché said yes. The Science Attaché, like the RO, has not seen the UK press report. The US Science Attaché will receive two copies of this report and will forward one copy to the appropriate S&T [Science & Technology] Agency in Washington."

It is a pity that the DIA report, which was prepared by Colonel Melvin J. Nielsen, does not expand upon the reference to "confidential British files on this subject." However, the fact that the Americans were keeping a close watch not just on UFOs and those members of the public implicated in the mystery to varying degrees, but were also carefully monitoring the activities of foreign governments in relation to UFOs, is extremely eye-opening.

One of the most intriguing instances of apparent official monitoring of UFO research groups in the 1950s and 1960s lies in the curious saga of the National Investigations Committee on Aerial Phenomena (NICAP) and its head, Major Donald E. Keyhoe, Marine Corps (Ret.), who unrelentingly challenged the blanket of official secrecy that was widely believed to surround the UFO subject in the 1950s. In addition, Keyhoe authored no less than five books that chronicled his battles with the Air Force as he sought to uncover the truth behind the UFO puzzle.

Although it is clear that NICAP attracted people from intelligence agencies—including the Central Intelligence Agency—who had a wholly personal interest in UFOs, the fact that so many "retired" CIA personnel did ultimately join its ranks has been viewed by many UFO commentators as not only highly suspicious, but as a clear example of outright infiltration of the organization.

As author Patrick Huyghe noted, "The CIA appears to have had a protracted interest in NICAP, which was founded in 1956 and utilized by Keyhoe as an organizational tool for challenging the alleged Air Force cover-up on UFOs. Both the CIA and the Air Force were upset by NICAP's wide-ranging influence. Its prestigious board of directors included, among others, Vice Adm. Roscoe Hillenkoetter, the first CIA director (1947–1950)."[13]

Huyghe continued, "The sixties saw further CIA interest in NICAP. After a flurry of Washington-area sightings in 1965, the agency contacted NICAP about seeing some of its case files on the matter. Richard H. Hall, then NICAP's assistant director, chatted with a CIA agent in the NICAP office about the sightings, NICAP's methodology, and Hall's background. The agent's memo on the visit suggests that the CIA had some role in mind for Hall, predicated upon his being granted a security clearance. Nothing apparently came of the suggestion. A later set of CIA papers reveals an interest in NICAP's organizational structure and notes that 'this group included some ex-CIA and Defense Intelligence types who advise on investigative techniques and NICAP-Government relations.'"[14]

Ray Fowler, a long-time UFO researcher who had filed extensive and painstakingly detailed reports with NICAP in its heyday, had interesting comments to make concerning NICAP and the official world: "NICAP seemed to tell its members that they were anti-Air Force and anti-secrecy, and pushed for Congressional hearings to expose this. On the other hand…they were also cooperating with the CIA and the Air Force. Unknown to us, the forms that were given to us to use in our investigations had been supplied by the Air Force."

Fowler added, "I lean toward the idea that there was cooperation between the government and NICAP. It would be a wonderful way to collect information…if there was serious government interest in the problem, and at least we had some evidence there was in the early days, it's logical that they would have moles within civilian groups that collect this information. It's just a logical thing to do."[15]

It was also in 1965 that the FBI became tangentially involved in an investigation that centered upon a source at the National Aeronautics and Space Administration (NASA) that was allegedly leaking classified data on UFOs to a number of flying saucer researchers in Pittsburgh. Notably, NICAP were referenced in the FBI's investigative files on this case. Although heavily censored, the currently available documentation suggests that the data was of a highly sensational nature and that the FBI was keeping a close watch on the situation. It reads as follows:

"On August 9, 1965, a source advised that the [Deleted] which has headquarters at [Deleted], Washington, D.C., 20036, has an informal chapter in Pittsburgh, Pa. [Deleted], an [sic] University of Pittsburgh graduate student, and one [Deleted] are members of the Pittsburgh organization. They are acquainted with a NASA employee, one [Deleted] (phonetic), and have stated that he furnishes them information by mail about unidentified flying objects (UFO) which he obtains from NASA files. The source believes that the information furnished may be classified. The source said, for example, that [Deleted] had seen a motion picture film showing a missile separation and an [sic] UFO appearing on the screen. Prior to the flight of Gemini 4, [Deleted] informed [Deleted] to watch out for something interesting because the space ship had devices aboard to detect UFOs. [Deleted] furnished the information received from [Deleted] to the headquarters of the National Investigations Committee on Aerial Phenomena. [Deleted] have informed the source that [Deleted] posts his letters in a mail box away from NASA and puts hairs in the glue of the envelope so that the addressee can determine of the envelope was opened. This source stated he had no reason to believe that the information secured by [Deleted] was going to any foreign power."

Here, then, is further proof that both the CIA and the FBI were closely watching the activities of NICAP in the mid-1960s.

Following Keyhoe's forced resignation from NICAP in December 1969 by its Board of Governors, a new leadership took control. As the author and researcher Richard Dolan observed, "John L. Acuff, an outsider to NICAP and not a UFO researcher, was suddenly elected to serve on NICAP's board. In May 1970, he became the new director. For some time, Acuff had been executive director of the Washington-based Society of Photographic Scientists and Engineers (SPSE). SPSE had already cooperated with NICAP informally in the area of photographic analysis. It was later discovered that SPSE had significant intelligence connections: many members were photo-analysts within the various intelligence components of the Department of Defense and CIA. The group had also been the target of KGB espionage."[16]

In a 1979 article written for *The New York Times Magazine*, Patrick Huyghe noted that "There are presently three former CIA employees on the NICAP board of directors, including Charles Lombard, a congressional aide to Senator Barry Goldwater, who is himself a NICAP board member; and retired U.S. Air Force Col. Joseph Bryan III. Bryan feels, as he did back in 1959 when he joined the board, that UFOs are interplanetary. NICAP's current president is Alan Hall, a former CIA covert employee for 30 years."[17]

Serious mismanagement problems would ultimately lead to the downfall of NICAP—the one organization more than any other that had caused major headaches for officials when it came to the UFO controversy. Some would argue that the downfall of NICAP had been the ultimate intent of the CIA from the beginning.

If the following case is not a hoax—and I personally do not believe it to be so—then, in early 1974, officials engaged in saucer spying had the tables turned on them when alien visitors were apparently doing some secret surveillance of their own. The date was early 1974 and the setting was the Marconi facility at Frimley, England. At the time of the event, Hannah Green was employed in the facility's Central Services Branch—having previously served an apprenticeship in the Royal Navy.

On arrival at work one particular morning, she was surprised to see an inordinate number of Ministry of Defense personnel swarming around one specific building that had been cordoned off. Although she was aware that something of significance had occurred, it was not until later that she was able to tackle a trusted colleague, who was a manager at the base.

"Something very serious has happened, hasn't it?" asked Green.

"Yes," came the reply. "We've had a break in; I can't say anymore."

Over the course of the next few weeks, further pieces of the puzzle began to fall into place. It transpired that the break-in was much more that simply an unauthorized entry. What had supposedly occurred was nothing less than the penetration of a guarded research station by a living, breathing extraterrestrial creature.

Green stated that the incident occurred at night, and the prime witness was a security guard who had been patrolling the building as part of his routine duty. While walking along a particular corridor, the guard was startled by a dazzling, blue light that emanated from a room. But this was no ordinary room: it was a storage facility for Top Secret documentation generated by Marconi as part of its work on behalf of the British Government, much of which related to classified radar-related defense projects.

Realizing that no one should have been within that area at that late hour the guard burst into the room and was confronted by a shocking scene: there, literally sifting through pages of classified files, was a humanoid (but distinctly nonhuman) entity that quickly dematerialized before the guard's eyes. Although severely traumatized by the event, he was able to give a description of the being to his superiors, and noted that the blue light emanated from a helmet that encompassed the head of the being.

By the following morning, the guard had suffered a near-complete nervous collapse and was taken—under military guard—to an unspecified hospital for intensive therapy. He was not seen again. Some weeks later, Green had occasion to overhear snippets of a conversation that took place within the office of her superior, a Mr. Bevan. According to Green, the conversation went along the lines of, "We have no way of keeping these beings out; we just don't know what to do next. If they can get in here, they can get in anywhere."[18]

Are James Bond-style extraterrestrial-spies infiltrating our most protected research stations and stealing our defense secrets? As outlandish as such a theory may sound, it does receive a degree of support from official sources. For example, consider the following, extracted from a 1972 report titled "Controlled Offensive Behavior— USSR," that was prepared for the U.S. Defense Intelligence Agency:

"...Before the end of the 1970s, Soviet diplomats will be able to sit in their foreign embassies and use ESP (extrasensory perception) to steal the secrets of their enemies...a spy would be hypnotized, then his invisible 'spirit' would be ordered to leave his body, travel across barriers of space and time to a foreign government's secure facility, and there read top-secret documents and relay back their information... the Soviets are at least 25 years ahead of the us in psychic research... [and] have realized the immense military advantage of the psychic ability known as astral projection (out-of-the-body travel)."[19]

Bizarre? Most definitely, but military agencies throughout the globe are always keen to exploit new and radical intelligence-gathering techniques. The method described above is simply one of many that have been examined by the Governments of the United States, the United Kingdom, and the former Soviet Union. Perhaps elsewhere in the universe, such techniques were perfected centuries ago to the extent that a living organism can now literally come and go at will, completely unhindered by our seemingly rigid, physical laws.

On the night of 26 September 1974 a father and son, Walter and Dan Richley, saw a strange object hovering high above their farm in Lynchburg, Ohio. Since there was a powerful searchlight mounted on the family's pickup truck, Walter and Dan decided—"as an experiment"—to try to get a better view of this object that was taking so much interest in their farm.

As the beam of light touched the UFO, the Richleys found themselves bathed in an equally bright beam of red light that emanated from the craft. Frightened out of their wits, both father and son ran for the safety of their home. As they did so, the UFO began to retreat over the horizon until it finally disappeared from view. At 11:00 p.m. on the following night, Dan was sitting up in bed reading, when he was suddenly jolted by a loud noise coming from outside. As he ran to the window he was amazed to see a large helicopter descending.

"I then got dad out of bed," said Dan. Mr. Richley quickly assessed the meaning of the helicopter's presence: "I think I put my light beam on something that was a military secret. That 'copter came here to warn me." UFO researcher Leonard Stringfield, who conducted a personal investigation of the case, asked Walter Richley if he had received an apology for the damage caused by the helicopter as it blew debris around his yard. "No, and I'm not about to press it; I'd rather forget it," replied Richley. It is highly likely that Richley's suspicions were correct: the military was letting him know in a distinctly less than subtle fashion that this was an incident he would be wise to forget.[20]

6

COSMIC KIDNAPPERS

I f extraterrestrials are indeed visiting the Earth, then the biggest question of all must surely be: Why are they here? Countless theories have been posited: to destroy us, to offer us spiritual guidance, to plunder our planet for its resources, or to one day invite us to join what some believe to be a galactic federation or brotherhood—not unlike that suggested by elements of the Contactee movement of the 1950s. However, many UFO researchers suspect that the definitive answers to the ongoing UFO presence will be found within the truly astonishing body of data that exists on the so-called "alien abduction" mystery.

Determining when the first alleged alien abduction of a human being occurred is no easy task. Most scholars within the field would probably agree that the phenomenon was relatively unknown until 19 September 1961. On that night Betty and Barney Hill, a married couple from New Hampshire, were driving home from Canada when they were subjected to a terrifying experience. Until their arrival home, there was little to indicate that anything untoward had happened during the journey. It later transpired, however, that approximately two hours could not be accounted for. After some months of emotional distress, the couple sought assistance from Benjamin Simon, a Boston-based psychiatrist and neurologist. Subjected to time-regression hypnosis, both Betty and Barney recalled what had taken place during that missing two hours. Astonishingly,

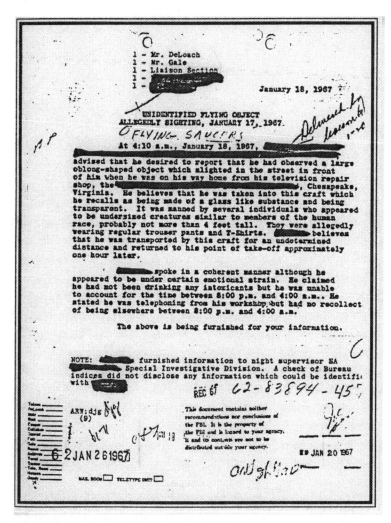

1 - Mr. DeLoach
1 - Mr. Gale
1 - Liaison Section
1 -
1 -

January 18, 1967

UNIDENTIFIED FLYING OBJECT
ALLEGEDLY SIGHTING, JANUARY 17, 1967.

O FLYING SAUCERS

At 4:10 a.m., January 18, 1967,

advised that he desired to report that he had observed a large
oblong-shaped object which alighted in the street in front
of him when he was on his way home from his television repair
shop, the ████████████████████████████████, Chesapeake,
Virginia. He believes that he was taken into this craft which
he recalls as being made of a glass like substance and being
transparent. It was manned by several individuals who appeared
to be undersized creatures similar to members of the human
race, probably not more than 4 feet tall. They were allegedly
wearing regular trouser pants and T-Shirts. ████████ believes
that he was transported by this craft for an undetermined
distance and returned to his point of take-off approximately
one hour later.

████████ spoke in a coherent manner although he
appeared to be under certain emotional strain. He claimed
he had not been drinking any intoxicants but he was unable
to account for the time between 8:00 p.m. and 4:00 a.m.. He
stated he was telephoning from his workshop but had no recollect
of being elsewhere between 8:00 p.m. and 4:00 a.m.

The above is being furnished for your information.

NOTE: ████████ furnished information to night supervisor SA
████████ Special Investigative Division. A check of Bureau
indices did not disclose any information which could be identifie
with ████.

REC 61 62-83894-45

ARV:djg
(9)

This document contains neither
recommendations nor conclusions of
the FBI. It is the property of
the FBI and is loaned to your agency.
It and its contents are not to be
distributed outside your agency.

62 JAN 26 1967

MAIL ROOM ☐ TELETYPE UNIT ☐

59 JAN 20 1967

Officials have created files on alleged abductees since at least 1967.

they provided very close accounts of encounters with alien beings who had taken the pair on board some form of craft and who had subjected them to a variety of physical examinations.[1]

Since that day, literally hundreds of similar accounts have appeared throughout the world. A turning point came in 1981 with the publication of Budd Hopkins's book, *Missing Time*. Detailing a number of accounts, Hopkins put forward a strong case suggesting that at least one extraterrestrial species was involved in the routine abduction of human beings. Hopkins's later work revealed a potentially more sinister link to the abductions namely, that the aliens were taking people as a part of some genetic operation, the goal of which was the production of a half-alien, half-human hybrid race.[2]

What is perhaps more remarkable than the abduction events is something that has a direct bearing on the theme of this book: the official surveillance of abductees by a whole variety of Government, Military, and Intelligence agencies. One of the most interesting events comes from Tammy, who was abducted at the age of twenty-four on 6 March 1973 near Waco, Texas. Tammy was later plunged into a bizarre world packed with Government spooks, phone-tapping operations, and intense monitoring not only of her but of her family as well. Today, Tammy is a fifty-seven-year-old grandmother, who, with her husband and daughter, manages a modestly sized restaurant in El Paso. Three decades on, she is comfortable about discussing her apparent out-of-this-world experience; and she has, to her credit, learned to accept it and move on with her life.

It all began when Tammy was finishing her late-night shift as a waitress at a diner that was situated around 25 to 30 miles from Waco. It was 2:00 a.m. on the date in question, and she was headed toward the city to her small apartment. On a quiet stretch of road, and after having driven for perhaps 15 minutes, Tammy began to "feel strange." The engine of the car seemed muffled, a slight sense of dizziness or light-headedness came over her, which was suddenly—

and alarmingly—followed by a violent feeling of intense vertigo. Despite feeling distinctly ill, Tammy told me she tried to get back to the comfort and safety of her home. However, her plans were suddenly changed—and changed radically. Without warning a bright glow enveloped the car, its headlights and engine failed, sharp pains surged throughout Tammy's body, and, fighting nausea brought on by the vertigo, she brought her vehicle to a quick halt on the shoulder of the road.

But that was the least of her worries. Situated in a field to the right of her at a distance of a couple of hundred feet was a small domed-shaped object that looked pale pink. From it, two small humanlike figures were heading toward her. Tammy scrambled to open the door and make a run for it. Alarmingly, as the creatures closed in, she began to feel very drowsy and her arms and legs began to feel weak and unresponsive. The next thing she knew, dawn was breaking and she was sitting in the front passenger seat of her car.

Scared, disoriented, and still feeling groggy, she headed home, took a long bath and collapsed into a long deep sleep. It was around 9:00 p.m. that night that she finally awoke. Tammy elected to tell no one about what had occurred, and aside from having a vague memory of seeing the strange object in the field and the two figures that approached her from it, she had no real recollection of anything substantial. Yet over the course of the next few nights, she would have a series of vivid dreams that seemed to fill in the blanks.

The dreams would always be the same. Tammy would see the figures approach the car. As they closed in, she could see that they were around five feet in height and had "thin faces and cheeks." They were both dressed identically in light blue, one-piece "uniforms" and a tight-fitting cap. In the dreams, Tammy could only sit in the car unable to move as one of the figures opened the driver's side door. The two of them then hauled her out of the car, and carried her by her ankles and wrists to the craft. Tammy's next memory was of being stripped of her clothes and laid out on a cold hard table with five or six similar "people" standing around her. She recalled that some sort of metallic object—"like a lead-colored tube"—was placed into her vagina. There was no direct pain associated with the procedure but there was a feeling of discomfort, which lasted until the device was removed several minutes later. A similar but much smaller device was placed into her right nostril and again removed after a few minutes. All this time, a large device "like a big eye" hovered over the table. A deep, continuous, resonating hum emanated from the "eye." Tammy's next recollection was of being dressed, then carried back to the car and placed into the passenger seat. She also had a vague recollection of a man in a military uniform sitting in the driver's seat looking intently at her. At this point the dream would usually end.

Over the course of the next few weeks, Tammy began to experience a completely different type of dream: a vivid, nightmarish vision of a truly apocalyptical nature. The dream depicted that Earth in the near future would be reduced to ruins from a combination of localized atomic skirmishes, pollution, over-population, starvation, and the ravages of a manufactured lethal virus that had laid waste much of the Middle East and was now spiraling out of control and spreading fast across the rest of the planet. Judgment Day, Armageddon, the end of all things, and a disturbing afterlife in which various gray-like entities of several types fed—vampire-style—on human souls dominated Tammy's every sleeping moment. But even stranger things were to follow.

About three weeks after her experience, Tammy received a knock on the door of her apartment at midday. When she opened the door a man dressed in a brown suit stood before her. Tammy said, "He could have passed for a marine—a big guy, very short hair." The man said that he was doing a "survey" for the police department on car crime and flashed an identity card at her that, Tammy added, "looked real, but back then I was real quiet and I should have asked to see it again, close up, but didn't."

Tammy felt somewhat uncomfortable and declined to let him in. So, looming over her in the doorway, the man fired off a whole series of questions: "Have you been the victim of car crime in the last month?" "How long have you owned you car?" and, most intriguing of all: "Are you concerned about being kidnapped from your car?" It was this latter question that particularly unnerved Tammy and she slammed the door shut with the man still shouting questions from the other side.

"I'm calling the police," she shouted, at which point the questions ceased. Some time later, Tammy opened the door and the man was gone. In the weeks that followed, she said, two other people called on her on three occasions. Both were "military men, but not in uniforms," said Tammy, adding, "they were real friendly with me and identified who they were and where they were from—Kirtland Air Force Base [which is situated in New Mexico]." According to Tammy, one of the men admitted that her previous visitor had been "with us" but that he had "gone way over the top." The pair apologized for his actions and then came the true bombshell: they knew about the abduction experience that Tammy had undergone and asked if they could discuss it with her.

"They were real friendly and okay with me," said Tammy, "and made me feel okay about talking to them." According to Tammy, her two visitors entrusted in her some startling facts: over the course of the previous twenty years, sporadic reports had reached officials that suggested that human beings—across the entire planet—had been kidnapped by otherworldly entities for purposes unknown. However, they added, since 1971, such kidnappings were increasing at alarming rates, and particularly in New Mexico, Texas, and Arizona. As a result, the military had established a highly secret operation to monitor not just UFO activity in these particular states but abductees, too, as part of a specific effort to determine the motives behind the "kidnappings." At the time, said Tammy, "they never mentioned the word abductions like you hear today—just kidnappings."

The men impressed upon Tammy that if she cooperated in answering their questions, she would be helping resolve an issue that was one of profound concern from a national security perspective. "So I said yes," explained Tammy. With her consent obtained, the pair reeled off a number of truly strange questions: Since the "kidnapping" had Tammy felt the urge to become vegetarian? Was she an adherent of Buddhist teachings? Did she believe in life after death, or had her views on the subject changed or been modified "since the kidnapping"? And most disturbing of all: Was she of the opinion that after death "we would all be judged by a higher-power?"

An amazed Tammy proceeded to tell the two Air Force men about her nightmares. They, in turn, expressed deep concern and confided in her that a number of other kidnapped citizens had been discreetly approached "by the project" and had told similar stories. This would lead to alarming developments. Tammy said that her mysterious visitors guardedly informed her that some of the personnel at Kirtland who were working on this particular surveillance operation of abductees were convinced that the kidnappings were the work of aliens. Others, however, had concluded that the "aliens" were in reality something very different: that they were deceptive, demonic beings whose point of origin was somehow connected with the realm of the dead and the afterlife, and that the creatures derived sustenance from the human life force—namely, the soul.

Tammy also learned of a dark and disturbing scenario: senior figures within the U.S. Intelligence community were convinced that these creatures were manipulating and infiltrating human society. They speculated that creatures were kidnapping and "programming" people for specific future tasks and that the ultimate intent was to bring on a nuclear Armageddon. This, they thought, would allow the beings to then "harvest" and feast upon the souls of the— potentially—billions of people that would be killed in the radioactive holocaust. Of most concern to Tammy to this very day is the fact that the Air Force men advised her that certain people within the U.S. political arena had been kidnapped by the creatures, and that "after their return" they were "speaking about the apocalypse, the end of the world, and why we needed to attack Russia quickly, while we had the chance." The stark reality, Tammy was told, was that the ultimate aim of these "aliens" was to deliberately try and instigate World War III. Then, when the carnage was over, their immense "soul-feeding" would begin in earnest.

The two men asked Tammy—"I was never ordered, only asked," —if she would be willing to undergo a thorough physical examination at Kirtland. Tammy said yes, and met the men at her home on two more occasions. Again questions were asked about the nature of her dreams, her thoughts on life after death, and—notably—her views on life after death in the animal kingdom. Ultimately, the physical examination never occurred and, after the last meeting, Tammy never heard from them again. She did experience something else: countless interruptions on her telephone for several more weeks from strange, rapid, and unintelligible voices that unnerved her considerably.

To this day she continues to muse upon her bizarre experience and asked me, "Do you remember how Reagan was obsessed with aliens and was always talking about them? Then he wanted to get that Star Wars system? I remember how he was into all that stuff about the end of the world and astrology, too. I think he could have been one of those politicians the Air Force told me about who the aliens—or whatever they are—had gotten to, and that he really wanted to start the War." A sobering thought.[3]

In the early-to-mid-1990s, researcher Ray Boeche established contact with two operatives from the Department of Defense who wanted to discuss his research into eschatology—a branch of theology that is concerned with such issues as death, judgement, heaven and hell, and the end of all things. Those same two DoD operatives later contacted the investigator and author Linda Howe, and advised her that the "non-human entities" or NHEs (as they described the beings that have become popularly known as the Grays) were both manipulative and deceptive. The pair, however, declined to elaborate upon the issue of precisely what the beings were and where they were from. They did state that, "The ultimate diversionary tactic…is the UFO abduction scenario. The concept of these events, real though they are, being the result of extra-terrestrial beings is a masterful piece of disinformation to divert attention away from the real source of the NHEs…the causal source of the UFO and UFO abduction phenomena is not extra-terrestrial." Disturbingly, Howe was advised that the NHEs were "neither benevolent nor neutral." Whatever the true nature and origin of the NHEs, Howe's and Boeche's informants were certain that a "grand deception" was in place that was most definitely not going to benefit the human race.[4]

We may never know whether or not Tammy was subjected to official disinformation, or if her mysterious visitors from Kirtland were honest with her about the nature of the abduction mystery. But what seems certain is that, at an official level, someone—or some entity—is keeping a close watch on those seemingly abducted by otherworldly visitors. Before we leave Tammy's case, it is worth noting that the FBI has declassified a document that may have a direct bearing on her experiences.

According to the document, on 9 March 1973—only three days after Tammy's experience—a Sergeant Stigliano of the USAF's Recruiting Office at Waco informed the San Antonio FBI that an individual (not identified in declassified FBI memoranda) had contacted the night shift supervisor at a Waco-based newspaper, and had "inquired regarding any information [the newspaper] could be able to furnish him concerning any unidentified flying objects observed in the Waco, Texas, area."

Sergeant Stigliano continued that the individual had identified himself as a captain in the U.S. Air Force and had in his possession a folder marked Top Secret that contained photographs of various military installations. "No specific information concerning these photos could be provided by Sergeant Stigliano," reported the FBI at San Antonio, adding, "The individual did not act in any strange manner, and did not attempt to obtain anything other than information from the newspaper. Sergeant Stigliano advised that this information was being furnished to the proper authorities only for information purposes as they do not suspect any unlawful activity."

Taking into consideration that this occurred only three days after Tammy's experience and in her home city of Waco, the possibility cannot be dismissed that the unknown "captain in the U.S. Air Force" may very well have been one of Tammy's mysterious visitors.

On 5 May 1973, only two months after Tammy's experience, Myrna Hansen was driving to her Eagle's Nest, New Mexico, home from a trip to Oklahoma along with her young son. Hansen suddenly found herself in a nightmarish world. Under hypnosis she recalled a classic alien abduction in which she was taken on board a UFO, undressed, and subjected to a physical examination. While on board she also witnessed a "struggling cow sucked up into its underside in some sort of 'tractor beam.' " More controversially, Hansen stated that after the abduction, she had been taken to an underground base, had seen "body parts" floating in vats, and felt that some sort of "device" had been implanted in her body so that the aliens could monitor and control her thoughts. When details of Hansen's description of the underground base were relayed to Kirtland Air Force Base security, it was immediately recognized that she was describing a classified section of one of its facilities: the Manzano Weapons Storage Complex, at the time the largest underground repository of nuclear weapons in the Western world. Here, then, was another case that linked Kirtland Air Force Base with alien abductions in 1973.[5]

It will be recalled that in Tammy's case (as in numerous so-called alien abductions), her experience occurred on a quiet stretch of road late at night after her car engine mysteriously failed. Subsequently, she received a firsthand visit from officials deeply interested in her experience. There are several officially documented examples from Britain where military personnel have undertaken firsthand, personal investigations of so-called "vehicle interference" UFO events that have occurred late at night and in the early hours of the morning. Perhaps the apparent pressing need to officially investigate these cases in person was due to a suspicion that they may have been part of a bigger abduction-style event that had been erased from—or buried deep within—the minds of the witnesses in a typical "missing-time" scenario. Consider the following document prepared by Sergeant C.J. Perry of the British Royal Air Force Police in 1962:

"At Aylesbury on 16th February, 1962 at 1530 hours I visited the Civil Police and requested information on an alleged 'Flying Saucer' incident. I was afforded every facility by the Civil Police authorities and although no official report had been made, details of the incident were recorded in the Station Occurrence book.

"The details are as follows: Mr. Ronald Wildman of Luton, a car collection driver, was traveling along the Aston Clinton road at about 0330 hrs. on 9th February 1962 when he came across an object like a hovercraft flying approximately 30 feet above the road surface. As he approached he was traveling at 40 mph but an unknown force slowed him down to 20 mph over a distance of 400 yards, then the object suddenly flew off. He described the object as being about 40 feet wide, oval in shape with a number of small portholes around the bottom edge. It emitted a fluorescent glow but was otherwise not illuminated.

"Mr. Wildman reported the incident to a police patrol who notified the Duty Sergeant, Sergeant Schofield. A radio patrol car was dispatched to the area but no further trace of the 'Flying Saucer' was seen. It was the opinion of the local police that the report by Mr. Wildman was perfectly genuine and the experience was not a figment of imagination. They saw that he was obviously shaken. I spoke to Sergeant Schofield and one of the Constables to whom the incident was reported. Both were convinced that Mr. Wildman was genuinely upset by his experience."

A copy of Sergeant Perry's report was forwarded to the Air Ministry, who, in its two-page report on the case, admitted that, "… this incident is one for which there can be no indisputable solution." In response to newspaper inquiries, the Air Ministry ventured the possibility that Wildman had merely viewed a cloud illuminated by the headlights of his car. This suggestion was not accepted by Wildman, who was convinced that he had seen a solid object of some sort: "It was oval-shaped and white with black marks at regular intervals round it, which could have been portholes or air vents. It was about twenty to thirty feet above the ground and at least forty feet wide across [sic], which in my estimation was fantastic. The object, which was silent, kept ahead of me by approximately twenty feet for 200 yards, then started to come lower. It continued like this till it came to the end of the stretch. Then a white haze appeared round it, like a halo round the moon. It veered off to the right at a terrific speed and vanished; as it did so it brushed particles of frost from the treetops on to my windscreen. It was definitely a solid object because the reflection of my headlights was thrown back from it."[6]

Four years later, British officials were still undertaking firsthand investigations of late night UFO encounters where the witness had reported a degree of vehicle interference. In a painstakingly detailed report, Corporal R.A. Rickwood of the Provost and Security Services (P&SS) Special Investigation Section related to his superiors the facts concerning a UFO incident he had personally investigated in late 1966:

"On 10th November 1966 a telephone message was received from Flight Lieutenant Williams, RAF Shawbury, reporting that a Mrs. Foulkes of White House Cottage, Great Ness, Shrewsbury, had complained that her daughter had been frightened by an object in the sky while she had been driving along the A5 road near Great Ness at 2355 hours on 8th November 1966. This object had emitted brilliant lights and radiation beams. On arriving home her daughter had been in a distressed condition and she had discovered marks on the car, which she considered were burn marks. On 14th November 1966, Miss Diane Foulkes, aged 22 years, a typist employed in Shrewsbury was seen at her home in the presence of her parents. She stated that she had received a letter dated 11th November 1966 from RAF Shawbury signed by a Flight Lieutenant Penny informing her that no service aircraft had been flying in that area at the time of the incident. She was now satisfied that the incident was in no way connected with the Royal Air Force or the Armed Forces. She then went on to relate her experiences connected with this enquiry. There had been two similar incidents. The first occurred two years ago in November 1964, when she had been driving from Shrewsbury to her home along the A5 road. This was at about 0200 hours as she neared the Montford Bridge over the River Severn. Approximately midway between Shrewsbury and Great Ness a brightly lit circular object appeared in the sky above her car. She had been frightened and had accelerated along the road. The object had kept pace with her remaining at the same height until she arrived home. She had told her mother and father who also watched the object. She described the object as an especially bright light in the sky which remained stationary due west from their home for about half an hour. It had then rapidly diminished in size and they assumed it had accelerated away from them. No sound was heard from the object. The light was yellow in color and became red as it diminished.

"The second incident occurred on the 8th November 1966 at 2355 hours and again while she was returning from Shrewsbury on the same road. The object had again appeared at Montford Bridge but this time it was much lower in the sky and on the north side of the road. On this occasion she could see rays of light shooting from the object which had again appeared to keep station with her car until she arrived home. At one time during the journey the object traveled near her and the rays seemed to come towards the right hand side of her car. She felt a bump against that side as if they had struck it. At this moment she felt as if she had received an electric shock and had felt a severe pain in her neck. The left-hand side headlight of the car also went out. This made her extremely frightened. When she got home she felt very ill and had complained to her parents. The object again remained stationary in the sky north of her home and had not been seen initially by her parents. They had noticed it for a short time before going inside her home. There had been no sign of the object on the following morning.

"Miss Foulkes's parents confirmed seeing an object in the sky on both occasions as described by their daughter and agreed with her descriptions of these. Miss Foulkes further stated that she believed that the objects could be associated with a Mr. Griffin who lived in the area and who is reputed to have made contact with these objects and actually entered one and met one of the occupants. He is also alleged to make his contacts with them at Montford Bridge.

"The local civil police had no information or reports of sightings of objects in the sky. There is no evidence to associate the incidents complained of with the Royal Air Force and the complainant Miss Foulkes is now satisfied that the incidents are unexplainable and are in no way connected with the Armed Forces."[7]

Key aspects of this case very closely parallel those of Tammy's experience: the light that enveloped the car of the witness; the electric shock-like pain that surged through her neck as the vehicle was bathed in the beam of light; the loss of power from the car's headlights; the comment to the effect that the encounter had left the witness feeling "very ill"; and the significant fact that she was interviewed at her home by military officials. Also, the Provost and Security Services' reference to a "Mr. Griffin" who had reputedly "made contact with these objects and actually entered one and met the occupants," sounds like a classic example of official interest in alien abduction-style events.

In the United States, official documents that demonstrate interest in alien abductions are rare—publicly, at least—but they do exist. Such an example can be found within the archives of the FBI. Dated 18 January 1967 one document states: "At 4:10 a.m., January 18, 1967 [witness' name and address deleted by the FBI] advised that he desired to report that he had observed a large oblong-shaped object which alighted in the street in front of him when he was on his way home from his television repair shop, the [deleted], Chesapeake, Virginia. He believes that he was taken into this craft which he recalls as being made of a glass like substance and being transparent. It was manned by several individuals who appeared to be undersized creatures similar to members of the human race, probably no more than 4 feet tall. They were allegedly wearing regular trouser pants and T-shirts. [Deleted] believes that he was transported by this craft for an undetermined distance and returned to his point of take-off approximately one hour later.

"[Deleted] spoke in a coherent manner although he appeared to be under certain emotional strain. He claimed he had not been drinking any intoxicants but he was unable to account for the time between 8:00 p.m. and 4:00 a.m. He stated he was telephoning from his workshop but had no recollect of being elsewhere between 8:00 p.m. and 4:00 a.m."

Although the reference to the creatures' humanlike attire is highly curious, this particular official report contains all of the ingredients of what has become known as the typical alien abduction: the initial sighting of a UFO; a period of missing time; recollections of small, apparently alien beings; and the transfer of the witness to an object or craft. Of potential significance is a note attached to the FBI report that shows a copy was forwarded to another agency for study. To this day, the identity of that agency—most probably a department of the Air Force—has not been revealed.

Betty Andreasson, an abductee whose experiences have been chronicled at length by researcher and author Raymond Fowler, has also been the subject of apparent official monitoring. In early 1980, when UFO investigator Larry Fawcett was working as the chief investigator for Ray Fowler on the book *The Andreasson Affair: Phase Two*, mystery helicopter events plagued Betty and her husband, Bob Luca. According to Fawcett and his writing partner, Barry Greenwood, "They reported that their home was over flown numerous times by black, unmarked helicopters of the Huey UH-1H type and that these helicopters would fly over their home at altitudes as low as 100 feet. The Luca's described these helicopters as being black in color, with no identifiable marking on them. They noticed that the windows were tinted black also, so that no one could see inside. During many of the over flights, Bob was able to take close to 200 photos of the helicopters."

On 8 May 1982 Bob Luca sent a letter to the Army's Office of the Adjutant General demanding an answer as to why he and Betty were being subjected to such low-level and repeated visitations by the mystery helicopters. The only response came from the Army's Adjutant General, Major General John F. Gore, who stated: "It is difficult to determine what particular aircraft is involved or the owning unit."[8]

Abductee Debbie Jordan, who has reported longstanding alien abduction experiences with an apparent genetic link, has also been harassed and monitored by the mysterious helicopters: "These... could be seen almost daily around our houses. They are so obvious about their flights it's almost comical. On occasions too numerous to even remember, they have hovered around my house, above my house, and above me for several minutes at a time, not trying to hide themselves or the fact that they are watching us. Even when I am outside and obviously watching back, it doesn't seem to bother them. They just sit there in midair, about sixty-to-ninety feet above the ground, whirling and watching. They are completely without identification and are always low enough so that I could easily see the pilot, if the windshield were clear glass. But the windshield is smoky black, with a finish that makes it impossible to see who's inside."[9]

From the investigator Peter Hough comes a truly remarkable account of alien abduction that resulted in official surveillance of—and interest in—the witness. Of the many and varied cases that Hough has investigated, one concerns a police officer, "Philip Spencer," who in 1987 literally stumbled across an apparent alien creature on Ilkley Moor, Yorkshire, England. While there is some evidence to suggest that Spencer had suffered a degree of "missing time" that was somehow tied in with an "abduction"-style experience, the most notable aspect of the controversy was an amazing piece of evidence that Spencer had at his disposal: a solitary photograph displaying a small, dark-colored creature striding up a grassy slope on the moors.

In an attempt to try and determine what had occurred during the period of missing time, Spencer was hypnotically regressed and recalled being taken on board a "big silver-like saucer thing" where he underwent some form of examination and was given a warning about a future ecological disaster that would affect the Earth.

The regression allowed Spencer to accurately recall in his mind the image of the alien: "It's quite small. It's about four-foot [tall]. He's got big pointed ears; it's got big eyes. They're quite dark. He hasn't got a nose. He's only got a little mouth. And his hands are enormous, and his arms are long. He's got funny feet. They're like a V-shape, like two big toes. It's got three big fingers, like sausages. Big sausages."

But that was not all. On a Friday evening in January 1988, events took an even stranger turn. Hearing a knock at his front door, Spencer opened it and found "two middle-aged men dressed smartly in business suits." Both flashed Ministry of Defense identity cards bearing the names Jefferson and Davies.

Spencer invited the men in and listened as Jefferson announced that they had come to interview him about his UFO experience. Even odder was the fact that Spencer had only discussed his encounter with three civilian UFO investigators; yet the men from the Ministry apparently knew all about his experience and fired off a barrage of pointed questions and demands at the perplexed officer: "Tell us about your UFO sighting. Did you take any photographs?"

Perhaps mindful of the fact that he was dealing with officialdom, Spencer admitted to taking one photograph, but stated that it was in the possession of "a friend" (in reality, the negative was in Peter Hough's hands at the time in question). With this, the two men lost all interest in further communication and quickly left as mysteriously as they had arrived. "Was this because they realized they were too late to retrieve Spencer's evidence of his abduction?" asks Peter Hough, perceptively. To this day, where Jefferson and Davies really came from remains a mystery.[10]

Melinda Leslie claims to have experienced classic abductions undertaken by aliens since 1993, as well as follow-up abductions undertaken by elements of the U.S. Military. As an example, she states that in November 1993 she was kidnapped and drugged by two men dressed in camouflage who took her to an unknown military facility. There, she was interrogated by a red-haired officer who was not only deeply interested in her alien abduction experiences, but in any data that she could supply on the aliens' technology: "What have they asked you?" the officer demanded to know. "Tell me about their technology. Tell me about the drive system, the drive mechanism. You tell me about what they told you to do. What did they ask you to do? Tell me, tell me, tell me. You know you are not theirs; you are ours." After the interrogation, Leslie said that she was taken—by military personnel—to a hangar where she saw large, unmarked helicopters, before being released.[11]

Similarly, Casey Turner, the husband of the late abductee Karla

Turner, stated that on one occasion he was drugged and transported to an underground installation and subjected to an in-depth interrogation by military personnel. Also, according to Turner, there were a number of other people there—all drugged for interrogation. Turner added, "They are all sitting there, sort of in a daze...I keep getting the feeling that there's a military officer who's real angry... I'm not cooperating and they're real perplexed...I get the feeling they want to know, maybe they're trying to find out what it is we know..."[12]

UFO researcher Greg Bishop has an interesting account to relate concerning Karla Turner: "Mail tampering is the darling of clinical paranoids, but nearly every piece of mail that the late researcher/abductee Karla Turner sent to [my] PO Box looked like it had been tampered with or opened. Since this is easy to do without having to be obvious, we figured someone was interested in her work enough to make it clear that she was being monitored. She took to putting a piece of transparent tape over the flap and writing 'sealed by sender' on it. Karla pretty much took it for granted after awhile, and suggested I do likewise."[13]

While there are literally dozens of similar accounts on record that suggest deep and ongoing surveillance of abductees, for our purposes one more will suffice. From Irene Bott, formerly the president of Britain's Staffordshire UFO Group, there comes a notable account, implicating the Men in Black in the alien abduction controversy.

Shortly after establishing her group in 1995, Bott found herself in a situation involving a witness to a UFO encounter—a witness who may very well have also undergone a period of so-called "missing time." The witness desired to learn more about what had happened and contacted Bott. He told her that he saw a brightly lit aerial object one morning in 1995.

The witness was certain that there was far more to the case than he could consciously recollect, and requested help in unraveling what had taken place. As a result, Bott referred the witness to a colleague in her group and the two discussed the details over the telephone. Shortly after returning home from work one day, the witness found that a note had been pushed through his letterbox warning him not to proceed further with his investigation.

Naturally concerned, the man asked his neighbors if they had seen anyone lurking in the vicinity of his house that might have conceivably been responsible for the strange and somewhat unsettling note. Fortunately, one such neighbor had seen something unusual that day. After the witness had set off for work, a black car had pulled up outside his house. A man dressed entirely in black who carried a briefcase exited the vehicle, marched up the driveway, shoved a piece of paper through the letterbox, returned to the car, and drove off at a high speed. One of our mysterious abduction monitors had struck again.[14]

The cases cited above seem to demonstrate that there are officials who are interested in unexplained alien abduction incidents. There is, however, another aspect—one that is in some ways even more controversial than the extraterrestrial angle. There are those who think that alien abductions actually have nothing whatsoever to do with the activities of real extraterrestrials, but are the result of clandestine work undertaken by the U.S. Military. The military uses the alien abduction motif as a carefully camouflaged cover to allow for the testing of new technologies, mind-controlling drugs, and sophisticated hypnotic techniques on unwitting citizens.

An example of a case that falls into this category comes from Alison, a thirty-six-year-old woman from Arizona, who lives on a ranch not too far from the town of Sedona. From the age of twenty-seven to thirty-one, Alison was subjected to at least five abductions that bore all the hallmarks of alien kidnappings. On each occasion, she was in her living room reading or watching TV when her two pet dogs, Lucy and Summer, began to act in a distressed fashion—pacing around the room and whimpering. At that point, things always became a blur and Alison would later find herself in a different part of the house with several hours having passed. She would always feel groggy, with a pounding headache and dry mouth.

For days after the weird experiences, she would dream of the moment when things began to go awry—which always resulted in a complete loss of electricity inside the house, a deep humming noise emanating from outside the large living room window, and powerful and intensely bright lights enveloping the room. In her semiconscious state Alison would see small shadowy figures scuttling around the room. They would then carry her outside onto a small craft where she was subjected to a gynecological examination and some form of nasal probing. She would then be returned to another part of the house and the aliens would leave. It was only after the aliens had departed that the intense humming noise would cease.

On what Alison believes to have been the fifth abduction, however, the mysterious humming sound abruptly came to a halt only a few seconds after her cosmic visitors had entered the room. At that point, Alison recalled—not in a later dream on this occasion but in real time—she began to slowly regain her senses and the feeling of disorientation eventually eased and finally vanished. And so did the aliens. In their place were not a group of frail-looking alien "Grays," but a number of large and burly men in what looked like black fatigues.

According to Alison, one of the men screamed into a microphone something like: "What's happened?" Suddenly, the men backed away slowly and, as Alison began to regain her senses, one of them held his hand up "as if to say 'stay where you are,'" and uttered the word "sorry" in her direction. Alison made her way to the window in time to see the men jump into not a state-of-the-art alien spacecraft but a very terrestrial-looking black unmarked helicopter. At a height of several hundred feet, a powerful lamp was suddenly turned on that lit up the dark sky around her property.

Alison firmly believes that as a result of a combination of subliminal hypnosis, mind-altering technologies, and perhaps even non-lethal weaponry designed to temporarily disable her nervous system and bodily movement, she was made to think that she was an alien abductee, but that, in reality, she was merely a guinea pig for the testing of sophisticated weaponry designed to affect and manipulate both mind and body.[15]

Is it possible that, as the stories in this chapter suggest, there may indeed be several reasons for the apparent official surveillance of abductees? Researcher Helmut Lammer, certainly seems to think so: "…one group may be interested in advanced mind- and behavior-control experiments…these experiments are similar to the experiments reported by survivors of the MKULTRA mind-control programs…A second group seems to be interested in biological or genetic research…a third group seems to be a military task force… This group appears to be interested in the UFO/alien abduction phenomenon for information gathering purposes…It seems to us that the leaders of this military task force believe that some alien abductions are real and that they have national security implications. If this is the case, it would be likely that the second and third group would work together, sharing their interest in genetic studies and their findings from alleged alien abductees."[16]

7

IN SEARCH OF APEN

I n the latter part of 1973, unusual events began to quietly unfold above the green fields and rolling hills of northern England. They subsequently triggered a strange and possibly ongoing operation coordinated by an elite division of the British Police Force. Remarkably, that operation was designed to carefully monitor the activities of certain key players within the public UFO research arena in Britain. And it all began with something known as the "phantom helicopters."

Precisely who was flying oddly elusive and unmarked helicopters around the United Kingdom in the dead of night was never fully resolved—at least not to the satisfaction of the public and the media. Numerous theories were formulated within the corridors of power, however. Much of the attention was focused upon the possibility that the many and varied helicopter sightings were linked with the clandestine, terrorism-based activities of the Irish Republican Army (IRA).[1]

Following a series of phantom helicopter encounters in and around the area of Buxton, Derbyshire, the Metropolitan Police Special Branch initiated an operation to try and resolve what was taking place. The Metropolitan Police Special Irish Branch was formed in March 1883, initially as a small section of the Criminal Investigation Department (CID) of the Metropolitan Police. Its purpose was to combat, on a national basis, the Irish campaign of terrorism that was prevalent on the United Kingdom mainland at the time. Subsequently, the term "Irish" was dropped from the Branch's title, as over time it took on responsibility for countering a wide range of extremist and terrorist activity.

Currently, Special Branch gathers, collates, analyzes, and exploits intelligence on extremist political and terrorist activity. It initiates, develops, and conducts intelligence operations against terrorists and political extremists; disseminates intelligence for operational use to law enforcement agencies at local, national, and international levels; and provides armed protection for Ministers of State, Foreign VIPs, and other persons at threat from terrorist or extremist attack. Special Branch polices the ports within the London area to detect terrorist or criminal suspects traveling into or out of the country. Special Branch also assists other Government agencies to counter threats to the security of the United Kingdom from public disorder. It also protects against the proliferation of weapons of mass destruction—whether nuclear, biological, or chemical—espionage by foreign powers, subversion of the democratic process, terrorism by Irish or international groups, and sabotage of the United Kingdom's infrastructure.[2]

That Special Branch was deeply involved in the phantom helicopter affair, and that the subject is considered one of on-going controversy and concern, can be amply demonstrated. In 2001 UFO researcher David Clarke made inquiries with the British Government's Home Office and learned that a file on these events, titled "Alleged Unauthorized Helicopter Flights In Derbyshire And Cheshire," remains closed and exempt from public disclosure until at least 2006. Clarke was further advised that "only a relatively small part of the content of the file" relates specifically to the phantom helicopter sightings, while the remainder "deals with matters, some of which remain sensitive." What may have prompted that carefully worded statement—and how it ties in with the UFO controversy—will become clear in a future chapter.[3]

Sightings of the phantom helicopters continued through March 1974. A meeting was held at Horseferry House, London, on the twenty-first of that month that was attended by senior officers from the Derbyshire and Cheshire constabularies, Special Branch, the

Home Office, and the Ministry of Defense. While plans to utilize Harrier Jump-Jet aircraft and Ministry of Defense helicopters in response to phantom helicopter encounters were intriguing, they were deemed too costly and ultimately impractical. A unanimous agreement was reached for a continual monitoring of the situation, if indeed such action was considered necessary. As it transpired, however, no further reports were filed and the Home Office asserted that "the helicopter and the pilot were never identified."

A report by Chief Superintendent of "B" Squad, Special Branch, summarized the conclusions: "In the event there were found to be only three 'hard' sightings and no useful pattern of timing or positioning was discernible; in addition, no crimes were reported at the times of the alleged flights. I was able to report that the Metropolitan Police Special Branch had no hard information to place potential subversive activities in the area."[4]

And at a stroke both the sightings and the investigations came to a close—all too conveniently, some suggested.

At the height of the phantom helicopter wave, an event occurred on the Berwyn Mountain range in North Wales that for some within the UFO researcher community has come to be known as the definitive British Roswell. As investigator Andy Roberts noted, "…on the evening of 23 January 1974 an event took place on the Berwyn Mountains that was to perplex locals and spawned a veritable cascade of rumours, culminating in an incredible claim that, if true, would irrevocably change our view of history and make us revise our plans for the future of both our planet and our species. The claim was that a UFO piloted by extraterrestrials crashed, or was shot down, on the mountain known as Cader Berwyn and that the alien crew, some still alive, were whisked off to a secret military installation in the south of England for study."[5]

Roberts's in-depth research suggested strongly that no such "crash" of a UFO occurred on the mountains. In reality the mythology and lore surrounding the case was borne out of a combination of the misidentification of an earth tremor and a meteor shower—both of

AERIAL PHENOMENA ENQUIRY NETWORK

REF : F.?.(?)-?.?./?A?-01

ORIGINAL

Northern Control
(PRESTON)

Dear Sir/Madam,

    We have just received a directive from our Central Control to circulate a message tape to several U.?.?. groups in your region.

    This will be done within the next few days and we hope that you can use the information contained on your copy of the tape.

    We have heard quite a good deal of encouraging news regarding you/Association and the work it is doing re. UFO. We wish you every success.

Sincerely

R. A. Rose.

NORTHERN CTL.
UNIT 15

In 1974, a mysterious fascist group known as APEN attempted to infiltrate and manipulate the British UFO research community.

which occurred in broadly the same location and timeframe—plus there were poachers out on the hills armed with powerful lamps. Despite the fact that Andy Roberts undoubtedly solved the major aspects of the Berwyn Mountains "UFO Crash" of 23 January 1974, shadowy forces would surface in the wake of the "incident" that seemed curiously intent on spreading the tale that something strange and of a distinctly UFO nature did occur on Cader Berwyn. As Roberts stated:

"Within months of the event, UFO investigators in the north of England began to receive official-looking documents from a group called the Aerial Phenomena Enquiry Network (APEN). These documents claimed that an extraterrestrial craft had come down on the Berwyns and was retrieved for study by an APEN crash retrieval team [that] had been on the scene within hours of the event. More significantly APEN claimed there had been a key witness to the UFO crash who they were recommending for hypnotic regression. Hypnotic regression was at that time virtually unknown in the UK UFO community. In fact besides having being used in the 1961 Betty and Barney Hill 'abduction,' hypnosis was not used within ufology at that time."

Roberts further noted: "If APEN were hoaxers, then they displayed an uncanny and detailed knowledge of both ufology in general and the Berwyn Mountain incident in particular. Some researchers have speculated that APEN may have been part of a government cover-up, using UFO mythology to spread disinformation and so divert attention from secret weapons testing. APEN also issued similar enigmatic communications in conjunction with other UFO events, notably the Rendlesham Forest case [of December 1980]."[6]

And thus in the wake of APEN, a bizarre operation—comprised of elements of the British Government and Special Branch—placed most of the key players in the British UFO research arena of the mid-1970s under close surveillance.

Researcher Jenny Randles has a deep knowledge of the APEN controversy.

"How did you first hear about APEN?" I asked Randles in an interview.

"I was aware of the [Berwyn Mountains] case at the time it occurred because there had been various media stories published, and I'd just become really interested in UFOs about a year earlier. But the stories had never really connected it with anything significant. The event had simply been written off as a meteorite.

"Well, at about the same time as [the Berwyns incident] occurred, I was involved in setting up an organization known as the Northern UFO Network, or NUFON. The original concept of NUFON was to be kind of a liaison scheme to bring local groups up and down the North and the Midlands together; and it was really formed by about three groups—one from Manchester, one from the Wyrral, and one from Nottingham, who decided that there was too much isolation amongst the groups.

"And at that time, the British UFO Research Association, BUFORA, the national organization, was very remote and distant and only based in London. And what was needed was some opportunity to bring people together and share information. So the magazine *Northern UFO News* was created as that sort of sharing information medium. But there was more to the organization at that stage. There were plans to have annual conferences; for several years they did happen. It was never a unification: every group would remain independent. There were lots of grand plans. So I think it was more than a coincidence that as that was happening APEN came onto the scene; because part of the ethos of APEN always was that they would promote this unification. They would stress NUFON; they would put people directly into contact with me.

"The first thing that I ever got was a cassette tape that was very bizarre because it began with what was later identified as a Nazi war march. The tape was filled with lots of voices shouting and screaming, heavily accented people—some Welsh, mostly American and some guy calling himself James T. Anderson, the Supreme Commander."

Randles continued her recollections of APEN's activities:

"Over the next few months it gradually dawned on us all that several of us in ufology, at the time, had been sent similar tapes. And then towards the end of 1974, letters started to arrive on APEN stationery. There were all kinds of silly James Bond-style coding. But these letters had been posted from all across the country; we could never track them down.

"Never any address; there was never any contact address given or any way of tracing them. The postal information on the letters they sent was scattered here, there and everywhere; they came from all over the country. There was never any sort of consistency with that regard so you could pin down what town they were coming from, if it was individual who was doing it. And there were always different names given. And I think that most of us within NUFON just thought that they were a bunch of crackpots that were going to the trouble to do this and that if we ignored them they would go away. I kept saying that several times in *Northern UFO News* and then dropped the whole story; but, I think one or two other people got rather fired up about this and saw it as a mystery, and pursued it more thoroughly than I did."

And what was the link between the mysterious APEN and the Berwyn incident?

According to Randles, "It was towards the end of 1974 that a letter arrived from APEN, which suggested that there had been a UFO landing in North Wales in January 1974 and that APEN were considering whether or not to send me to the full report on the case. It was going to be through 'all the chains of command,' they said.

"APEN claimed that this UFO had landed rather than crashed; it was an alien craft. There was also supposed to be a former military officer who lived in a remote cottage on the mountain that was allegedly involved. This was all quite bizarre.

"Now, I was aware of the Berwyn or Llandrillo case, of course, in the sense that there had been media stories at the time and I'd just become really interested in UFOs about a year earlier, so it was something that had crossed my mind. But the story had never directly connected with anything significant; it always looked to be something like a meteor. It had been written off as a meteorite, so nobody that I can recall within the UFO community had ever proceeded to do any real investigation.

"There was a short article in *Flying Saucer Review* at the time, written by Eileen Buckle. And there was also an article written by Tony Pace for BUFORA. But that was really the only things [sic]. Nobody considered the case to be of any significance. But this letter from APEN suggested that there was a landing case in North Wales and they were considering whether to send a full report of this to me; it was going through all the chains of command etc., etc.; the usual. I just dismissed it out of hand completely; well, if it happens, it happens. If it doesn't, it doesn't, and it probably won't. If it does, we'll not know what credibility to make of it.

"It would have been around about early January or February in seventy-five that the APEN so-called report on the case arrived. It was very difficult to make any sense of because it was full of this daft coding and information about how they had this huge organization and could get access to things like Land Rovers, theodolites, sending in new staff, bizarre claims that this UFO had landed on the mountains rather than crashed and that it was an alien craft. They didn't give any date for that. And I've never been able to trace any specific incident that that might relate to, or how the aliens had supposedly given the APEN ex-directory telephone number to this military officer that lived on the mountainside—who they directly contacted—so that you should only communicate with them, of course explaining why nobody's ever heard of this military witness. Nobody's ever been able to find anybody that might fit that bill.

"The only thing that makes it clear that it is the case is that it gives the date—which was the same—and it starts off by saying it was in North Wales. And I only really got to see that there was anything of significance with the APEN case about three or four years later, when I, by pure chance, spent some time in Llandrillo.

"About a year later, around February 1976, I moved house. Literally nobody knew the new address, but when we arrived at the new house, sitting on the doorstep was a card saying, 'Welcome to your new home.' And inside was a sticker with the APEN sign on saying, 'Never call anyone bigger than yourself stupid.'

"In the meantime, towards the end of 1975, APEN had made what I believe was the only ever direct contact with anybody. This was with a chap by the name of Peter Bottomley, who briefly came onto the UFO scene around about that time as a new BUFORA investigator. He'd literally just joined the group two or three months earlier and then APEN came to see him, saying that they wanted him to act as a go-between between themselves and the UFO community, and they'd picked someone who was fairly naïve and didn't know the scene and so on and so forth and no axe to grind, for that reason.

"He thought that they were totally sincere. They wouldn't give him any names: they told him that if he took on this job, what would happen was they would give him a special telephone number that he could use, but he must sign an agreement that he would never reveal it to anybody else and that was in effect it. He was never offered any money or anything like that.

"Their argument always was that they were some sort of super organization which was created from within the UFO community but had decided that secrecy was the only way to make real progress because it was the only way to make contact with the Intelligence Community. It wasn't very clear, because they were never terribly forthcoming about themselves. But I never got the impression that they were alleging they were part of the Government, but more that they were a sort of select group of ufologists who had chosen this path to be closer to Government sources of information. But that could be a misunderstanding, because, as I say, it was never clear. But that was the innuendo, anyway, of what they told him.

"He contacted Gordon Clegg, who at that time was the BUFORA Regional Coordinator for the northwest area, because Peter Bottomley lived in Manchester. And when Bottomley said, 'I've been contacted by this organization called APEN. Have you ever heard of them? Should I work with them?' Clegg didn't react very enthusiastically, Peter Bottomley said, and Clegg suggested immediately that he contact me.

"He did and I told him what little I knew about APEN. And two colleagues of mine at the time who were in the local UFO group, which was then called MUFORA, Peter Warrington and Geoff Porter—both of whom are now are not really active within the UFO community at all but both were for quite a long time, about ten or fifteen years—went to see him, gave him all the information and said, 'It's entirely up to you how you play this.'

"His wife said, 'If you want to be a serious ufologist, the last thing you should do is get mixed up with these clowns. They're obviously very childish and immature; it isn't worth your time.'

"So he opted to not to do so. And they actually did call him back, as they'd arranged to do on the phone. He told them that he'd decided to not to participate; they said, 'Fine, thank you.' They didn't try to coerce him and they never attempted this sort of thing again, so far as I know, with anybody else. So it was the only direct contact, as far as we know.

"Over the years, the APEN saga continued. It didn't fizzle out, as you might have imagined a little crackpot thing that wasn't getting very far would have done. They continued to contact groups up and down the country and even now I still hear from organizations that say, you know, 'We have this mysterious contact.' It's obvious that they've been contacted by APEN and I'd never known about it. I've heard about instances of APEN contact as recently as about five or six years ago, so it has been going on for more than twenty years, by the sounds of it."

"Didn't they surface in the Rendlesham Forest case as well?" I asked, in reference to the famous, alleged UFO landing incident near RAF Bentwaters, Suffolk, England, in December 1980.

Randles replied, "They did. That's the last direct contact I've ever had with them. By direct I mean they didn't actually write or send me anything but they contacted somebody who contacted me and asked for my association with it. In effect, it was the local group in Crewe, which went by the name of FUFOR, the Federation for UFO Research, who were one of the NUFON-affiliated groups in the late seventies, early-to-mid-eighties. This would be around about…must have been about eighty-five, six, something like that. It was after *Skycrash* had been published [*Skycrash*, co-written by Randles with Dot Street and Brenda Butler, was the first full-length book on the Rendlesham Forest affair]. So it probably must have been around about eighty-six.

"But they came to me and they said that this APEN organization, who they'd heard of, had contacted them and said that the Rendlesham Forest case related to something which was not UFO-orientated. I think the innuendo of it was that it was something to do with a nuclear missile, and that they had all this information to impart and they wanted a meeting with me. And the meeting was to be on Crewe Railway Station at 2 o'clock in the morning, which quite naturally I declined. FUFOR wouldn't explain how they were able to get into contact with APEN; they didn't say that APEN had been to see them. I assume it was similar with Peter Bottomley, and they were going to phone them back. But at that point, after ten years of APEN shenanigans, I'd had all kinds of stories about them from different people, and had seen how dangerous they could be."

"What do you mean by dangerous?" I asked.

Randles replied, "They weren't just crackpots; they had got up to some fairly nasty tactics. For example, there was one group in Leicester, where they got into trouble with the police because what APEN had apparently done was they'd called up the police, sent them out to a UFO sighting, which didn't happen, and APEN reported themselves as the local group. And then the local group was hauled in for wasting police time. And then after that they got letters from APEN saying: 'This was just to tell you that we're around and you should watch out for us.'

"Then that group and several other groups in the East Midlands started to get letters from APEN telling them—this must have been around seventy-seven, seventy-eight—telling them that there was a sort of bogus APEN going around claiming to be them who weren't really them. So in the future what they were going to do was to send out APEN identification cards showing what their agents looked like and only if you are contacted by one of these people should you accept that it's APEN.

"And they did send out, sort of like passport photographs, with what I presume were made up names, and nobody was ever able to trace any of the names, or had ever heard of any of these individuals as ufologists. That's one of the biggest arguments against them being part of the UFO community: the names, maybe a dozen or twenty names I've heard connected with APEN, not one of them has ever been a ufologist that anybody's been able to trace or ever had a minor involvement with the subject.

"So there were tactics like that. There was also a claim that they broke into a building in, I think, it was Nottingham, where some UFO files were housed and ransacked the place and again sent a calling card letter to the group afterwards, saying, 'Just to notify you that we're around.' So they were apparently getting up to nasty tactics.

"There were several other incidents. For example, I started to get phone calls, around about 1980, I think, from people saying, 'I'm phoning up your number and asking how I can join APEN?' And I said, 'Well, how should I know?' They replied, 'Well, because there's an advertisement in a newspaper in Cambridge saying, Join APEN and phone this number.' And it was my telephone number.

"But a lot of these things I've, over the years, suspected that it was almost like what happened in the crop circle phenomenon: people jumping on the bandwagon of the APEN scenario and just trying to get in on the act and coming up with all kinds of tricks and tactics, which may not have been directly related to whoever was behind APEN in the first place. And there were lots of sort of things like that that went on.

"My surmise has always been that the most likely explanation for APEN is that it is some kind of prank like UMMO that took off. Then, the bigger it got, the more fun it got for those who were doing it. And that it looks bigger than it is—primarily because a lot of people on the periphery of the UFO community have recognized its legendary status. Rather than just being a one-off hoax by a few individuals it's become sort of a series of hoaxes all using the APEN name. But that is no more than a surmise. I really don't know.

"You do have to wonder if some of the sinister things that they did would really have been perpetrated just for the sake of it. I think that the most serious aspect was that it did attempt to destabilize NUFON. I've no doubt whatsoever that that was the case. At the time, when BUFORA were attempting a similar initiative—trying to bring in local groups, a group liaison system that they operated—they also started to get similar APEN letters, basically telling them not to contact BUFORA. And also in the late seventies, when BUFORA, through their then-chairman, Roger Stanway, attempted a direct liaison with *Flying Saucer Review*, exactly the same thing happened vis-à-vis *Flying Saucer Review*.

"I don't know whether you're aware of this but [the late editor of *Flying Saucer Review*] Gordon Creighton wrote a few nasty things in *FSR* about APEN and me. But he completely misunderstands the situation. The story of what happened is this: I don't know if you've seen the full account that I wrote of APEN in 1986 in a magazine called *The Unknown*. But that was the first time that I ever actually told this story about Sanderson Sign & Print in Reading. What happened was, there was a guy called Brian Ratcliffe, who lived in Nottingham at the time. He actually wrote a letter to the magazine after my articles, attacking my articles for not being explicit enough and not openly accusing *Flying Saucer Review* of having faked all of this APEN [sic]. He seems to be convinced that the whole APEN affair was actually created by Gordon Creighton.

"Gordon Creighton was a bit strange, to say the least, and I can't for the life of me understand why he would do that and I never had any suspicions that that's the case. But I think that *Flying Saucer Review* was set-up in exactly the same way as a number of us were set-up. What really did happen was Brian Ratcliffe was investigating APEN like some people have done down through the years periodically—and going to get to the bottom of it, and he decided he was going to track down the source of the APEN-headed stationery.

"And somehow or another by something to do with the watermark in the paper, he alleged that he tracked it down to the printers, Sanderson Design & Print in Reading, and spoke to them and they told him that *Flying Saucer Review* had ordered it. Now, I thought this was absurd; because at that time I was actually on the *Flying Saucer Review*…not on the Board as such but I was what was called Secretarial Assistant, I think it was. I was working quite closely with Charles Bowen, and doing quite a bit of work for them. I did attend occasional board meetings; and we were working very closely to forge a direct liaison with BUFORA. The intention was that Roger Stanway, who was then BUFORA's chairman, would go on to the *FSR* board; that BUFORA would get a double-page spread in every issue of *Flying Saucer Review*, in which BUFORA's better cases would be published. So, in other words, it would be a profitable link up between what were then Britain's two major UFO outlets. *Flying Saucer Review*, at that time, was a respectable, serious magazine. It didn't have to contend with the rather strange editorials produced by Gordon Creighton.

"Anyway, I think that there were destabilizing tactics by somebody who wanted to scupper that. It never happened for a whole host of reasons; which again may or may not be directly relevant. Basically, Roger Stanway left the field overnight; he was warned off, so some people claim. He told us within BUFORA that he had got religion and that was the reason. And we never heard from him again. He literally just walked out of the field overnight. He was one of the best investigators in the country. And if he had stayed with BUFORA, British ufology would have taken an entirely different course. So you can understand the arguments of some people for, you know, that somebody got at him. I honestly don't think that that was the case. Knowing Roger as I did at that point, I think he was probably just sincerely one of these people who became a sort of born-again Christian and didn't see that as being compatible with the UFO community.

"But it came at a very bad time. And it did scupper the plans. What happened ultimately was that UFOIN emerged from the ashes of what was going to be a joint BUFORA-*FSR* initiative, doing some of the same things but not as effectively as it would have been if there had been this direct BUFORA-*FSR* liaison.

"But I did check with Sanderson Design & Print. I phoned them up and they told me on the phone that, yes they did print the APEN stationery; and, yes it was paid for by *Flying Saucer Review*. I couldn't believe it when they confirmed that to me over the phone. But that apparently is the case. But my understanding of the situation—and this is why Brian Ratcliffe wrote this letter to *The Unknown*—was that what had happened was that APEN had slipped their order on the coat-tails of the regular *FSR* order and gone in and collected the stationery and it had not gone out to the normal address or whatever; and that FSR had simply never realized that they'd paid for this additional stationery.

"Brian Ratcliffe says that that is impossible; his argument is that according to what Sanderson Design & Print told him, it was paid for and collected by *Flying Saucer Review*, which, of course, would make a fundamental difference if that were true. But I cannot verify that. That is not my understanding of what Sanderson Design & Print told me.

"Obviously, going back to a memory of a phone conversation twenty-odd years ago is difficult but that is my understanding of what it was. But I have never believed that Gordon Creighton or *Flying Saucer Review* were behind APEN, as Gordon Creighton seemed to think I do. My view is that they were being used by whoever APEN was, for the direct purpose of sewing seeds of disruption and confusion within the UFO community. This has always been the intention of APEN."

I asked Randles for clarification, "You mean they may have actually used *Flying Saucer Review*'s name to order the material?"

"Yes, I do," Randles replied. "I'm sure they did. Because that's clearly what Sanderson Design & Print—the printers—told me. I know that they did tell me that. There's no argument about that: APEN stationery was paid for on an *FSR* account. That is clearly what the printers told me. I understood from what Sanderson Design & Print told me that it was just part of a series of regular orders and that someone came in and collected as opposed to it being delivered to whoever they normally delivered the *FSR* material to. So they didn't regard it as anything strange. They just thought, well…didn't cross their mind to question why *Flying Saucer Review* were having some letterheads printed with Aerial Phenomena Enquiry Network on.

"And *Flying Saucer Review* might not have noticed it on the page; because if they didn't itemize the bill—I never asked them if they did—but that was certainly the implication of what they told me, that what had happened was that APEN had slipped the order in using *FSR*'s name, that therefore they didn't have to pay for it, they came in and collected it, so it never actually went out to *FSR*; so *FSR* would never have known that this material had been paid for and collected under their name.

"But Brian Ratcliffe says quite the opposite. He is adamant that that isn't what happened. But I can only tell you what Sanderson Design & Print told me at the time. And it does make a fundamental difference, in that regard, if he's right. But I have seen the tactics that APEN has employed down through the years and the way that they have tried to implicate different people.

"And, not long after that, I discovered that a number of people that hadn't been talking to me for some time, weren't talking to me because they had received letters allegedly from me which were signed by a passing resemblance to my signature; but it wasn't my signature, in which they were offered jobs as part of the Government UFO investigation scheme, that should involve a company car, money and it was just ludicrous and obviously a joke, in that regard.

"But they'd taken it seriously and they thought I was part of a covert operation and therefore they weren't going to talk to me. I have no doubt in my own mind that the people who did that, whoever it was that sent out those letters, are the same people who are behind APEN and it's just an example of whatever it was that they were trying to do.

"Now this doesn't mean necessarily that it was some kind of MI5 mission or whatever. If you wanted to be very egotistical you could come up with that argument that they were trying to destabilize ufology. I couldn't actively refute it because I do believe that from time to time there have been intelligence operations against the UFO community; but I wouldn't rule it totally out of court. But knowing ufology as I know it and how it attracts crackpots and cranks like flies, I think you have to at first look to the UFO community itself as being the most likely home of whoever it was that was trying these destabilizing tactics.

"And I think the idea of the way in which the whole of the APEN ethos focused around this Nazism, points the finger towards the British Nazi party, who for some reason would want to try and destabilize ufology. I cannot understand why that would be true. It may just simply have been a group of individuals whose idea of a joke it was. But it was a long-running one, that's for sure; and it went to a lot of trouble to cause trouble, if you see what I mean. But I'm absolutely certain and I do want to make this clear, that in my own mind nobody like Gordon Creighton or *Flying Saucer Review* was responsible for APEN: I think that they were as much a victim as everybody else."

In conclusion, I asked Randles, "Do you think it's in any way significant, the fact that the two cases that APEN really picked up on were the Berwyn incident and Rendlesham Forest, the two cases that could really be considered among the most controversial and significant within the history of UFO research in the UK?"

"Yes," she replied. "That's one of the few things about the APEN story that really makes me wonder about them. Because they did see the significance of [the Berwyn Mountain case] years before anybody else did; and of course they also recognized that Rendlesham Forest was more than it appeared to be on the surface; I think before many other people did, too. And that suggests an element of sophistication that normally you would not subscribe to elements within the UFO community. So, yes, I have to admit that's one of the things about APEN that does make me still take an interest in them and not write them off totally as crackpots."

And so who, exactly, were APEN? Were they deluded Walter Mitty-types on the fringes of the UFO research community? Were they government agents stirring the ufological pot to create division among those investigating the UFO controversy? Or, were they something else entirely?

For the answer, we have to turn our attention to none other than Special Branch, the elite division of the British Police Force implicated in the phantom helicopter encounters of 1973–1974.

8

ENTER SANDMAN

While conducting research into the saga of the mysterious APEN, the phantom helicopter wave of 1973–1974, and the controversy surrounding the Berwyn Mountains incident of January 1974, I came into contact with a man I will refer to as the Sandman. He served with the Metropolitan Police's Special Branch in the 1970s, was directly allied to investigations into these same controversies, and was able to unravel certain parts of the mystery, something that forces us to look at the collective situation in a whole new extraordinary light.

When APEN surfaced, the intense, official surveillance of practically the entire British UFO research community began in earnest. At the time of the phantom helicopter encounters and the event on the Berwyn Mountains, the Sandman was engaged in an operation that involved the Special Branch, Scotland Yard, and MI5 (the British equivalent of the FBI). This operation was designed to carefully monitor a number of low-profile individuals in the north of England, Nottingham, Cambridge, Birmingham, London, Leicester, and elsewhere, who were all tied (albeit not in an official sense) with underground and extremely ultra-right-wing fascist organizations in Britain.

"This began in mid-1973 and was carrying on right through the late 1970s and early 1980s," said the Sandman. "These were not your usual Nazi-skinhead-thug groups on the football terraces, nor were they even your average British Movement people, but a group of people who were trying to create a new, underground, right-wing group that had aims far more serious and subversive than what we had been used to. To describe some of these people as potential terrorists was not an exaggeration."

The Sandman explained that seventeen individuals were involved; they largely stayed in contact by telephone but would on occasion meet to discuss operations—most of which, the Sandman states in careful words, "might have led to the death of certain people in both Labor and Conservative politics at the time." But there was more.

The Sandman informed me that, as a direct result of the surveillance operation, it became abundantly clear to Special Branch that six of the people being carefully watched "for extremist actions" had a personal interest in the UFO controversy. Not only that but in the post–September 1973 period, those six individuals had deep and lengthy conversations about the phantom helicopter wave that was then in full swing.

"And this was what was so important and relevant," stressed the Sandman. "We had our team looking at right-wing groups, and there were some of our other boys that were looking at the helicopter invasions of the same time. And no one ever thought that the two could possibly be connected. If anything, the best guess for the helicopters was the IRA, but even that fell down. But there were people in the [right-wing] groups that were discussing the helicopters in a UFO context. They saw the helicopters as possibly UFOs, I mean."

The Sandman continued, "We didn't really know if we had something, or were even really on to something, but when you have these far-right-thinkers who we were watching, and they were all coordinating information on helicopter invasions that Scotland Yard thought might be terrorist plots, we saw what could be a direct link with the two, so it was studied further to see if it was connected."

And while no link between the phantom helicopters and those ultra-right-wingers within 1970s ufology was ever confirmed, the

Sandman stated that in late March 1974, a meeting was held at an address in Northumberland Avenue, London, that was attended by "us, [MI]5, and GCHQ [Government Communications Headquarters, the British equivalent of the National Security Agency]."

A careful study of the activities, correspondence, and telephone calls of these six people under surveillance led the intelligence community to reach a unique and fascinating conclusion: that the UFO interests of the six were in reality nothing more than a carefully created cover, behind which their extremist political aims and intentions could be discussed, planned, and acted upon.

"I'll tell you what we had," said the Sandman. "We had these six—who were very dangerous, very dangerous fascists with links to some very evil people who even the British Movement wouldn't touch with a barge-pole—keeping in touch, forging UFO links, traveling around the country, and meeting at UFO groups and seminars.

"Now, Special Branch does not investigate UFOs and we never have. But we have investigated people with UFO interests, but only where there is an overlap with other areas and usually political areas. Our boys sat in on several of these [Flying] Saucer meetings and these people were always deep in discussion, huddled together. But what if, we were thinking, what if these UFO meetings and lectures allowed these six people to meet up under the pretext of discussing UFOs? No one would ever know that there was something else—and something much more serious—that linked them and that they were really discussing: namely the fascist groups and setting up a new fascist group and network all across England. It was perfect cover."

The Sandman further advised me that four of these people (whose names he openly supplied and who were relatively well-known figures in Britain's UFO research community of the mid-1970s) were heard on several occasions on the telephone discussing two key issues that were of paramount interest to Special Branch.

"These guys were very clever and very devious; I must give it to them," said the Sandman. "They realized—as did we—that there were other people in the Flying Saucer study groups that were sympathetic to their right-wing views, and who they wanted to target

AERIAL PHENOMENA ENQUIRY NETWORK

REF :- T.E.(R)-N.C/RAR-O2.
Northern Control
(PRESTON).

-3 APL 1975

-3 APL 1975

Dear Sir,

Re. your telephone conversation of todays date with our ▬▬▬▬▬

    We understand you asked for help concerning "investigation methods"
plus evaluation of reports which are in your possession. I have issued
orders to our investigation staff to formulate brief instructions on these
two matters and these instructions should be in your possession very
shortly.

    We are sorry but we will be unable to send a representative to your
meeting but at the moment to do so would be contrary to our instructions
from Central Control. As soon as these instructions are withdrawn we will
gladly attend your meetings.

    A second message tape and a copy of one of our Initial Reports will
follow within a few days.

Yours sincerely,

R. A. Rose.
Northern Controller,
A.P.E.N.

N
CONFIDENCE

*In the mid-1970s, British Intelligence closely monitored the activities of
the Aerial Phenomena Enquiry Network.*

for recruiting to their fascist links—and to do it all by hiding behind a UFO research group recruitment pretext. But they also realized—and, again, so did Special Branch after we targeted most of your UFO people at the time—that to do so, they had to gain control of the research groups and hold sway over them."

It was at this point, says the Sandman, that the six hatched a truly ingenious plan to create a new group that was designed with two specific purposes in mind: It would carefully target influential UFO research groups around Britain—such as BUFORA, NUFON, and *Flying Saucer Review* magazine—and pitch them against each other by way of smear campaigns and faked gossip, with the express intent of destabilizing those same organizations. In theory, the new group would take control of the entire British UFO research community and it would also subtly foster the idea that it had quasi-Governmental connections, thus ensuring that many targeted would "sign up immediately or at least tow the line, because they wanted to get on the inside of what the government knew about UFOs," stated the Sandman.

"We learned quick that UFO people will do almost anything to get on the inside of the UFO secrecy that they think exists," the Sandman added. He then stated that the new group was none other than APEN—the Aerial Phenomena Enquiry Network.

"Can you see how easy this could have worked?" he asked me. "There would be this ultra-right-wing organization that no one in authority would be able to find. And why wouldn't we be able to find them? Because they wouldn't be advertising themselves for what they were: they would be hiding behind the cover of a UFO research group and would be secretly and carefully manipulating and recruiting new people—particularly younger, disaffected people—from inside that UFO community, rather than recruiting from known and identified far-right groups. It was a very clever plan."

The Sandman also stated that extensive and classified files existed on the phantom helicopters, the Berwyn controversy, and the saga of APEN, and they were housed in the archives of the Home Office, MI5, and Special Branch. However, he warned me, "Now before you rush to print, be aware that we looked into the helicopters, and if anything, it was probably a terrorist thing that was shut down after we got close to them, and not a UFO thing at all. We also looked into the [Berwyn] mountain and the UFO story—because APEN were talking about that, too—and found that there was nothing there, nothing at all. And APEN was just planned as a deep cover for the recruitment of people to right-wing groups. It had nothing to do with being a part of a secret government UFO group.

"So, I'm saying don't presume that because we have classified files on the mountain story that this means we have files on crashed spacemen. We don't. We looked into all this because these were the allegations that APEN was making about landed UFOs on the mountains; so we looked at the stories, nothing more."

But this was not the "most bizarre" aspect of the APEN affair, stated the Sandman. And if he is not actively spreading either official or personal disinformation—and I do not believe that he is—then I have to agree with his "most bizarre" assessment. According to the Sandman, as the APEN team began formulating their plan to subvert British ufology and directly recruit from its ranks people that could be "useful to the right-wingers," they began sending out anonymous letters to sow the seeds of discontent within the flying saucer research community.

"This was very clever," he said. "They would send out letters saying this researcher or that researcher works for MI5 or at the Ministry of Defense. Or they would say this researcher is keeping subscription money for UFO magazines and using the money to go on holiday to Spain. Or they would say that the person they were writing to had been selected to 'work for the government' and had to sign up with APEN and renounce all other UFO group links. Just creating divisions."

According to the Sandman, the people behind APEN even hatched an ingenious plan to have their paperwork printed by a certain company that also printed *Flying Saucer Review* magazine at the time—just as Jenny Randles had concluded. The idea, he said—and as Randles had suspected—was to then carefully reveal this to influential elements of the UFO research community and thus hopefully make people think that *Flying Saucer Review* and APEN were connected. This would then create even more ufological divisions that APEN could exploit as part of its determined plan to destroy, rebuild, subvert, and subsequently plunder for covert political reasons, the collective British UFO research community.

And further, according to the Sandman, the process "probably would have worked," except for one truly startling thing, as he revealed. "We decided at Special Branch and GCHQ that there was one way we could stop this: we began creating our own APEN letters, and began sending them out.

"The plan was to make the 'real' APEN seem even more sinister, but also less than credible at the same time, which would hopefully make the Saucer groups keep away from it. We also sent out tapes and letters that purposefully amplified the right-wing aspects of APEN, and that we hoped would worry some of the leading UFO people so that they kept away from anything connected with APEN of a political note.

"I must tell you that it raised a lot of laughs in the Met [The Metropolitan Police] when these APEN people realized that there was another APEN—us—subverting them. I don't think I'm wrong in saying it worked. We watched what was said in the magazines and on the phones, and everyone—by everyone, I mean the UFO people—came around to what we wanted them to think: that APEN were extreme right-wing lunatics with delusions of grandeur—which was all true; they were. But the main thing we wanted—and which worked—was to close down or lessen the influence of the APEN people that intended using UFO conferences and meetings as cover places for recruiting people to their right-wing organizations."[1] It will be noted that in some ways this mirrors the comments of researcher Jacques Vallee concerning the way in which the KGB had possibly manipulated for its own purposes the UMMO cult.

Quite by coincidence and without knowing what the Sandman had told me, Andy Roberts emailed me in 2004 to say that he had obtained a batch of letters written by a source from mid-to-late

1970s ufology who was pursuing an identical theory: that APEN and a number of well-known figures within the British UFO research community at the time were utilizing the UFO subject as a smokescreen for conducting ultra-right-wing activities that somehow implicated the British Movement in the whole sorry affair. Roberts sent me the originals of all of the correspondence and, indeed, it collectively sits very well with the assertions of the Sandman.

There is another example of apparent official monitoring of British UFO researchers in the late 1970s—but this time by American authorities. In 1977, the late Graham Birdsall—editor of the now-defunct British-based *UFO Magazine*— and his brother Mark, investigated a major UFO sighting near Harrogate, North Yorkshire, England. The sighting involved a number of witnesses who had seen strange aerial objects in the vicinity of Menwith Hill—a vast "listening-post" controlled by the U.S. National Security Agency (NSA). The Birdsall brothers duly approached the staff at Menwith Hill for comment and, at one point, were actually allowed on base. This led to a curious series of events. Soon after visiting the base, Graham received a telephone call from a Mr. Mills, the senior NSA security officer at the base, who had just taken up his post at Menwith Hill and was keen to cement good local relations. Graham engaged the NSA official in conversation for approximately one hour.

Within a short space of time the Birdsall family began to notice an "awful lot" of interference on the telephone that Graham had used to speak to Mills. This continued for days, then weeks. On one occasion, Graham was speaking with Mark when several clicking noises were heard on the line, followed by their voices repeating back the very same words they had spoken only minutes before.[2]

One year later, American authorities were still apparently engaged in watching the activities of UFO researchers. One of the strangest episodes in the saga of official surveillance of UFO investigators in the United States surfaced in 1978, but had its origins in Cuba's airspace more than a decade previously. In March 1967, according to a "security specialist" who was assigned to the 6947th Security Squadron at Homestead Air Force Base, a unit of the U.S. Air Force Security Service (AFSS), the Spanish-speaking intercept operators of Detachment A at Homestead heard Cuban air defense radar controllers report an unidentified "bogey" approaching Cuba from the northeast.

The UFO apparently entered Cuban airspace at a height of about 10,000 meters and "sped off" at nearly 660 mph. The operators then scrambled two Russian-built MIG-21 jet fighters, which were guided to within three miles of the UFO by ground-based radar personnel. The flight-leader then radioed that the object appeared to be a "bright metallic sphere with no visible markings or appendages."

When an attempt at radio contact failed, Cuban air defense headquarters ordered the flight leader to arm his weapons and destroy the object. The leader reported his radar was locked onto the "bogey" and his missiles were armed. Only moments later, however, the wingman "screamed" to the ground controller that his leader's jet "had exploded." The wingman added that there was no smoke or flame and that his leader's MIG-21 had simply disintegrated. Cuban radar then reported that the UFO had quickly accelerated, climbed above 30,000 meters, and was last tracked heading toward South America. An Intelligence Spot Report was reportedly sent to the National Security Agency's headquarters, since AFSS and its units were under NSA operational control.

UFO researcher Robert Todd sent Freedom of Information Act (FOIA) requests concerning the Cuban incident to the Air Force, CIA, NSA, and the Navy between February and July of 1978, but all without success. Then, on 10 March 1978, the CIA suggested that Todd "check with the Cuban government for records on the incident." On 14 July Todd notified both the NSA and the Air Force that because neither agency wished to cooperate, he would indeed contact the Cuban government as per the suggestion of the CIA.

Then on 28 July 1978, between 5:30 and 6:00 p.m., Todd's mother answered a knock at the door. Two men, one older than the other, asked for Todd. When Todd came downstairs, both flashed identification cards that revealed them to be with the FBI. The FBI men read Todd his rights, though he waived his right to silence because he felt that he did not have anything to hide. One of the men then began to read the espionage laws, being careful to add that those laws carried a penalty of life in prison or death. Both agents hinted at the possibility some indictments would be issued, although ultimately, that did not happen. There was also a discussion that Todd's phone might be tapped.

Todd soon filed a request with the Air Force to obtain copies of his FOIA case file on the matter. Colonel James Johnson, Executive Officer of the Air Force's Office of the Judge Advocate General, replied in a 14 September 1978 letter stating: "...You are advised that the Air Force can neither confirm nor deny the authenticity of this statement, nor the existence of any records concerning the incident described therein However, if authentic, I am advised the statement would be classified Secret in its entirety."

Does this mean that the event involved a genuine UFO? According to Tom Deuley, formerly of the National Security Agency, and who served with one of the watch officers from Homestead Air Force Base, the answer is "probably not." There was a theory, said Deuley, that the incident was not UFO-related, but referred to the attempts by the Cubans to shoot down a high-flying American spy plane. The "bogey" actually was an SR71 Blackbird and not a UFO. The fact that the intercepting aircraft exploded, Deuley asserted, was attributed to the attempts by the Cubans to use what was referred to as a "Chandell climb." This meant achieving a higher speed and a higher altitude, and involved the Cuban pilot putting his aircraft into a dive, then pulling out of the dive and "hitting the afterburners" to secure maximum speed and height. The assumption, said Deuley, was that when he hit the afterburners, the pilot blew himself up.

To what extent this particular theory will ever receive ultimate validation—or not—is a matter that, for now, remains unknown. Indeed, the fact that the initial report described a "bright metallic sphere with no visible markings or appendages" suggests that even today we are not in possession of the full story. However, it should not be forgotten that UFO means—quite literally—"unidentified flying object." It does not always mean "alien spacecraft."[3]

9

BETA AND BEYOND

In the late 1970s, physicist Paul Bennewitz began digging deep into Air Force and National Security Agency secret projects at Kirtland Air Force Base, New Mexico. He believed they were connected to the activities of sinister extraterrestrials and UFOs. In reality, what Bennewitz had really tapped into were classified operations that specifically focused upon NSA communications systems, test flights (and possibly crashes) of early prototype stealth aircraft and unmanned aerial vehicles, and Air Force technologies designed to track the orbital movements of space satellites launched by the former Soviet Union.

As a result, Bennewitz was put under surveillance by the U.S. Military and Intelligence services, and fed a mass of disinformation, faked stories, and outright lies in order to divert him from his research—which worked. In fact, it worked too well, and led to his mental disintegration. As history has shown, U.S. Intelligence did not care that Bennewitz thought that their secret operations were UFO-related—precisely because the UFO connection was one of Bennewitz's own making. However, there was deep concern on the part of officials that by digging into classified activities at Kirtland in search of UFOs, Bennewitz would inadvertently reveal—to the Soviets, in a worst-case scenario—information and technology that had to be kept secret at all costs, even if those costs included Bennewitz's own sanity.

Bennewitz believed that aliens were mutilating cattle as part of some weird medical experiment, that they were abducting American citizens and implanting them with devices for purposes unknown, that those same aliens were living underground in a secure fortress at Dulce, New Mexico, and that very soon we were all going to be in dire trouble as a direct result of this brewing intergalactic threat. And so a plan was initiated: Break into Bennewitz's home while he was out, learn the essential parts of his theories, and confirm to him that they were all true. Of course, this was all just a carefully planned ruse to bombard Bennewitz with so much faked UFO data in the hope that it would steer him away from the classified military projects of a non-UFO nature that he had unwittingly uncovered.

It worked. When Bennewitz received conformation (albeit carefully controlled and utterly fabricated) that yes, he had stumbled upon the horrible truth and that yes, there really was an alien base deep below Dulce, the actions of the Intelligence community had the desired effect: Bennewitz became increasingly paranoid and unstable, and he began looking away from Kirtland toward the vicinity of Dulce. There, his actions, research, and theories could be carefully controlled and manipulated by the Government.

U.S. Intelligence even brought Bill Moore (coauthor with Charles Berlitz of the 1980 book, *The Roswell Incident*) into the scheme and asked him to keep them informed of how their disinformation operations against Bennewitz were working. In return, Moore was promised—and was provided with—data and documents on alleged super-secret, official UFO projects, crashed saucers, dead aliens, and more.

Moore largely retired from the UFO scene after he informed a shocked and outraged audience at the 1989 Symposium of the Mutual UFO Network of his involvement in keeping the Intelligence community informed of how their disinformation campaign against Bennewitz was working. The official disinformation operation that targeted Bennewitz resulted in his hospitalization after he was driven to a complete mental collapse. This may have been the full intent all along: to completely crush Bennewitz, and to keep Moore busy

COMPLAINT FORM

ADMINISTRATIVE DATA

TITLE	DATE	TIME
KIRTLAND AFB, NM, 13 Aug 80, Possible Hostile Intelligence Intercept Incident, Frequency Jamming.	14 Aug 80	0730

PLACE: AFOSI District 17 B1D, Kirtland AFB, NM

HOW RECEIVED: [X] IN PERSON [ ] TELEPHONICALLY [ ] IN WRITING

SOURCE AND EVALUATION: 1960th Communication Officer

RESIDENCE OR BUSINESS ADDRESS: 1960 COMMSq KAFB, NM — PHONE: 4-5098

CN _____ APPLIES

SUMMARY OF INFORMATION

REMARKS

1. On 13 Aug 80, 1960 COMMSq Maintenance Officer reported Radar Approach Control equipment and scanner radar inoperative due to high frequency jamming from an unknown cause. Total blackout of entire radar approach system to include Albuquerque Airport was in effect between 1630-2215hrs. Radar Approach Control back up systems also were inoperative.

2. On 13 Aug 80, Defense Nuclear Agency Radio Frequency Monitors determined, by vector analysis, the interference was being sent from an area (V-90 degrees or due East) on DAF Map coordinates E-28.6. The area was located NW of Coyote Canyon Test area. It was first thought that Sandia Laboratory, which utilizes the test range was responsible. However, after a careful check, it was later determined that no tests were being conducted in the canyon area. Department of Energy, Air Force Weapons Laboratory and DNA were contacted but assured that their agencies were not responsible.

3. On 13 Aug 80, Base Security Police conducted a physical check of the area but because of the mountainous terrain, a thorough check could not be completed at that time. A later foot search failed to disclosed anything that could have caused the interference.

4. On 13 Aug 80, at 2215hrs., all radar equipment returned to normal operation without further incident.

5. CONCLUSION: The presence of hostile intelligence jamming cannot be ruled out. Although no evidence would suggest this, the method has been used in the past. Communication maintenance specialists cannot explain how such interference could cause the radar equipment to become totally inoperative. Neither could they suggest the type or range of the interference signal. DNA frequency monitors reported the interference beam was wide spread and a type unknown to their electronical equipment. Further check of the area was being conducted by Technical Services, AFOSI.

6. High command interest item. Briefings requested IAW AFOSIR 124-4 be completed at HQ AFOSI/IVOE. HQ CR 44 and 51 items.

DATE FORWARDED HQ AFOSI

AFOSI FORM 95 ATTACHED [ ] YES [ ] NO

An official example of the mysterious activity reported in the vicinity of Kirtland Air Force Base in 1980, which led researcher Paul Bennewitz to believe that there was an alien presence in the area. Bennewitz's research resulted in deep surveillance of his activites by the USAF and the National Security Agency.

chasing officially created lies and half-truths about UFOs. After all, both men were digging deep (and at precisely the same time) into official secrets. In Bennewitz's case, scientific and technical projects at Kirtland Air Force Base, and in Moore's case, what had really happened at Roswell.[1]

Published in 2005, Greg Bishop's book, *Project Beta: The Story of Paul Bennewitz, National Security, and the Creation of a Modern UFO Myth*, provides UFO research with what is certainly the most complete and accurate account of the Bennewitz saga. In early 2005, I met with Bishop for dinner in Burbank, California, and later that night conducted an interview with him in a Hollywood bar. What was it that had prompted Bishop to dig into this particularly dark and disturbing affair?

"Well," Bishop began, "the main thing was that I knew Bill Moore. I was at the MUFON Symposium in 1989 when Bill made that speech about how the Air Force had him report back to them about how effective their disinformation operations on Bennewitz were. And I figured I had to know the complete story of what was going on. Over the years I just kept asking Bill certain questions; and as things developed, he would answer more of them. Now, I think Bill got to the point where he told me as much as he possibly could. And just as the mystery grew and I got more answers to my questions, I got more interested in it."

Bishop continued, "I'm tired of what I call UFO porno—case after case just being discussed without real answers. But one of the avenues where someone might know the answers is the government. And that's a huge subject; and the [Bennewitz case] is a little tiny corner of it. I think I was lucky that I was around the story and definitely around the players in the story enough so that I could contact them, those that were still alive. The fact that it was pretty much an ignored story—apart from in the UFO research community—didn't make that much difference to me. And the fact that it has all these implications for Ufology—that was just a fringe benefit of it. I wasn't on any kind of crusade. I just wanted to find out for myself what was going on, or to get as close as I could get to the truth about what happened to Bennewitz. And I tried—and hopefully succeeded—to be impartial."

I continued my questions: "There is no doubt that [your research] absolutely demolishes certain cornerstones of the UFO subject, and specifically some of the tales in circulation in the 1980s about underground alien bases at Dulce, New Mexico, and alien-induced cattle mutilations. Did this make you wonder how much else of the UFO history and the lore that we have to work with is real or faked, too?"

Bishop replied, "Those underground base stories started out with Bennewitz's own beliefs in the late '70s and were based at least partly on abductees he'd researched who claimed to have been taken to underground bases. And the Air Force and the NSA then just amplified those beliefs to where that became his main obsession and he began looking away from Kirtland towards Dulce, which is what they wanted, as it was hundreds of miles away.

"The majority of the things he talked about were underground bases, how to fight the aliens, how they affected our history, and what kind of threat they posed. These were the things that seemed immediate to Bennewitz at the time. It was basically a combination of probably 75 percent of his perception of things and then 25 percent of the Air Force and the NSA egging him on.

"It was Bennewitz who brought up the alien invasion, so they only had to expand on it. When he first brought up the subject of an underground base at Dulce, that made the NSA and Air Force very excited and very pleased. To draw his attention over there and away from Kirtland was their entire reason; and to point his nose in that direction was all they could have hoped for, so that's where all their effort went."

Bishop was careful to add, "That doesn't mean there couldn't be underground UFO bases; but it does mean that there is a very good likelihood that it was all just a rumor that started spreading, as that is the thing people wanted—and still want—to hear. But I don't think this was a one-off situation."

"Do you have other examples of the Intelligence community watching UFO researchers and feeding them disinformation?" I asked.

"The most recent one, I would personally think, was probably much of the MJ12 stuff that was leaked to Bob and Ryan Wood. When things like that happen, I start to wonder how much of that is steering them in some direction that the disinformation people want them to go and completely away from the answer. And it does make me wonder and ask: how much of this is actually true?"

The MJ12 documents are a collection of what are purported to be official, leaked top-secret Government files that claim an alien spacecraft crashed at Roswell, New Mexico, in 1947. Championed by some as the real thing, the documents are viewed by others as officially created disinformation, designed to further cloud the murky waters of the Roswell affair.

"And what about the animal mutilations that became a part of Bennewitz's whole scenario?" I pressed.

"There were reports in the Dulce area in the late 1970s and early 1980s of a weird craft that was seen. In fact, Gabe Valdez, a highway patrol officer in Dulce, New Mexico, and some of his deputies saw one and actually tried to surround it before it floated off and out of sight. But what was interesting is that this object had kind of a lawnmower-type engine noise and sounded like a little surveillance drone with an internal combustion engine.

"Now, while I don't think anything that small would be able to pick up a cow, based on my research I'm fairly certain that the cattle mutilation thing has to do with some sort of pathogen that got out into the animal population in the 1960s and somebody is trying to track it down and figure out what it is before it gets too far and it ruins the beef industry and starts killing people. I think there is a government group—or quasi-government group—that do most of the mutilations."

"I was impressed that you got a lot of retired insiders to speak to you," I said to Bishop.

He nodded and replied, "I've had former USAF Intelligence people tell me the book is pretty much on the mark as far as they knew. There were only a couple of people who asked me not to use their names. One was a physicist in the Air Force Weapons Lab. I asked him at the time what he thought they were covering up and he said: 'There were a lot of things going on at the base at that time.' I knew that he was involved in the Bennewitz case so I knew that he knew. So instead of pressing him on it we moved onto other things.

"But the next day we went to the Kirtland base and he drove me around on the base with his ID card, which, I guess, was still good. And he was showing me various things from the main road inside the base; he pointed at the Star Fire Range and said: 'That was an interesting area; there was a guy named Bob Fugate who figured out how to watch satellites; and it was a big deal at the time and everyone was excited about it.' And I realized that what he was doing was answering my questions from the day before without having to sit there and say something. I find that a lot of intelligence people, if they can't answer something directly but they really want to help you, then they'll tell you in another way, but you have to pay attention. So the Star Fire Range is one of those things that I think they were trying to steer Bennewitz's attention away from."

"Who do you sympathize with in this story? Bennewitz, because he really thought that he was on to some hot UFO data, or the Government, because it was trying to protect its Cold War secrets?" I wanted to know.

Bishop replied, "You know, I get asked that question and it's funny because a lot of the things that appear evil are, in fact, things done by people in a mundane way. That doesn't make them not wrong. But from the Government and Intelligence point of view, it was protect this information at all costs and if a person has to go crazy, that's fine. And in Bennewitz's case, he was unfortunately primed that way already because he wouldn't listen to anybody that tried to lead him away from that idea. He really didn't help his case any. But if I'm asked if I have a moral problem with anything in the book, when they knew he was kind of going around the bend, they didn't really change anything. They kept feeding him disinformation and letting it go where it was going to go. And they figured at all costs that was more important. Protecting the projects at Kirtland and sources in the Soviet Union was more important than one person ending up in a mental institution; and that I have a problem with."[2]

In 1998 after the publication of my book *The FBI Files*, I was contacted by a man who served with the FBI when it was investigating the MJ12 documents, and who had knowledge of the official interest shown in them. Greg Bishop mentions these documents as potential Government-created disinformation. According to the man, the FBI had actually been aware of the intricacies of the MJ12 saga some two years before British author Timothy Good published the documents in his 1987 bestseller *Above Top Secret*. However, I was advised, the investigation was intensified after the documents were publicized in the U.S.. I was further told that initially there was a fear on the part of the Air Force and the FBI's Foreign Counter-Intelligence people that the MJ12 papers had been fabricated by Soviet intelligence personnel who intended them as "bait."

That bait was to be used on American citizens who had a personal interest in UFOs but who were also working on sensitive defense-related projects—including the Stealth fighter. The FBI and AFOSI suspected that by offering the MJ12 papers to targeted sources within the American defense industry, the Soviets would receive something of value of a defense nature in return. The man was unsure precisely how the investigation concluded. He did know that no charges were brought against anyone.[3]

This was an ingenious scenario, but my source reiterated that the Soviet theory was simply that—a theory and nothing more. It was, he said, one of several avenues actively pursued by the FBI at the time—including, interestingly enough, the possibility that the MJ12 documents had been created as disinformation by the U.S. Government to hide the facts concerning secret "human experiments" undertaken by the military in the immediate post–war era. Gerald Haines, historian of the National Reconnaissance Office, made a similar comment in his controversial paper, "CIA's Role in the Study of UFOs: 1947–1990." In a section of the report that dealt specifically with CIA involvement in UFO investigations in the 1980s, Haines commented that "Agency analysts from the Life Science Division of OSI and OSWR officially devoted a small amount of their time to issues relating to UFOs. These included counterintelligence concerns that the Soviets and the KGB were using U.S. citizens and UFO groups to obtain information on sensitive U.S. weapons development programs (such as the Stealth aircraft)."[4]

On an identical track, Greg Bishop stated that "Former Special Agent Walter Bosley was assigned to counterintelligence duties with two detachments of the AFOSI from 1994 to 1999. He says his office was proudest of the fact that for years, UFO stories (among others) were part of a program to keep various stealth technology projects under wraps, and usher any meddling inquiries behind the laughter curtain." On the issue of official agencies secretly watching those people with interests in UFOs, Bosley expanded on this to Bishop: "I also initiated an investigation to look at hostile intelligence services and their use of unwitting U.S. citizens to collect info on defense technology. We went to a few UFO events around Southern California to check this kind of thing out."[5]

There is further evidence that the FBI has more information in its archives pertaining to MJ12 and the related Roswell controversy. Indeed, that evidence reinforces the fact that many of the key UFO researchers that were investigating Roswell and MJ12 in the 1980s were the subjects of official interest and surveillance. On 16 November 1988, UFO researcher Larry Bryant (who was the subject of an FBI investigation in the 1960s) wrote to Ms. Hope Nakamura of the Center for National Security Studies and advised her that the bulk of the FBI's dossier on Bill Moore (that amounted to no less than fifty-five pages) was being withheld for reasons directly affecting the national security of the United States. Bryant went on to explain that Moore was attempting to find legal assistance to challenge the nondisclosure of the majority of the FBI's file. In a determined effort to lend assistance to Moore, Bryant drafted a lengthy and detailed advertisement that he proposed submitting to a number of military newspapers for future publication.

Titled "UFO SECRECY/CONGRESS-WATCH," the ad specifically addressed the fact that the Bureau's file on Moore was classified at no less than Secret level, and that at least one other (unnamed) U.S. Government agency was also keeping tabs on Moore and his UFO pursuits. In particular those pursuits related to certain "whistle-blower testimony" that Moore had acquired from a variety of sources within the American Military and Government. Bryant urged those reading the advertisement to contact their local congressman and to press for nothing less than a full-scale inquiry into the issue of UFOs.

Bryant's advertisement was ultimately published in the 23 November 1988 issue of *The Pentagram*, a publication of the Army. Yet as spirited as it was, it failed to force the FBI to relinquish its files on Moore. By 1993, the FBI's dossier on Moore, still classified Secret, ran to 61 pages. Moore had gained access to a mere six.[6]

In 1989 Bryant, mindful of the FBI's surveillance of Moore, attempted to force the Bureau to release any or all records on Stanton Friedman, another leading UFO researcher in pursuit of the MJ12 and Roswell stories. On 2 August of that year, Bryant received the following response from Richard L. Huff: "Mr. Friedman is the subject of one Headquarters main file. This file is classified in its entirety and I am affirming the denial of access to it."

Bryant's efforts on Friedman's behalf came after Friedman had filed FOIA requests with the Bureau and the CIA. The CIA's response was that it had no responsive files—except for a "negative" name check from the FBI, which subsequently refused to reveal details of either the size of the file or its security classification.

On 28 August 1989, Bryant filed suit in the District Court for the Eastern District of Columbia. "My complaint," explained Bryant, "seeks full disclosure of the UFO-related content of the FBI dossier on Stan Friedman. Neither Stan nor I have been able to convince the U.S. Federal Bureau of Investigation to loosen its grasp on that dossier, which Bureau officials assert bears a security classification." Fortunately, in Friedman's case, a "small portion" of the FBI's file pertaining to him was eventually released on 13 November 1989 as a result of Bryant's actions. The remainder of the FBI file on Friedman has never surfaced.

Greg Bishop also has been the subject of what sounds like Government-orchestrated chicanery. On 3 September 1999, Bishop stated the following in an email exchange with Jim Keith, an author of numerous books on UFOs and conspiracy theories who died, under circumstances that some see as highly suspicious, only four days after he and Bishop exchanged emails:

"I turned on my computer [the last week of August, 1999] and found that all of my article and work in progress files had been deleted. Luckily, I had backed them up. What was weird was the fact that the articles were not only 'trashed,' but were also deleted from the trash AND erased from the trash sector of the hard drive, making them unrecoverable. This takes a few steps of which I would have most likely been aware, and certainly don't remember, if indeed I was the culprit. There are a few possibilities: I was hacked through the modem, I was given a virus that only affects my article folder and no other Word files, or someone broke in the house and deleted them. I guess I'll believe the story that makes me feel best."[7]

And this odd affair was not a singular event as Bishop astutely noted: "Mail problems…cropped up with a cattle mutilation researcher. Our postal and even email exchanges were often a marvel of missed and misrouted communications. He recently suggested that we back off our discussions for a while for reasons he would not talk about. Then there were the endless hang-up calls. *69 never worked with any of them. These came in sometimes five to ten times (or more) a day. If we picked up the receiver, there was static or silence."[8]

Whatever the truth behind the murky saga of Paul Bennewitz, MJ12, and Roswell, the key point is that the controversies led to intense, official surveillance of leading elements within the UFO research community in the United States—reinforcing the fact that wherever the flying saucer investigators go, the Government is never far behind.

Another classic example of this surveillance is the way in which Government, Military, and Intelligence agencies monitor conferences on subjects related to UFOs. One such example demonstrates that in the late 1970s, the FBI was taking a keen interest in those who investigated cattle mutilations, including Officer Gabe Valdez, who was a central player in the Paul Bennewitz saga. And the FBI even went as far as dispatching agents to attend a conference on the subject that was held on 20 April 1979, at the Albuquerque Public Library.

A report to FBI headquarters from Albuquerque, dated 25 April 1979, outlined the flavor of the conference, and addressed the various opinions of those in attendance: "Forrest S. Putman, Special Agent in Charge (SAC), Albuquerque Office of the FBI, explained to the conference that the Justice Department had given the FBI authority to investigate those cattle mutilations which have occurred or might occur on Indian lands.

"Gabe Valdez, New Mexico State Police, Dulce, New Mexico, reported he has investigated the death of 90 cattle during the past three years, as well as six horses. Officer Valdez said he is convinced that the mutilations of the animals have not been the work of predators because of the precise manner of the cuts. Officer Valdez said he had investigated mutilations of several animals which had occurred on the ranch of Manuel Gomez of Dulce, New Mexico. Manuel Gomez addressed the conference and explained he had lost six animals to unexplained deaths which were found in a mutilated condition within the last two years. Further, Gomez said that he and his family are experiencing fear and mental anguish because of the mutilations."

The FBI's conference document also focused on diverse lectures given by a range of speakers: "David Perkins, the Director of the Department of Research at Libre School in Farasita, Colorado...said, 'The only thing that makes sense about the mutilations is that they make no sense at all.'

"Tom Adams of Paris, Texas, who has been independently examining mutilations for six years, said his investigation has shown that helicopters are almost always observed in the area of the mutilations. He said that the helicopters do not have identifying markings and they fly at abnormal, unsafe, or illegal altitudes. Dr. Peter Van Arsdale, Ph.D., Assistant Professor, Department of Anthropology, University of Denver, suggested that those investigating the cattle mutilations take a systematic approach and look at all types of evidence [sic] is discounting any of the theories such as responsibility by extraterrestrial visitors or satanic cults. Richard Sigismund, Social Scientist, Boulder, Colorado, presented an argument which advanced the theory that the cattle mutilations are possibly related to activity of UFOs. Numerous other persons made similar type presentations expounding on their theories regarding the possibility that the mutilations are the responsibility of extraterrestrial visitors, members of Satanic cults, or some unknown government agency. Dr. Richard Prine, Forensic Veterinarian, Los Alamos Scientific Laboratory (LASL), Los Alamos, New Mexico, discounted the possibility that the mutilations had been done by anything but predators. He said he had examined six carcasses and in his opinion predators were responsible for the mutilation of all six.

"Tommy Blann, Lewisville, Texas, told the conference he has been studying UFO activities for twenty-two years and mutilations for twelve years. He explained that animal mutilations date back to the early 1800's in England and Scotland. He also pointed out that animal mutilations are not confined to cattle, but cited incidents of mutilation of horses, dogs, sheep, and rabbits. He also said the mutilations are not only nationwide, but international in scope. Carl W. Whiteside, Investigator, Colorado Bureau of Investigation, told the conference that between April and December 1975, his Bureau investigated 203 reports of cattle mutilations."

After the conference, a closed-to-the-public meeting convened in Albuquerque that was heavily attended by elements of the FBI, local law enforcement officers from New Mexico, and official investigators from Nebraska, Colorado, Montana, and Arkansas. One of the more notable highlights was the revelation that in Arkansas, authorities had investigated twenty-eight cases of cattle mutilation, all of which "were the work of intentional mutilators and not of predators."

As a result of the ongoing controversy, in May 1979 Santa Fe's District Attorney's Office received a $50,000 Law Enforcement Assistance Administration grant, allowing a comprehensive review of the evidence to proceed. The investigation was limited, however, to a study of those livestock found solely on Indian land in New Mexico. Intriguingly, an FBI memorandum of 1 June 1979 stated that, following the announcement that an official investigation was to begin, "there have been no new cattle mutilations in Indian country." By the summer of 1980, a final report—"Operation Animal Mutilation"—was published and copies were circulated throughout the FBI. The final entry in the FBI's cattle mutilation file reads: "A perusal of this report reflects it adds nothing new in regard to potential investigation by the Albuquerque FBI of alleged mutilations on Indian lands in New Mexico." The matter was laid firmly to rest along with conclusions and assertions that the mutilations were merely the work of predators.

Despite whoever or whatever is responsible for the cattle mutilations, it is worth noting that at the same time the Air Force Office of Special Investigations was monitoring the activities of Paul Bennewitz and bombarding him with fake UFO tales, the FBI was taking note of Officer Valdez's cattle mutilation investigations. Valdez was also acquainted with Bennewitz. In other words, at an official level it seems that all of the central players in this story—Bennewitz, Valdez, Bill Moore, and Greg Bishop—were, on various occasions, the subjects of official interest and surveillance.

From 1992 and 1993, come three examples of official monitoring of conferences that had UFO themes or connections. For example, U.S. Government agents were in attendance at the first European meeting of the Society for Scientific Exploration (SSE). Held on 7–8 August 1992 in Munich, SSE had the UFO subject on its agenda. A three-page document pertaining to the conference, originally classified at the Secret level, was made available to me under the terms of the Freedom of Information Act by the Defense Intelligence Agency in 1993. Its contents make for interesting reading: "The expressed aim of the SSE meeting was to promote the exchange of ideas, results and goals among researchers in various fields of anomalies, and inform the public of the discussion among active scientists concerning current controversial issues. Papers and communications were in English, and German language abstracts of the various parapsychology (PS) papers presented were distributed at the beginning of the meeting.

"The conference sessions examined PSI [psychic abilities] and other extraordinary mental phenomena, crop circles (were they messages or hoaxes), geophysical variables and their influences on human behavior, astro-psychology, the Earth and unidentified flying objects (UFO), and additional highlights, to include near death experiences (NDE)."

Similarly, on 8 October 1993 following a routine FOIA request submitted to the Defense Intelligence Agency, I received a number of UFO records that had then been recently declassified by the State Department. One of those documents—dated 1992—dealt with an official reference to a UFO conference in China that was the subject of interest to the U.S. Intelligence community. According to the document:

"China Unidentified Flying Object (UFO) Research Organization hosts national conference in Beijing on 11 May. The organization hopes that China will be selected to host the first world UFO conference, which is scheduled for 1993. More than 200 Chinese researchers are attending the conference to study reports of flying saucers or 'Fei Die' in China. About 5,000 UFO sightings have been reported in China in the past 20 years."

Copies of this document were forwarded to a number of departments within the U.S. Government, Intelligence community, and Military, including the National Security Agency, Wright-Patterson Air Force Base, the CIA, and the American Embassy in Beijing. Most notable of all, the DIA also flashed a copy of the report, via electronic signal, to the British Ministry of Defense's Defense Intelligence Staff (DIS) in London.

An integral part of the MoD, the DIS was created on 1 April 1964 out of the amalgamation of the pre-1964 service intelligence branches and the Joint Intelligence Bureau. DIS now serves as a unified body able to serve the MoD, the Armed Forces, and a variety of other Government departments. Broadly speaking, the DIS carries out the same functions as that of its predecessors—Army, Navy and Air Intelligence—and provides the MoD with a central and unified intelligence organization for objective assessments of defense intelligence matters in both peacetime and wartime. Its primary function is to give warning of preparations for war by a potential enemy. Much of the DIS's work is devoted to military issues such as tactics, orders of battle (known as ORBATS), and weapons and capabilities. Other areas are covered to ensure a more complete picture, and these include science and technology, nuclear, chemical, and biological capabilities, arms traffic, and the control, verification, and economic aspects of defense.[9]

In 1989 Clive Neville of the MoD told me that "…we are only interested in reported [UFO] sightings which occur in the airspace of the United Kingdom." Therefore, this raises an important question: Why was the MoD's Defense Intelligence Staff receiving official briefings relating to UFO conferences held on the other side of the world? Not surprisingly, the DIS refused to discuss this matter with me.[10]

Thus, having unsurprisingly failed to secure a reply from the DIS, I directed the same question to Nick Pope, who investigated UFOs at an official level for the MoD between 1991 and 1994. In 1996 Pope wrote a book on UFOs titled *Open Skies, Closed Minds*. Pope's response of 11 October 1993 was typically bureaucratic in nature: "I am afraid that it is not our policy to discuss the distribution of UFO data within the Ministry of Defense, beyond saying that [we] are assisted by specialist staff with responsibilities covering the Air Defense of the UK. These staff examine such data routinely as part of their normal duties. Their task—like ours—is to look for evidence of any threat to the UK. If no such evidence is found, no further action is taken."[11]

Although not without interest, Pope's carefully worded reply did not reveal a great deal. Five months later, however, and during a tape-recorded interview with him, Pope provided me with a slightly modified response: "I've not seen this document arrive to us, apart from you sending it; so I don't know what happened with it."

Did this not imply that the DIS had an interest in monitoring UFO conferences and researchers on the other side of the world? I asked. Pope's reply was intriguing: "I don't know. That's a whole area that I don't want to comment on, and it's not anything to do with the UFO subject per se. One doesn't talk about intelligence divisions or their role in relation to any subject."[12]

Examples of official interest in UFO conferences continue. In 1989 I had begun to conduct extensive research on claims that elements of the British Intelligence community routinely monitored certain people involved in the promotion of animal-rights organizations. While I was able to put together a convincing body of evidence, I was soon taken up with other matters and shelved the project. However, during the course of my research, I hooked up with an official from the British Government's Ministry of Agriculture, Fisheries, and Foods (MAFF), who was able to provide some useful leads.

In 1992 over drinks in a London bar, the official asked me what I was currently working on, and during the discussion I mentioned that I was liaising with a researcher of UFOs and conspiracy theories named Mary Seal. She made the headlines in early 1993 when she rented the Wembley Indoor Arena in London to hold a conference with the intent of exposing the "machinations" of what she termed a "global elite" who had been responsible for manipulating the human race for centuries.

My acquaintance asked a few questions, I gave a few answers, and we soon got on to another topic. Shortly after our meeting I received a package in the mail. Inside was a transcript of a telephone conversation between Seal and a well-known and controversial UFO researcher variously known as both Henry Azadhedel and Armen Victorian. The conversation centered upon Seal's decision to feature the late American UFO- and conspiracy-researcher Bill Cooper at her Wembley conference.

As this information had been given to me anonymously (but almost certainly directly or indirectly by my MAFF source), I thought long and hard about what to do. Eventually, when invited to Seal's home not long afterward, I gave her the details of the phone conversation she had with Azadhedel/Victorian, without, of course, revealing the name of my source. Faced with this piece of evidence, Seal looked at me dumbfounded.

"I knew it," she seethed. "The bastards have got me monitored, haven't they?"

It certainly appears so.[13]

10

DEEP THROAT OR
DISINFORMATION?

I n 1987 British UFO author Timothy Good published in his
best-selling book *Above Top Secret* a collection of documents
that allegedly originated with the super-secret MJ12 group, as
described in the previous chapter. An unnamed source with purported
official connections had given Good the collection of documents. As
with all of the collective MJ12 papers, they reinforced the allegations
that an alien spacecraft crashed at Roswell, New Mexico, in the
summer of 1947, that extraterrestrial bodies were found, and that
a cover-up of cosmic proportions was put into place. Needless to
say, the documents provoked a huge storm of controversy that still
rumbles to this day—albeit, twenty years on, to an ever-dwindling
degree.[1]

What is less well known is that in 1986 the prolific UFO writer
Jenny Randles was approached by a former British Army source who
offered her—quite literally out of the blue—a huge mass of allegedly
Top Secret U.S. Military documents. Their description sounded
suspiciously similar to the MJ12 papers provided to Timothy Good
less than twelve months later. Whereas Good's documents amounted
to only a handful of pages, Randles was offered hundreds of pages.

At first glance, one might assume that Randles's source was a Deep
Throat-like individual who wished to reveal the U.S. Government's
most classified UFO secrets. However, a careful analysis of the data
strongly suggests that for some time before the offer was made to

Randles, she had been the subject of official surveillance by both British and U.S. authorities. The purpose was to swamp her with bogus documentation on crashed UFOs and dead aliens and keep her away from something else that she had been digging into—distinctly terrestrial events, possibly of a nuclear nature that were being hidden behind a UFO smokescreen by officials on both sides of the Atlantic.

In an interview with Randles, she told me, "I got a phone call from a complete stranger asking me if I was the writer Jenny Randles. This would be late October 1986. It was a very strange conversation; it was a very hesitant call, and not the kind of thing you would expect from anybody full of confidence. I assumed at first that it was just a UFO witness who was reluctant to talk about a sighting, as they sometime are, and was just testing the water before they ventured into it. But after I confirmed who I was, he said that he had some information which had been given to him by his superior officer—a major—in the British military forces, and he needed to see me to talk about it. Was I willing to do so at a prearranged location?

"I said to him: 'That's fine; but I want someone to come with me.' He was reluctant, and said no. I pointed out to him that if he wanted the meeting on that day—which he did, in fact, more or less within an hour or two—I couldn't get there because I don't drive, and therefore I needed someone to come with me. He reluctantly accepted that. This wasn't only true: it was a very useful excuse for me to have someone else there."

According to Randles, she made arrangements to meet the mysterious caller at a pub in Eccles, England, some ten miles from where she was living at the time. Randles then quickly telephoned a colleague—Peter Hough—and both set off in Hough's car for the meeting. When they walked into the pub, it was lunchtime and the pub was swarming with customers.

"We had no idea who we were looking for," said Randles. "We just assumed that he would find us. We went and sat down and at first we thought that no one was coming because no one immediately came up to us. But, shortly after, this guy walked up to our table.

TOP SECRET/MJ-12

DRAFT

Directive Regarding Project BLUE BOOK

Project BLUE BOOK will continue in its current intelligence
collection activities and counterintelligence functions as
specified in current NIE. Reference to BLUE BOOK is authorized
only when responding to public and congressional inquiries.

TOP SECRET/MJ-12

*In the 1980s and 1990s, a number of high-profile UFO investigators
received "leaked" documents that were allegedly Top Secret.*

He was, I would say, in his late twenties. There was nothing strange about him particularly. In fact, Peter and I were surprised by the credibility level that particular afternoon, because we hadn't gone there with any great expectations, to be perfectly honest.

"He said that he'd hesitated before coming over because he'd been given a photograph to identify me, and it was one taken about ten years earlier in which I had much longer hair and which had been used in the book *UFOs: A British Viewpoint*. He sat down, we talked, and he went through his entire story. We must have spent about three or four hours going through it, and Peter and I both took about twenty pages of notes each. He was very forthcoming; he never failed to answer a question and was certainly convincing in that regard.

"'Robert,' as I'll call him, said that until early 1985, he had served with a particular British Army unit. But towards the end of his tour of duty, his commanding officer [CO]—the major—had befriended him and several others within the unit over the space of a few months. In retrospect, although it wasn't obvious at first, what his commanding officer was doing was sounding them out for interest in, and awareness of, UFOs." Indeed, it would seem that this issue of "sounding them out" was directly related to the surveillance of Randles that was already underway at that time—as will become apparent.

Randles stated that "His CO would say things like, 'What do you think about this case? Have you read about that incident in the newspaper?' And the CO seemed to home in on not those who were interested, but on Robert, primarily, it appeared, because of his lack of enthusiasm for the subject. He wasn't entirely dismissive, but was willing to listen without being too critical.

"It was some months into this whole scenario when Robert's CO showed him a photograph of what looked like a UFO, and asked him for his comments on it, while at the same time informing him that the UFO had been tracked on radar, and had been seen both from the ground and from a commercial airliner. 'Well,' Robert replied, 'you can fake anything these days.'

"'What if I were to tell you that things like this have been tracked on radar and chased by airplanes?' said the CO. 'What if I were to tell you that they've also been recovered and we've got bodies, and things like that?' Robert replied: 'Well, I'd need to see evidence to prove that.' At that time, his CO didn't say anything more and just let it drop.

"Some months went by, and things only really took off when Robert was leaving his tour of duty in the Army, and was getting ready to go into civilian life. It was at this stage that Robert was told by his commanding officer that he had some information which he wanted Robert to get out to the world at large. It was too dangerous for the CO to do it; and he had decided that Robert was the person to trust."

The carefully planned and executed operation to target Jenny Randles had officially begun: "Robert's CO told him that, while in America, he had become friendly with a U.S. Air Force officer stationed at Wright-Patterson Air Force Base in Ohio. This man had been serving as a records officer, and had 'accidentally' intruded into Top Secret U.S. Government UFO files while he was doing some repair work on the computer system. The result of this was that he had discovered these UFO records and had managed to print out over six hundred pages of material.

"He recognized the significance of what he'd got, and managed to spirit it away without anybody knowing. However, he evidently triggered some sort of alarm and was eventually found out and was subsequently arrested. Although the files weren't recovered, he was sure they ultimately would be. And before he was hauled before a court martial, he decided that he wanted the British CO to take the files out of the country. He told the CO where to get the material, how to pick it up, and to get it out of the U.S. quickly, because he didn't think it would be there for much longer. The CO did pick it up and did bring it back to Britain without detection. But shortly afterwards, this computer operator died before the court martial in what was alleged to have been a car accident involving drunk driving. The CO said he was always suspicious of this and thought it was a set-up."

At that point in his dealings with his CO, Robert had not yet personally seen the files, Randles explained, and that remained the case until he left the British Army in 1985. Ten weeks before he telephoned Randles, Robert was invited to a reunion with his CO and once again the issue of the mysterious files surfaced. Little did he know it at the time, but Robert was about to become the conduit in this operation to ensnare Randles in a military plot. Robert's CO explained that he was due to take on a new position within the British Army and he needed to offload the UFO files. Was Robert the man for the job? Robert could see his CO's predicament and agreed to help. The files were at a specific location and Robert was given instructions on how to pick them up. On doing so, Robert finally had the opportunity to peruse their contents. As Randles told me:

"It was blatantly obvious to both Peter and I that much of what the files referred to was the Roswell crash. Robert said that there was mention of a UFO which had crashed somewhere in the western United States in 1947, and that wreckage and bodies were found. Robert wasn't saying this in an overenthusiastic way; it was all done very methodically and matter-of-factly. And that was one of the most convincing aspects of what he was telling us. But you could hear the awe in his voice, as if he'd never come across any possibility like this before.

"There was lots of material about Roswell, including photographs of the UFO and of the aliens; and one of the most detailed files was an autopsy report on one of the bodies recovered from the Roswell crash. Robert remembered the name of the doctor who had written it. His name was Dr. Frederick Hauser, a name I'd never seen connected with UFOs in any way whatsoever. Robert said that there was a very detailed account that was mostly filled with medical jargon about the autopsy which he didn't understand, and there was a photograph of this entity with a slit right down the middle from the neck to the navel.

"One of the things Robert said was, the aliens were very human-looking. He said that the head was completely bald, but the most unusual feature of the face was the nose, which was almost flush into the face—almost unnoticeable. He couldn't tell from the photographs, but the autopsy report made it clear that the beings were slightly smaller than average human size—about five feet in height. In addition to this, Robert said that the other biggest single file in the report was one with a rather disturbing title: 'Elimination of non-military personnel.' He said that this was a document discussing the ways in which witnesses who had come into possession of too much information on UFOs were to be silenced.

"And although this sounds very much like something out of a spy film, from his detailed discussion of a number of case histories in the file, the one tactic that was used most often—particularly with people in influential positions—was to offer them high-paid jobs in government departments. They had pretty much determined that, where money was concerned, people usually comply.

"But there was also a discussion of the so-called Men in Black—people going around warning people about national security and intimidating them into silence. However, Robert told us that this tactic was only used on those whose instability was considered to be significant enough that, if they ever told their story publicly, it would not be considered credible." But, if all else failed, there was one ominous option: termination. Although Robert told Randles and Hough that this tactic wasn't employed too frequently, those charged with carrying out such dubious activities were well trained to ensure that any "UFO-related deaths" appeared to be due to suicide or an accident.

Randles added, "There were also a number of other specific case histories, including a case which, Robert said, involved a UFO which had crashed somewhere in England in 1980. Robert couldn't remember where exactly in the country this was supposed to have been, but he said that there were definitely photographs of the object and it was incredible. It was at night, it was a disc, and it was surrounded by lights. Some of the things that Robert said about it suggested the Rendlesham Forest case. For example, he said that the crash was in connection with a military base, which was nearby. That's why it was covered up so effectively.

"Robert told us that, for his own protection, he'd separated the material into about twenty or thirty piles so that there was no complete document anywhere. In other words, if anyone found any one batch of material, it wouldn't make much sense because everything was scattered about in different locations in his house. Robert decided that he would have to 'think about what to do next.' So, Peter and I arranged to meet him about a week later at a covert location—which was actually a country park in the middle of nowhere—where the documents would be handed over to us. We were suspicious because Robert hadn't brought with him to the pub one scrap of paper to support his case, but he was very credible. Come the day of the meeting, Peter and I went to the park, but Robert failed to turn up, which was not exactly a great surprise to us.

"A few days later, I was surprised when Robert wrote me a letter. In it, he alleged that in the week between our meeting at the pub and when we were supposed to be handed the documents, he had been contacted by what he termed his 'former employers,' and that they had taken him to a military base somewhere in southern England. He didn't say much more than that, but specified that they had interrogated him for forty-eight hours. The military were clearly aware of everything that had happened, including our meeting at the pub. And they knew all about the six hundred pages of documentation, which they ordered him to hand over, pointing out that he had a wife and children, and it was they who would suffer if he didn't.

"Apparently, Robert was told that the files were nothing more than a prank on someone's part, and they were to be transferred to a U.S. Air Force base in England, before being flown back to America, where they were to be destroyed. Robert's letter was full of apologies, saying things like: 'I know this means now that you will never believe a word I say. There is nothing I can do about that. But I am telling you that I am going to spend the rest of my life trying to prove that this is true. And if I get proof, I will contact you. All I can do is ask you to think of me kindly. But I have to think of my family. They have to be my priority.'"

Even though Randles and Hough would not see their informer again, they were not beyond doing a bit of surveillance of their own as they sought to verify that Robert was who he claimed to be. They watched Robert drive away from the pub so that they could write down his license plate.

"We did this because we could use a friend of ours in the Police Force to track Robert down. As a result of that, during the intervening week between that meeting and when we were supposed to meet with him in the park, we were actually able to do quite a bit of digging into Robert. It turned out that what he told us proved to be correct: the name he had given us was his real name; he lived where he said he lived; he had recently been in the Army; and his car had been registered in the area he worked in precisely the same month that his Army career had come to an end. We even used a bit of subterfuge to get to speak with his employers. In fact, we lied through our teeth and pretended that we were making inquiries about Social Security matters."

While Randles's and Hough's inquiries certainly seemed to suggest that Robert was exactly what he claimed to be, Randles was convinced that his revelations were nothing less than a disinformation ploy aimed directly at her. She had noted the apparent ease with which the alleged records officer at Wright-Patterson Air Force base uncovered, downloaded, and provided to Robert's commanding officer, highly classified files on crashed UFOs. "This is one of the parts of the whole story which I find totally unbelievable. He had discovered these UFO records and had managed to print out over six hundred pages without anybody noticing, which I think would have taken ages. And, anyway, wouldn't you rather just make a disk of it?

"Then he managed to get this material away from Wright-Patterson without anyone knowing—despite the fact that he had apparently triggered an alarm of some sort. And then Robert's CO somehow miraculously got all of this material out of the country and back to Britain. And why would Robert's superiors need to interrogate him for two days to get him to hand over the files? Presumably, they could have simply marched into his house on a pretext of national security and removed them.

"I think that Peter and I more or less mutually decided between ourselves that the most likely explanation was that Robert had been set up by someone, and that he really did have this documentation. If it was a hoax, then Robert certainly wasn't guilty of it. And I'd probably still have to say that today.

"In retrospect, it's fairly obvious from the detailed notes we took of what Robert told us that what he was describing was very similar to the Majestic 12 documents which Tim Good released in 1987, and the appendices to those documents which have still never surfaced. It's clear from those MJ12 papers that have been released that those half a dozen pages are just the tip of the iceberg, and there were masses of other data which were never released."

Randles had an interesting theory to explain what may lie behind the MJ12 documents and why her research may have led her to become the target of official interest: "The MJ12 documents surfaced in May 1987. Tim Good had received them at some point after our meeting with Robert, and published them—more or less at the last minute—in *Above Top Secret*. I thought that what was happening was this: someone had first approached Moore, Shandera, and Friedman with these papers. And because they'd sat on them for a couple of years and hadn't published them, they had given up on them. It was not unknown in October 1986 that I was then writing *The UFO Conspiracy*—which dealt with government investigations of UFOs— and that maybe they were hoping that by feeding this story to me, I'd publish it in [the book].

"But when Peter Hough and I started to make inquiries and checks, someone, somewhere, got cold feet and the offer was withdrawn. When we didn't pass the test, Tim Good was the next option. He was writing *Above Top Secret* at the time and didn't ask as many questions. I should stress that this is all surmise, but it was curious the way it all came out. I'm absolutely certain that the MJ12 documents are disinformation. The fact that [they] were released to people in strategic positions—and by that I mean people who could relate the account in a book—was important. The whole point was to discredit the question of delving into the UFO phenomenon."

Randles made a further important point—possibly the most crucial point of all: "Another thing to bear in mind, which I think is possibly significant and which maybe has been overlooked is that the paperback version of *Skycrash* [the first published book devoted solely to the alleged UFO landing at Rendlesham Forest, Suffolk, England, in December 1980] had been released just a few weeks before I was approached with this offer of the files. Now, in the paperback, there was a whole new chapter addressing the possibility that the UFO crash story was a smokescreen for something else—possibly a nuclear missile or a Russian satellite. Perhaps this might have alerted someone to the need to destabilize me in some way. If they could make me look less credible, people might take what I had to say less seriously.

"I'll give you an example: when *From out of the Blue*—my second book on the Rendlesham Forest case—was released, I remember it was reviewed by Nigel Watson in *Fortean Times* magazine. In that book, I had mentioned my experience with Robert and the files, and Nigel homed in on this and said: 'Jenny is taking ludicrous stories like this seriously,' and dismissed the whole book as a consequence of that. So, in other words, even in that one instance, if this was a disinformation exercise, it worked."[2]

Randles is likely correct; publishing a book that suggested that a nuclear accident might have occurred on British soil in 1980 would certainly have attracted official interest, on both sides of the Atlantic. Throughout the early-to-mid-1980s the Campaign for Nuclear Disarmament (CND) was a high profile organization in Britain that had widespread support and called for the U.S. nuclear presence to be removed from the United Kingdom. If the Rendlesham event was even remotely connected to something resembling a nuclear accident, it is not at all beyond the bounds of possibility that a plan would have been put into place to try and discredit the source of the story—in this case, Jenny Randles. Particularly if the accident was the result of the clandestine activities of Americans.

And what better way to do discredit Randles than to carefully watch her, follow her research, and then employ the talents of a useful patsy to feed her seemingly official-looking documents on crashed

UFOs and dead aliens that would the be widely denounced and dismissed as hoaxed material upon publication? The result? Anything that Randles might have to say in the future on UFOs in general, but on Rendlesham in particular, could be similarly denounced as a hoax.

To their credit, Randles and Peter Hough did not fall for the ruse and instead elected to dig deep into the background of Robert and his military history. It is perhaps significant that at this point the operation was terminated. Doubtless it quickly became clear to officials that Randles was not falling for their spurious ufological bait, and the alleged whistleblowers and their carefully crafted "Top Secret files" on crashed UFOs vanished back into the darkness from which they had originally emerged. Moreover, in early 2002 I was able to speak personally with Frederick Hauser—the person that Robert had claimed had participated in an alien autopsy. Hauser quickly asserted that his path had never crossed with that of the UFO in any capacity.

The controversy surrounding classified computerized files on crashed UFOs and dead alien bodies supposedly held within an underground fortress at Wright-Patterson Air Force Base—as well as official surveillance of those that dared to dig into such controversies—was far from over, however.

11

HACKING THE HANGAR

"The subject of UFOs is one that has interested me for some long time. About ten or twelve years ago I made an effort to find out what was in the building at Wright-Patterson Air Force Base where the information is stored that has been collected by the Air Force, and I was understandably denied this request. It is still classified above Top Secret." Intriguing words—and they are made even more intriguing by the fact that they were written in a 28 March 1975 letter to UFO investigator Shlomo Arnon by none other than the late Senator Barry Goldwater, formerly the chairman of the U.S. Senate Intelligence Committee.[1]

For years it has been rumored that there exists a highly classified (and decidedly off-limits) series of rooms, aircraft hangars, and underground chambers at Wright-Patterson Air Force Base, Dayton, Ohio, where the preserved remains of a number of dead alien creatures are stored along with the wreckage of their crashed and recovered spacecraft. In specifically generic and folkloric terms, the location of this astonishing evidence has become popularly known as Hangar 18.

Of those who attempted to force open the doors of Hangar 18, the late Leonard Stringfield was certainly the most active. A United States Air Force Intelligence officer during the Second World War, Stringfield collected a huge amount of data that, if true, suggests that there existed an absolute wealth of UFO material, debris, and even alien bodies locked away from prying eyes at Wright-Patterson Air Force Base.

Of the many accounts that were brought to Stringfield's attention, two came from researcher Charles Wilhelm. As Stringfield recalled, "In 1959, a lady living alone in Price Hill, Cincinnati, had hired young Charles to cut her grass all summer. She knew of his interest in the UFO [subject] but said little about it until she became ill with cancer. Knowing that she had a short time to live, she called Charles to her bedside to reveal a startling story. She said that she had had a Top Secret clearance in her past work at Wright-Patterson and had seen two saucer-shaped craft in a secret hangar. One craft was intact; the other, damaged. She also knew of two 'small creatures' preserved inside another secret building, and had personally handled the paperwork on their autopsy report. She told Charles, 'Uncle Sam can't do anything to me after I'm in the grave.'"[2]

The second revelation came to Stringfield from Wilhelm following his acquisition of sensitive intelligence data in 1966. "Wilhelm got the story from a friend in the Army Reserve whose father worked with Project Blue Book at Wright-Patterson Field and held high security clearance," stated Stringfield. "On his deathbed, he related to his son that he had seen two disc-shaped craft, one intact and one damaged, and four preserved, small alien bodies 'packed in chemicals.'"[3]

Where had Wright-Patterson acquired this incredible material evidence? Much of the witness testimony suggested that its point of origin was the New Mexico desert, circa July 1947: Roswell.

There are long-standing allegations to the effect that during the summer of 1947, a UFO crashed in the deserts of New Mexico and, along with its dead crew, was whisked away under cover of overwhelming secrecy to Wright-Field (later renamed Wright-Patterson), where both the UFO and the alien bodies were placed into storage for preservation and analysis.[4]

For example, an ex-military man named Norman Richards, formerly of the U.S. 25th Tropic Lightning Division, recollects events that occurred in the post–World War Two era: "In 1950, I was in the ROTC program of the Air Force at Indiana University. We were sent to Lowry Air Force Base for six weeks training that summer. One day, we had a lecture by a colonel from Wright-Patterson AFB. He outlined many changes and new experimental aircraft being tested. During the question and answer session, he was asked if UFOs were real. He got very excited and said we better believe it. He went on to tell us of the crash, and retrieval of the parts, and the humanoids found at the site. He said they were under investigation at Wright-Patterson after being flown from Roswell, New Mexico."[5]

As Leonard Stringfield's inquiries into Wright-Patterson's involvement in the crashed UFO issue deepened, other sources came forward with additional data. Citing one such source, Stringfield asserted, "My informant is self-employed after serving a long career with the Air Force, retiring with the rank of major. During one of

Computer hacker Matthew Bevan was the subject of a major investigation by U.S. and British Intelligence after he hacked into the computer systems of Wright-Patterson Air Force Base in search of data on crashed UFOs.

our several discussions of the UFO problem, when I cited some of the medical information relative to the recovered alien humanoids, he confided in me that in 1952 he had attended a high-level secret meeting at Wright-Patterson AFB and saw in an underground chamber one of the deceased alien bodies in deep-freeze preservation. The body was about four feet tall. The head was large by human standards, and the skin on the face appeared smooth and gray. No bone structure was evident; eyes were open, no hair. The feet, he said, were like an orangutan."[6]

What was without any doubt the most fantastic account related to Stringfield, concerned an allegedly live alien on the loose at the Air Force Museum in Fairborn, Ohio. It had supposedly escaped from its confines within the bowels of Wright-Patterson. On a Sunday in 1965, "R.M." and his wife had decided to pay a visit to the museum. While his wife examined a German V-2 rocket, R.M. wandered off and headed down a corridor with a double door marked OFF LIMITS.

As he opened the door, R.M. was suddenly confronted by "a being so incredible looking that all he can remember in his numb state was saying 'Hi,' to which he got no response." The creature was small and its eyes were large under a heavy brow. There was no nose and only a slit for a mouth. Standing in stark amazement, R.M. could only stare in awe as the creature shuffled toward him and pointed its elongated fingers into his face. At that point, alarms began to scream, lights flashed, and R.M. made a hasty retreat. Military police were everywhere, ushering people to the exits.

"The cause for the emergency evacuation [R.M] opined, was without question the creature who probably had escaped from its confinement," said Stringfield. Intriguingly, according to a retired Air Force colonel known to R.M., at the time two live alien creatures were reportedly held at Wright Patterson—American scientists having developed an "incubative [sic] atmosphere" to sustain them.

As Stringfield stated, "Live aliens! Loose in the Air Force Museum? Fantastic, of course, but the Wright-Patterson complex is vast and so are its underground facilities. It is conceivable, if truly live aliens exist, that one may have slipped by the guards into the passageways and surfaced in an upper chamber of the museum."[7]

Stringfield was not alone in collecting incredible data. Victor Marchetti, a former executive assistant to the Deputy Director and Special Assistant to the Executive Director of the CIA, recalls that during his tenure with the Agency, UFOs came under the category of "very sensitive activities." More significantly, Marchetti states that he heard from "high levels" within the CIA that the bodies of an undisclosed number of "little gray men" and their crashed UFO were stored at the Foreign Technology Division (FTD) of Wright-Patterson Air Force Base.[8]

This is not the only occasion that the FTD was involved in the crashed UFO controversy. In 1993, commenting on data concerning crashed UFOs and dead alien bodies acquired from "half a dozen former and current intelligence sources," "M. Collins" wrote in *Far Out* magazine that "An extensive but little-known complex of underground bunkers, rooms, vaults and tunnels [at Wright-Patterson] did conceal such secrets up through the early 1970s, when following the close of USAF Project Blue Book, everything was moved to a 'consolidated location' elsewhere. According to these same sources, nothing 'alien' now remains at Wright-Pat except perhaps for some 'Special Control Channel' documentation and a few left-over scraps of wreckage material retained by the old Foreign Technology Division (FTD), which is now known as Foreign Aerospace Science and Technology Center (FASTC)."[9]

A number of other individuals have asserted that at Wright-Patterson there exists a huge bank of computers where the Government's UFO secrets are stored—secrets relating to crashed UFOs, dead alien beings, the exploitation of extraterrestrial technology, and the autopsies of alien corpses.

One such account that has a bearing on this issue came from a former United States Army Intelligence source, who related to Stringfield that, "Since 1948, secret information concerning UFO activity involving the us military has been contained in a computer center at Wright-Patterson AFB. At this base, a master computer file is maintained with duplicate support back-up files secreted at other military installations. Get the complete 'dump file,' both the master and the support back-up files and you've got all the hidden UFO data."[10]

Similarly, on 27 October 1992, *Dateline NBC* broadcast a segment on computer hacking that featured selected interviews with a number of self-confessed hackers. As one of the hackers talked about his ability to break into both Government and military computer systems, NBC flashed across the screen a variety of material apparently gleaned from Wright-Patterson's computer system, which stated in part, "WRIGHT-PATTERSON AFB/Catalogued UFO parts list, an underground facility of Foreign..." At that point the camera panned away and the remaining segment did not reference the text. However, it was later revealed that at least part of the material downloaded by the hacker did, indeed, reference alien autopsy data stored on Wright-Patterson's computers.[11]

In 1993 NBC broke its silence on this issue and Susan Adams, the producer of that particular segment of the program, expressed considerable surprise at the incredible response that NBC had received following the airing of the episode. The hacker, said Adams, wished to remain anonymous (primarily because much of his material had allegedly been acquired illegally from classified American Governmental and military computerized files and archives). Adams was at pains to point out that NBC lawyers had scrutinized the relevant piece "with a fine-tooth comb" and were convinced of the legitimacy of the material. Moreover, since the hacker was technically committing a felony, there was no way his identity could be revealed. "The hacker is aware of the interest his apparent UFO data has provoked, but does not wish to respond," Adams clarified.[12]

But Wright-Patterson AFB is apparently not the only place to hold computerized files on UFOs and alien bodies. Investigators Donald Schmitt and Kevin Randle have learned that such material may also be held at the North American Aerospace Defense Command (NORAD) at Cheyenne Mountain, Colorado Springs.

Commenting on those who had either direct or indirect access to actual crash-recovered exhibits of alien technology or alien remains,

Schmitt and Randle stated, "There are others, however, who have firsthand experiences, but who did not see the bodies. They, through their work with the military, saw files containing notes about the crashes and photographs of the bodies. One of those is a man who said he worked at NORAD in Colorado Springs. In the course of computerizing some of the files, he came across one labeled: USAAF (United States Army Air Force) Early Automation. The file dealt with the recovery of several small bodies and included black and white photographs of them. The man said the bodies were small, no more than four or five feet tall, with big heads."[13]

While the identity of NBC's UFO hacker may not have become public knowledge, the same cannot be said in every case. During the course of my research to uncover the UFO secrets of the British Government, I contacted Matthew Bevan, a self-confessed computer hacker who lives in Wales. Bevan, who went under the hacking name of Kuji, delved deeply into the secret world of Wright-Patterson, Hangar 18, crashed UFO accounts, and classified, futuristic aircraft.

It is clear that Bevan created considerable headaches for the Intelligence communities of both the United States and Britain, to the extent that one such Intelligence source referred to him—with apparent deadly seriousness—as "the greatest threat to world peace since Adolf Hitler." Indeed, it was this perceived threat that plunged Matthew Bevan into a distinctly bizarre world populated by covert sources within Special Branch, Scotland Yard's Computer Crime Unit, the United States Government, U.S. Air Force Intelligence, Chinese Military Intelligence, and a whole range of undercover surveillance and phone-tapping operations.

"I've been interested in computers probably since about the age of eleven," stated Bevan when I interviewed him. "I had a ZX81 for my eleventh birthday and upgraded several times and eventually got a Commodore Amiga 1200—which is the one I was using when I hacked Wright-Patterson back in '94. I was on the computer for hours at this time, but I didn't run up a big telephone bill because a friend had given me a black-market program that allows you to make calls for free. The way it works is that it uses tones within the computer that fool the telephone exchange into believing that there's no one using the line. This is called Blue-Boxing.

"In a nutshell, computer hacking is the art of getting into other people's computer systems without any prior permission. Basically, it's a criminal offence in the majority of countries if you have no permission; it's determined as unauthorized access. You need to start off with a fairly good idea of computer systems. At the moment, it's very easy for people to do because there are so many sources on the Internet with very detailed and explicit descriptions on how to actually hack systems. Well, I got a modem when I was about sixteen and began getting into it a few months later—early 1990s. First of all, I tried going for universities in the States, because I knew they were regularly hacked anyway and that I would be less likely to be prosecuted for hacking a university and it would be good experience.

"You see, people often tend to go with the same password for multiple systems; so, the chances are that if you can access their password for one system, then that password may well work on another system, too. But you certainly don't have to sit there and type in hundreds of different passwords until you get the right one. There are actually programs that will do this for you and will get you into the system. They literally search millions of words until they find the right one, and then you're in. Now, sometimes at these universities, you will have a professor who may be doing work for the military as well, and they may use the same password on both systems. For example, it only takes a few seconds to find out all of the publicly accessible files of say, NASA, which are on the Internet. However, if you hack a university and find out that a particular professor is doing work for NASA and you have his university password, you can find out a bit more about the material that isn't publicly accessible. Without getting too technical, if we take NASA as an example again, there are, as I said, the publicly available files that NASA puts on the Net. But these are by necessity connected to additional computers that are a part of their inner network—the classified material. But there have to be computers that are on the front line, as it were.

"Well, you get into the front line computers, and once you're into those, you can then begin to worm your way into their inner network. This is why the authorities and agencies always put out a statement saying that there is no classified material on the stuff they put on the Net. That's true; but they are connected to the classified network as well. Before we come to UFOs, one of the most interesting places I got into was called FLEX—Force Level Execution. This was at Rome Laboratories at Griffiss Air Force Base in New York. The official Air Force line was that this was a program designed to plan a U.S. military strike in the event of a war. But there was far more to it than that."

With a touch of humor and pride in his voice, Bevan stated, "As I got further and further into the system, it became clear that I could eventually have had access to the missiles themselves. This system was controlled by the Department of Defense and wasn't public knowledge at the time—they were actually still putting the finishing touches to it when I got in. Now, if you can get into the system and get the same access level as the administrator, you can change and delete anything you want. Well, if somewhere along the line you can change the controlling program, then you can gain access to those missiles. It wasn't a case of having a red button on my keyboard, but, effectively, if I had spent a few days working on something and then pressed Enter, there is a potential for doing something like launching a missile." Perhaps wisely, Bevan elected to concentrate on UFOs.

How and why did Bevan become interested in the secrets of Hangar 18? Was it due to his early (but nonetheless spectacularly successful) attempts to penetrate apparently secure computer systems?

"When I first started getting on the Net, I began looking at all the various bulletin boards that were available and began making friends with other users. One guy—in Australia—had on his bulletin board all these text files about UFOs. This was about 1994. Well, I'd never really been interested in UFOs. I'd seen *ET* and *Close Encounters of the Third Kind*, like everyone else, but that was about it and I certainly hadn't read anything in-depth on the subject. He had some very interesting files on there and I pulled down about five hundred of these and started getting into it. There was also a magazine called *PHRACK* that listed a whole host of military bases where people were looking for UFO stuff, and rumors were circulating that a group of hackers who had found something out about classified computerized UFO files had gone missing. I thought, if they've gone missing, maybe they found something. Maybe I can find something."[14]

Whitley Strieber, the best-selling author of *Communion*, has stated that the U.S. Government was indeed concerned that UFO researchers were possibly making unauthorized entries into classified computerized systems in the early-to-mid-1990s. In the latter part of 1993, less than one year before Matthew Bevan set about unraveling the mysteries of Hangar 18, Strieber had received an email that purported to identify the coded locations of Top Secret UFO data stored on the Defense Department's computer system.

"Spooks started prowling around my neighborhood upstate," recalled Strieber, who lived in New York at the time. "A business associate was accosted on an airplane by a group of young men who flashed badges, claimed to be with the National Security Agency, and questioned him about our activities for a couple of hours. They alleged that they were responsible for investigating intrusions into the Defense Department's secure computer systems."[15]

Time-wise, this seemed to coincide with Bevan's activities, as Bevan revealed: "I began looking at all these files and accounts to see if there was a common thread. Well, there was the Roswell story, this craft which crashed and which was taken to Wright-Patterson. You had the Stealth aircraft being tested by various defense contractors, and you had Area 51, where some of these contractors operated from and where it was also alleged that the U.S. Government was storing crashed UFOs. So, I was really picking out terms and places in all these stories that seemed important, and I began to see if I could hack the relevant systems.

"Wright-Patterson was a very, very easy computer system to get into. There was one account on one machine that was not even pass-worded. Once you're into the system and you've taken it over, you have control over all the files on that system. There are special files on the system for people's mail accounts; you can read anybody's email and look at their work. In a lot of these establishments, you have people who are working on various projects, and in each of their directories they will have files regarding what they're working on or developing and there is generally a flow of email between people which you can access.

"Now, on the one particular system that I got into, there was this flow of email back and forth in which there was a discussion about some sort of radical engine that was being developed—people were discussing it in a normal work-type environment. They were talking about this engine and I recall one guy mentioned that 'We've managed to sustain mach 15 and this thing is super-fast.' This was part of a discussion that was taking place between people at Wright-Patterson and there were explicit drawings, diagrams and so on, too. The files very clearly referred to a working prototype of an anti-gravity vehicle that utilized a heavy element to power it. This wasn't a normal aircraft; it was very small, split level, with a reactor at the bottom and room for the crew at the top."[16]

This is not the first time these types of claims have surfaced. In the late 1980s a very controversial character, Bob Lazar, claimed that he had for a relatively brief period of time been employed at the notorious Area 51 in the harsh desert of Nevada. Lazar also asserted that the United States Government stored no less than nine UFOs of extraterrestrial origin at Area 51. Most illuminating of all, Lazar stated that the spacecraft to which he was given access, utilized a super-heavy element (Element 115) to power it. This was extremely similar to that described in classified files at Wright-Patterson Air Force Base and accessed by Bevan. It must be stressed that the Lazar tale is a highly emotive one and attracts just as many disbelievers as it does believers. There are also those who think that the Lazar story was Government-sponsored disinformation designed to confuse the issue of what was really was going on at Area 51.[17]

After Bevan penetrated the inner sanctum of Wright-Patterson Air Force Base, perused secret files on strange and futuristic aircraft powered by nothing less than anti-gravity engines, he duly exited the system without detection. Or so he thought.

He explained that in 1996, "I was working at Admiral Insurance in Cardiff. It was a normal day and one of the finance managers called down and spoke to someone else about me, asked if I was there and what I was doing. Well, when he got off the phone, I thought I was in trouble; but he just said, 'Can you come and have a look at the managing director's computer?' No problem, I thought, and I trundled off with him to the M.D.'s office. But when we entered the room, all of the blinds were down.

"I looked around the room and there were seven or eight people in the room, all men. There was our finance manager and one of the other managers, but there were five or six other people who identified themselves as being from the local police and from Scotland Yard. One of them outstretched his hand and I shook it. 'Matthew Bevan?' he said. 'Yes,' I replied. 'My name is Detective Sergeant Simon Janes of Scotland Yard's Computer Crime Unit and I'm placing you under arrest for hacking NASA, Wright-Patterson Air Force Base, and Lockheed.'"

To find out how Scotland Yard succeeded in tracking down Matthew Bevan, we have to turn our attention to data that has been secured via the U.S. Government's Freedom of Information Act. Bevan's actions were the subject of at least three Government reports: "Security and Cyberspace," written by Dan Gelber and Jim Christy, and which was presented to the Senate Permanent Subcommittee of Investigations, and two General Accounting Office papers written by Jack Brock that extensively detailed Bevan's hacking history. The Gelber-Christy paper discussed Bevan's hacking activities in an eight-page appendix titled "The Case Study: Rome Laboratory, Griffiss Air Force Base, NY Intrusion."

One U.S. department that was involved in tracking Bevan, monitoring his activities, and implicated in the investigation to varying degrees was the Defense Information Systems Agency (who were notified once it became apparent that someone had hacked their way into Rome and Wright-Patterson). Also involved was a team from the Air Force Office of Special Investigations at the Air Force Information Warfare Center (AFIWC) in San Antonio, Texas. The AFIWC team was led by an Air Force computer scientist named Kevin Ziese, who provided a deposition to Scotland Yard on Bevan that officials steadfastly refuse to place in the public domain to this day.

The break-ins had been traced to a New York City-based internet provider, Mindvox, and the Air Force was then given permission to monitor all communications on the Rome Labs network. It appears, however, from examining data on the events, that the final and positive identification of Bevan came to the AFIWC via, ironically, a network of informants in the hacking community and not by identifying him directly via his own computer.

U.S. records show that on 14 April 1994, Bevan hacked into the Goddard Space Center system from a server in Latvia and copied data. The Air Force naturally assumed that this was a penetration by an unfriendly nation, who had used Bevan for doing some illegal snooping on its behalf. In hindsight it seems likely that this was simply Bevan's way of covering his tracks. The following day, AFIWC monitored Bevan as he entered the systems of Wright-Patterson AFB—and so the countdown to Bevan's subsequent and inevitable arrest began. Why two years went by before any arrest was made, however, is an issue that remains a puzzle to this day.

"Well, when I was arrested, I was taken to Cardiff Central Police Station and stuck in a cell. When I was taken for interview, I was persuaded not to have a solicitor present, so I co-operated for the first couple of interviews and was asked questions like, 'Did you hack this computer system? Did you hack that computer system?' Now, bear in mind that at the time I was doing the hacking, it was around 1994, but it was '96 when I was arrested so I honestly couldn't remember the exact details—mainly because I'd hacked into literally thousands of systems. My answers to the police were quite vague, but it was not due to avoidance."

Was Bevan questioned specifically about Wright-Patterson Air Force Base?

"Oh yes. For the last two interviews, I had a solicitor present and I was asked outright, 'Did you hack Wright-Patterson Air Force Base?' I said, 'Well, the password was literally handed to me on a plate.' I was then asked by D.S. Janes, 'What does the term Hangar 18 mean to you?' I replied, 'That's a hoarding place for alien technology.'

"And throughout the interview, they kept coming back to Hangar 18: Did I see anything on the Wright-Patterson computers? Did I download anything? Well, when Janes and his colleague Mark Morris asked me if I saw anything on the Wright-Pat computers, I said, 'Yes, an anti-gravity propulsion system.'

"The conversation then went like this, 'Did you download any files on the anti-gravity engine?' 'No.' 'Are you sure you didn't download anything?' 'Yes, I read everything on-line.' 'So you didn't download anything?' 'No!'

"Janes and Morris were pushing me on this throughout the interviews: Hangar 18, the anti-gravity engine and so on, but I just continued to tell them the same story, which was the truth. Now, a few months later, there was a hearing at Bow Street Magistrates Court. I was out on bail at the time. It turned out that the Americans were now claiming that certain things on the computers I had supposedly hacked into had been changed.

"My solicitor said, 'Fine. Show us how things were on the system before Matthew got in and show us how he changed them.' Of course, the Americans said 'No.' However, at the hearing there was a representative from U.S. Intelligence named Jim Hanson, and, basically, he took the stand and said that he was there to represent the U.S. Government. My defense continued to push for information to back up the claims of the U.S. Government that I had somehow altered their systems, but he would simply refuse to make anything available to us, to the prosecution, or to the judge. In fact, the judge actually ruled that he had no jurisdiction to order the U.S. Government to provide any evidence to back up their claims, which is really weird. In a murder case, for example, if there's no evidence, the case is kicked out.

"As the hearing continued, the prosecution asked Hanson what the American Government thought about my motives regarding my hacking at Wright-Patterson. 'We now believe that Mr. Bevan had no malicious intentions and that his primary purpose was to uncover information on UFOs and Hangar 18,' Hanson replied.

"Well, everyone had a bit of a laugh at that point. However, when the prosecution asked, 'Can you confirm if Hangar 18 exists or if it's a myth?' Hanson replied, 'I can neither confirm nor deny as I'm not in possession of that information.' But it was interesting that Hanson had traveled all the way from the States, and that he had specific knowledge of my attempts to find out information on Hangar 18."

Did the U.S. Government initially believe that there were far more sinister motives behind Bevan's computer hacking?

"Yeah. At the time the U.S. Senate had held a number of hearings on information warfare and in one of the hearings the hacking of the Rome Labs—where the FLEX system was stored—was cited as an example. The Americans knew that both Iraq and Russia were training teams of hackers to penetrate the U.S. military's computer files and, I suppose, thought that I was perhaps involved. In fact, in one of the interviews with Simon Janes and Mark Morris, I was asked if my hacking had any political motivations and it was quite funny because I'm not a spy—I'm just a normal guy. D.S. Janes, for example, said, 'Do you have any political motivation?' 'No,' I replied. Then Mark Morris said, 'Oh yeah, but you're a vegetarian.' 'Okay,' I replied, 'if that's a political motivation, then I'll plead guilty to that.' They even wanted to see my bank account records from the age of twelve."

What happened next?

"Well, as all of this was going on, there was a guy named Richard Pryce, who went under the hacking name of Data Stream Cowboy, and who was someone who I had been in touch with over the internet. However, we'd never personally met or spoken, in fact. But, as it turned out, Pryce and myself had been hacking into the same places. He eventually got a £1,200 fine in March 1997 after he admitted a number of offences. These resulted from investigations into penetrations of the Rome Labs' computer systems. Pryce pleaded guilty to twelve counts under the Computer Misuse Act and was fined £100 on each charge. As a result, the judge, in a later hearing, said that bearing in mind Pryce's sentence, he could not impose a custodial sentence on me, and really couldn't fine me any more than Price was fined. 'I suggest you think hard and long about this case,' he told the prosecution.

"Bear in mind, that the prosecution had changed their charges from straightforward hacking to hacking with intent to impair the operation of their computer system. Also it was estimated that the costs to prosecute me in a full court case were likely to be in the order of £10,000 per day. Well, as a result, the prosecution eventually came back, said that they weren't going to offer any evidence—the Americans, remember, wouldn't make anything available for the judge, my defense or the prosecution—and they dropped the case. This was on November 21, 1997."

Matthew Bevan's problems were far from over, however.

"As all of this was going on, the Americans stated that someone who had hacked into their systems had actually from there penetrated a nuclear institute in Korea. The worry was that the North Korean's would believe that it was the Americans doing the hacking when it was really a hacker using their system. Well, I began to get a series of funny phone calls. I would answer the phone, or my wife would answer the phone, and the person on the other end of the line would hang up. I then began to get a number of calls from a guy with the Chinese military. I would get my wife to answer the calls, but when I came to the phone he would hang up. My worry was that maybe the Chinese had got wind of this Korean situation and that they were either going to get me to work for them or shut me up. It was a very unstable time.

"We decided to get our phone number changed and applied to British Telecom for a new number. Well, they sent us a mandate that you sign and that gives you the details of your new number. In the meantime, this Chinese guy phoned again. My wife said, 'Stop phoning. Anyway, we're having our number changed.' But he just said to her, 'If you're having it changed to [the new number], don't bother because we already have it.' We just thought: let's move. So, we got a new place under an assumed name. In fact, the only person who then managed to track me down was a guy from the *Daily Mail* newspaper, so then we moved again."

Was Bevan of the opinion that his daily activities were monitored—by both U.S. and British authorities—at this critical time in his life?

"Yeah, it didn't surprise me at all. My barrister, in fact, had gone to court and spoke to the prosecution and told them to stop monitoring my calls. They said they weren't, but from the very next day, all the weird clicks, bleeps and noises we had been getting on the line suddenly stopped. I did find it all very sinister, though. When people got my number and I was getting calls from the Chinese military, I was genuinely concerned and that's why I kept on the move."

Does Bevan perhaps think that British and American authorities believed and perhaps still do believe that he had accessed additional data from the Wright-Patterson computer system on the strange, anti-gravity system?

"Absolutely. Maybe the cops and Jim Hanson didn't know—or maybe they did—but someone, somewhere, wanted to know what I had seen on the anti-gravity propulsion engine, simply out of worry. If I had been a spy, it would have been even worse. I was told by Scotland Yard that if I ever set foot in America, I'm going to be arrested on sight."

Would Bevan have still followed the same course of action, bearing in mind everything that he went through at the hands of Scotland Yard's Computer Crime Unit?

"What a good question. Yeah. Probably. It's done a lot for my career, I think. I now head a company called Tiger Computer Security and run a team of paid hackers. If someone—banks, finance houses and so on—wants to contract us, we will test their computer security via a brute force hack from outside; and if we get in, then we tell them how we got in and how to improve their system to prevent hacking from rival businesses, companies, et cetera."

And what would Bevan say was his ultimate goal as a computer hacker?

"It was really to try and get hold of the Roswell files, self-satisfaction, and the buzz and adrenaline of hacking a secret system. Nothing more."[18]

The Sandman, along with "at least twenty others," became part of a post–1994 operation to monitor a number of players in the British UFO arena on behalf of Special Branch, MI5 (Britain's FBI), Scotland Yard, MI6 (the British equivalent of the CIA), and the Government Communications Headquarters. "For most of the journey," said the Sandman, Scotland Yard's Computer Crime Unit was practically unanimous in the opinion that while Bevan was certainly "a blessed nuisance," he was nothing more.

"He's just an *X-Files* idiot," was how one Scotland Yard employee would describe Bevan, said the Sandman. However, the fact that the U.S. Government took a far more serious view, and believed that Bevan was possibly the witting or unwitting spy of a foreign nation, meant that, said the Sandman: "The [Scotland] Yard had to go along for the ride just to show the Yanks that they would punish Bevan and teach him a lesson. As it happens, though, the prosecution case fell apart. But once the Yard got into it all, they really were practically certain this chap was no spy."[19]

However, some senior elements within Special Branch and Scotland Yard were not quite so sure that Bevan was the innocent that he claimed to be. This especially was the case when it became clear that Bevan was also closely acquainted with a man named Matthew Williams, another South Wales UFO researcher. In 1994, (the same year that Bevan began his hacking activities), Williams started delving into claims that a crashed UFO and alien bodies were held deep below ground at a sensitive Royal Air Force installation in the southwest of England called RAF Rudloe Manor.

12

RUDLOE REVELATIONS

The buzz that had been bubbling quietly within certain factions of the UFO research community since the late 1970s was that the relatively innocuous-looking base known as Royal Air Force Rudloe Manor—which is situated within the green and pleasant countryside of the county of Wiltshire—sat atop a large, futuristic, underground installation. It was described like something straight out of an Austin Powers-style parody of a James Bond movie. Not only that, but deep within this cavernous and sinister underworld, some claim that the holiest of all ufological Holy Grails could be found: alien bodies from a crashed UFO.

British authorities have long asserted that the stories are all nonsense and little more than modern-day folklore. Needless to say, determining the truth of this seemingly endless affair has proven to be somewhat problematic. However, one thing can be said with certainty: The area of Wiltshire in which Rudloe Manor is situated is the source of what is known as Bath Stone. This type of stone has been quarried extensively for centuries, hence the existence of the huge underground openings, caverns, and tunnels that certainly do exist deep below Rudloe Manor and throughout the surrounding countryside.

Until 1998 the Royal Air Force's Provost and Security Services (P&SS) had their headquarters at Rudloe. Its duties included the investigation of crime and disciplinary matters involving RAF personnel, security vetting of employees, and the issuing of identity cards, passes, and permits. Far more significant, investigators attached to the P&SS are also trained in the field of counterintelligence (C/I). Such training is undertaken at the RAF Police School. Prospective candidates for counterintelligence work are required to take specialized courses in subjects such as computer security and surveillance. Before being considered for C/I work, personnel have to attain the rank of corporal within the RAF Police. C/I investigators are responsible for issues affecting the security of the RAF, which includes the loss and theft of classified documents, matters pertaining to espionage cases, and the protection of royalty and VIPs when they visit RAF stations. Also situated within the headquarters of the P&SS is a division known as the Flying Complaints Flight, which primarily investigates complaints of low-flying military aircraft in Britain.[1]

In addition, on 17 October 1996 the late Member of the British Parliament, Martin Redmond, had asked a number of questions in Parliament that provided more information on the workings of the Rudloe installation. Eleven days later he was informed by then-Defense Minister Nicholas Soames that, "RAF Rudloe Manor consists of a parent unit and five lodger units." Specifically these were:

(a) The Detachment of 1001 Signals Unit, which operated the British military's communications satellite system;

(b) No. 1 Signals Unit, which provided voice and data communications for the entire RAF, Royal Navy, Army and Ministry of Defense;

(c) The HQ of the P&SS;

(d) The HQ of the P&SS Western Region;

(e) And the Controller Defense Communications Network, a tri-service unit controlling worldwide communications for the military. Not only that but the DCN was situated 120 feet underground and was capable of housing no fewer than 55,000 people in the event of a national emergency.[2]

So much for the official story, but what else was possibly going on at Rudloe? Was the base really the British equivalent of the infamous Area 51? Certain researchers were convinced that it was and were determined to uncover the truth. Once again, it was this determination that led directly to additional surveillance of certain key players within the British UFO investigation field by Special Branch and others.

The story largely began just before the dawn of the 1980s and specifically with Graham Birdsall, the editor of *UFO Magazine*. According to Birdsall, "Late one evening back in 1979, I received a telephone call from a friend of long-standing which was to rank as one of the most important messages I have ever received while researching the subject of UFOs. The call came from Oxford, and my source and the information that was passed directly to me [were] to remain secret for a number of years. It concerned the location and activities of an establishment which was to be revealed publicly for the first time in Timothy Good's book *Above Top Secret*. I wish to make it absolutely clear that I was not the sole source of the

For years, Top Secret UFO research was undertaken from RAF Rudloe, Manor, England.

information on RAF Rudloe Manor that Timothy Good details in his book, but my information enabled him to complete the jigsaw in a puzzle that he was very close to solving at the time. I was one of two independent sources which revealed the whereabouts of an official Ministry of Defense establishment that handled UFO reports, and possibly much more. This establishment was not in London, but in Wiltshire, some one hundred miles away from Whitehall. This was the publicly known MoD department that supposedly dealt with all UFO reports."[3]

In his 1987 book *Above Top Secret*, Good revealed how, after having been tipped off that something strange and of a UFO nature was afoot at Rudloe, he visited the base and spent some time strolling around taking photographs. Unsurprisingly, Good was later detained by the police and asked specifically what he was up to and what his intentions were. Good duly revealed the truth: he had heard the UFO rumors and was determined to uncover the facts for himself. He was later released by a somewhat bemused Police Force with a warning to take extreme care when walking around the perimeter of a British military base in future.[4]

At the time Good's book was published, little more had surfaced. That situation changed as the years progressed. For example, in his 1991 book *Alien Liaison*, Good related the account of a former special investigator with the P&SS who claimed specific knowledge of its involvement in the UFO subject. "I am sure beyond any reasonable shadow of doubt," Good's source told him, "that all initial investigations into UFOs are carried out by investigators of the P&SS who are serving in a small secret unit with the Flying Complaints Flight based at HQ, P&SS, Rudloe Manor."[5]

Further corroboration came from a former counterintelligence investigator who informed Good's source that, "I had access to every Top Secret file there was, except Low Flying, because I understand they dealt with UFOs. We could get in anywhere, but not in that department. I remember they used to have an Air Ministry guard in the passage—you couldn't get past them. We could see the Provost Marshal's top secret files but yet I couldn't get into the place dealing with UFOs."[6]

Despite the fact that Good's sources wished to remain anonymous, there were those who were willing to speak on the record to me. Jonathan Turner served with the Royal Air Force for ten years as a medic and retired in 1993. While stationed at RAF Lyneham, Turner learned that reports of UFO sightings by military pilots were never recorded in the flight logs. Instead, details would first be channelled through to the Squadron Commander, who would then advise the Station Commander of the situation. From there, all relevant information would be forwarded to the P&SS for examination.[7]

The real coup came in 1993 when I located a file at the National Archive at Kew that conclusively proved that the stories of clandestine UFO investigations undertaken by the P&SS were true and dated back to at least 1962.

On the evening of 30 August 1962, the world was about to change drastically for Anne Henson. "At the time that this happened," Henson told me, "I lived on a dairy farm and was still at school; I was sixteen at the time. I actually moved back here with my family some years ago and we run a nursery business now. It was the middle of the night and something must have woken me up because I sat up in my bed and I could see through the window what looked like a round ball of light in the sky; my room over-looked the Brendon Hills. It seemed to change color from red to green to yellow and I could see a circle with rays of light coming from it.

"At first I thought it was a star, but it wasn't static. Then I thought that it must be a helicopter or something like that, but there was absolutely no sound from it. Well, it then began moving backwards and forwards and went from left to right. I was very intrigued by it because it was making fairly rapid movements. But it was the colors of its lights that attracted me first; they were nice bright colors. It would come towards me quite quickly and appeared to increase in size, and then reversed and moved sideways at a middle speed. But it always returned to its original position just above the hills.

"Over an hour or so, the light gradually receded until it was just like a pin-prick of light. Well, I went to sleep, but the next night I wondered if it might be there again—and it was. This happened on a few occasions and I got quite used to seeing it when it was a clear night.

"To be honest," said Henson, with a tinge of humor in her voice, "I got quite friendly with it, really. I didn't feel threatened by it, because although it came close to our farm, it didn't come that close. Now, when I'd seen it a few times, I decided that I would get a compass and graph paper and try to track where it was coming from because this was intriguing me. I thought: this is a bit different.

"After I saw the light for a few times and tracked the movements of it, I contacted RAF Chivenor. I told them what I'd seen and then I got a letter saying that my sighting was being looked at. Then this chap turned up at the house. It was an evening when he arrived for the first time, and he pulled up in this old black car, and when he came in the house he was wearing a black suit and tie. I would imagine that he was in his late thirties and I was most disappointed that he wasn't wearing a uniform. He announced himself as a Royal Air Force official and, of course, I took it as such. To me, he was an authority, put it like that. He actually came to visit me on several occasions. I assumed he was from RAF Chivenor; he didn't actually say so. I was a bit over-awed that somebody was actually coming to see me.

"Altogether," Henson explained, "he came on three nights. On the first night he came up to my bedroom and we sat there waiting for the clouds to clear. Unfortunately, that night and the next night he came, we couldn't see anything. So, he said that he would have to come back again. Now, on the third night, he saw it."

Did he have any opinion as to what the phenomenon was?

"No, none at all. He was just concentrating on looking at it. But he was very cagey. He wasn't very friendly, but he wasn't nasty either. But on this night he took some photos of the light. He didn't seem very surprised by what he saw. It was all very, very low-key, which I suppose is the way to play it if it was something unusual. If he'd have got excited, I'd have got excited. He then left and he took his camera and took my compass drawings and notes—and I never got them back. But before going he said that nobody else would believe what I'd seen and there was no point in me talking about it at school. At that age, you don't want to be laughed at—and my family had laughed at me, anyway."

Today, Henson remains puzzled about the bizarre experience: "I thought originally that it was some military object, but then the Ministry of Defense said it was a planet; although that didn't explain the way it moved. Now, it all hinges on whether or not you believe in UFOs. I can't see why there shouldn't be life on other planets. And if there is, why shouldn't they come here to have a look at us?"[8]

Anne Henson's case is a classic example of a Man in Black encounter as discussed in a previous chapter. It started with the sighting of a strange object, and was followed by a visit from a dark-suited authority figure who warned her not to talk about what she had seen and who confiscated her compass drawings and notes that displayed the movements of the phenomenon. But Henson's account differs in one striking aspect to other Men in Black accounts that remain unverifiable. Not only did I succeed in locating the official files pertaining to her encounter, but the file identified her mysterious visitor as an employee of the Special Investigation Section of the Provost & Security Services, who—the British Government is keen to assert—do not undertake UFO investigations.

That an organization of this caliber would take a keen interest in the subject of UFOs is intriguing to say the least. The Confidential report on Anne Henson's encounter prepared by Sergeant S.W. Scott of the P&SS's Special Investigation Section states: "MISS ANNE HENSON, aged 16, said that on 30th August, 1962 between 10.30 p.m. and 10.55 p.m. she opened the window of her room which faces N.N.E. and saw a diminishing star-like object with what appeared to be red and green colored flames coming from it. It was slightly larger than the average star and appeared to be round. After about 2 1/2 minutes it became very small and she could only see it with the aid of binoculars. She was quite sure that it was not the navigation lights of an aircraft because she had seen these many times and could recognize them immediately.

"She did not look for it again until 17th October 1962, when she saw the object again which was partially obscured by fog. With the aid of binoculars she compared the object with several stars and noticed that the stars were silvery white whereas the object was red and green. Near to and above the object she noticed another exactly similar but smaller object. She noticed a difference in the color of the original object which was now emitting green and orange flames in the same way as before.

"MRS. C. HENSON, mother of ANNE HENSON, said that she had seen the object described by her daughter. She could offer no explanation as to the identity of the object but was of the opinion that it was not a star. She declined to make a written statement.

"A visit was made on 1st November, 1962 when the sky was clear and all stars visible. MISS HENSON, however, said that the object was not in view on this particular night. Observations were maintained for one hour but nothing was seen. MISS HENSON was asked to continue her observations and on the next occasion on which she saw the object or objects to compile a diagram showing its position in relation to the stars. This she agreed to do.

"On 28th November, 1962, the next available opportunity, [the witnesses address] was again visited. However, although observations were maintained for 2 hours the sky remained obscured and nothing was seen. MISS HENSON was interviewed and said that she had seen the objects again on two occasions and although she had compiled a diagram she had omitted to note the date. She said that she would again watch for the objects noting times and dates and compile another diagram which she will forward by post to this Headquarters.

"MISS HENSON reports unidentified aerial phenomena and provides a diagram showing their position in relation to stars. The objects have not been seen by the Investigator who cannot therefore give an opinion as to their identity. It is considered that MISS HENSON is a reasonable person, although at 16 years of age girls are inclined to be over-imaginative. However, MISS HENSON is supported by her mother, a person of about 50 years of age, who seems quite sincere. The matter should be brought to the notice of [the] Department at Air Ministry set up to investigate such phenomena."[9]

A copy of Sergeant Scott's report was ultimately dispatched to an Air Intelligence office that concluded Anne Henson had simply misperceived a celestial body such as a star or a planet. That may indeed have been the case; however, there is a far more important issue to be noted. As this affair reveals, there are now documented and verifiable cases on record where dark-suited officials have visited the homes of UFO witnesses, have warned them not to talk about their UFO encounters, and have confiscated data pertaining to the incident at issue. More importantly, in Britain at least, those same dark-suited visitors appear to originate from within an elite division of the Royal Air Force that is trained in counterintelligence and espionage operations, and that for two decades was based at RAF Rudloe Manor.

Upon receipt of this file, which totaled eleven pages, I forwarded a copy to Air Commodore J.L. Uprichard, Director of Security and Provost Marshal (RAF), for comment. His reply of 4 May 1994 revealed, "The 1962 report to which you referred is a rare example of an alleged UFO sighting being treated as a low flying incident and investigated accordingly. Routinely, we neither investigate nor evaluate such reports."[10]

The importance of Air Commodore Uprichard's letter cannot be over-emphasized. Although he said such investigations were "rare," here was documented proof from the Director of Security and Provost Marshal that indicated that UFO encounters had been treated as low-flying incidents by the P&SS and had been "investigated accordingly." This was something that Timothy Good's sources had maintained anonymously for years.

Nevertheless, certain people were unwilling to accept the facts, including Nick Pope, a civil servant who investigated UFO encounters for the MoD at an official level from 1991 to 1994. "Members of the public, a lot of them, don't know the procedure for reporting a UFO. Some people will phone the press, some will phone us direct, some people—and this is the key point—will phone their nearest

RAF base. I suspect that someone has reported something to Rudloe Manor, as people can and do. Someone at Rudloe Manor has said: 'Yes, I'll take details of that,' and from there [the allegations] grew and grew. I know this story from *Above Top Secret* and I don't agree with the conclusions in there. I'm not aware of any secret research that they're doing or anything like that. As far as I'm concerned, they were just doing their job."[11]

Pope's comments failed to satisfactorily explain one glaring question: If there was nothing of substance to the claims, why were agents of the P&SS traveling around the country monitoring and interviewing UFO witnesses?

In late 1995 there was a surprising development in the Rudloe Manor controversy. On 19 November of that year, a Welsh UFO researcher named Chris Fowler wrote to the Ministry of Defense and inquired about the claims contained within Timothy Good's book *Above Top Secret* that clandestine research into UFO activity was undertaken at RAF Rudloe Manor. Rather than make an outright denial, MoD spokeswoman Kerry Philpott wrote in her 14 December reply to Fowler that, "In the past, Rudloe Manor was indeed the RAF coordination point for reports of 'unexplained' aerial sightings."[12]

What prompted this complete turnaround on the part of the MoD was never made clear. Philpott was Nick Pope's successor in Sec(AS)2a, but Pope had no awareness that Rudloe performed such a function and was openly skeptical of such claims. So one might ask: where did Kerry Philpott obtain information that apparently contradicted the assertions of Nick Pope, who had held the same position as she did?

In an attempt to answer that question, in early 1996 I made inquiries with Group Captain John Rose, Officer Commanding, P&SS (UK). Rose told me "I can confirm that Flying Complaints Flight was responsible for coordinating reports of unexplained aerial sightings until 1992. I have not been able to determine the date on which Flying Complaints Flight began to fulfill this role. Please note, however, that Flying Complaints Flight only moved to RAF Rudloe Manor (with the rest of HQ P&SS (UK)) in 1977. RAF Rudloe Manor itself would have had no role in the coordination of unexplained aerial sighting reports prior to the arrival of HQ P&SS (UK). Indeed, it is likely, although we are unable to confirm this, that Flying Complaints Flight coordinated such reports whilst at the previous location of HQ P&SS (UK) at Acton."[13]

Given that the P&SS was stationed at Acton from 1950 onward, this implies that the P&SS's Flying Complaints Flight could have been involved in the coordination of UFO reports for nearly half a century. Moreover, Group Captain Rose's assertion that Rudloe Manor had no role to play in UFO encounters prior to 1977 is incorrect. The researchers Andy Roberts and David Clarke learned that Rudloe Manor played a key role in a significant UFO encounter that occurred in British airspace in October 1952 that was of interest to the Government Communications Headquarters—the British equivalent of the National Security Agency.

That it was not until 1996 that Group Captain Rose talked to me about Rudloe Manor, suggests that officials chose to keep the public and the UFO research community ignorant of the facts. Nick Pope's comments would suggest that he too was kept in the dark. Perhaps Philpott was kept ignorant of the full story as well, as she was only able to provide Timothy Good with a definitive answer to questions similar to those posed by Chris Fowler after she specifically consulted with knowledgeable sources at Rudloe Manor.

The most fascinating revelation concerning possible post–1992 involvement on the part of RAF Rudloe Manor in the UFO puzzle came from a former British Government civil servant who had an interest in unidentified flying objects. This person caused major headaches for the staff at Rudloe, and became the subject of a Special Branch-controlled surveillance operation. It was none other than Matthew Williams, the close friend of computer-hacker, Matthew Bevan.

Within the tightly knit British UFO research community of the mid-to-late 1990s Matthew Williams was primarily known for his research into the intricacies of the Rudloe Manor saga. What is less well known is that Williams had an official background—one that was partly the reason why he was subjected to so much intense surveillance by Special Branch. After completing his education, Williams went to work for the British Government's Customs & Excise agency, first in its Personnel Division, and later in its Criminal Investigations Department. "I'm telling you something which breaks the Official Secrets Act," Williams said to me when I interviewed him about his Rudloe research. "When I was with Customs & Excise, we would receive what were known as the Suspect Index Telexes—this would be 'flash traffic' which would say something like: 'John Smith is coming into Heathrow; he's suspected of carrying drugs. Don't approach him. Inform us.' Now, the 'us' we were to inform would sometimes be London Customs; sometimes it would be the Criminal Investigations Unit; and sometimes it would say: 'Contact Rudloe Manor.'"[14]

That there was a direct relationship between Williams's department and Rudloe Manor was something later confirmed to me by Flight Lieutenant Andy Woodruff who told me "The Flying Complaints Flight has the responsibility for RAF liaison with HM Customs and Excise."[15] In other words, not only was Rudloe Manor working hand-in-glove with Customs & Excise, but the specific division involved at Rudloe that had the responsibility for such work was none other than Flying Complaints Flight. This was the element of the Provost & Security Services that (along with the Special Investigations Branch) investigated UFO encounters. Williams explained to me how he had become interested in the stories concerning UFOs and Rudloe Manor:

"The first time I went down to Rudloe was in January 1994. I'd gone down with the [UFO] researcher Paul Damon. We were just having a look around the outskirts of the base and were suddenly approached by armed guards who visibly threatened us. We told them, quite honestly, that we were interested in the UFO stories— we'd read Tim Good's *Above Top Secret*. What was interesting was that the guard asked for our names and made what was no more than a one-minute phone call from the guardhouse. Well, he came back and said our details checked out. But the speed with which they were able to do the check suggested that at Rudloe there is some sort of central computer where people's identities and personal details can be accessed immediately."[16]

This is highly plausible. In the same year, Jonathan Dillon of the National Union of Journalists had spoken with a former RAF Police Officer who informed him that Rudloe Manor employed personnel whose job it was in part to monitor both UFO researchers and RAF employees with "off-beat" hobbies, which included UFOs.[17]

Williams continued, "Because Paul and I had received so much hassle at Rudloe, this really spurred us on; and this was one of the reasons why we spent so much time in the area speaking with the locals. One of the things that came up was that there was a place at Rudloe which investigated UFOs. But a number of people, including people who worked there, said that UFOs were a taboo subject; you don't bring it up. One guy I spoke with was a flight lieutenant actually stationed at Rudloe. He had some interest in UFOs and asked his superior officer, who was a wing commander, what went on in the place which dealt with UFOs. The wing commander basically replied: 'I can tell you, or you can keep your job. What do you want to do?' Naturally he answered, 'I'll keep my job.'

"Another guy who approached me worked in the Command of the Defense Communication Network. His area was nuclear security—transporting nuclear materials, and so on. He had access to top-secret data, and was sometimes allowed to action things, sometimes not. But he was never allowed to deal with UFO data. He had to give this to very high-up sources. He didn't know what happened to the information, but he did know that there was somewhere at Rudloe which dealt with it all. As well as that, I had a contact who was acquainted with people employed in the Defense Communication Network [DCN]. They said that Rudloe has an extensive radar tracking system which extends to outer space, and there's apparently a huge room which is full of screens just monitoring Britain's airspace. When I put this to the DCN, I got what I would call a 'shocked denial.'"

A particularly notable addition to Williams's investigation of Rudloe Manor surfaced in May 1996, when he and a BBC television crew from the popular series *Out Of This World* traveled to the base to produce a segment for a forthcoming episode on the stories linking Rudloe Manor with clandestine UFO investigations. "First," Williams told me, "I should explain that at the base they have a number of unmarked cars which basically just drive around the area. On a number of occasions, I was stopped and questioned as to why I was there. One occasion, I was with Paul Damon and we stopped near the base—but in a car park; not right outside the gates, or anything like that. A car stopped by us. Immediately, I recognized that it had been fitted with a 'covert aerial.' I recognized this from my Customs & Excise days because we used to fit them. The next minute, our car was surrounded by Ministry of Defense people. It was no surprise at all to me that they started asking a lot of questions. I said to one of the RAF policemen that I knew his vehicle was fitted with a covert aerial—the radios were basically secured to prevent anyone from listening in—and he gave me a little wry smile. Time and again, we would have these little confrontations."

"But why," Williams continued, "should the level of security there be so much higher than at other military bases? I'd visited RAF stations when I was with Customs & Excise, including RAF Lyneham. Lyneham is like Heathrow for the military, but Rudloe's security is way above that. Through Customs & Excise, and documents I had access to, I learned that a lot of the function of Rudloe Manor revolves around military intelligence. Basically, they liaise with C&E, police, and Interpol amongst others. When I asked why all of this was so sensitive, I was told it was because of the other stuff—the UFOs. This was from people who worked there."

Williams then turned his recollections to the *Out Of This World* filming:

"The BBC knew I was doing these investigations into Rudloe, and asked me to help with *Out Of This World*, show them around the base perimeter, that sort of thing. When we arrived, we spoke with a guard who is normally stationed at the guardhouse. He'd been speaking quite freely with me—and the BBC's [presenter] Chris Choi—about the size of the facility, how many people worked there, and being quite amicable. But the moment we mentioned the word

UFO—which we left until last—he visibly shook and stopped in his tracks. His eyes widened, and he said, 'Sorry, I can't say any more.'

"With that, he turned around and walked back inside the guardhouse. He then made a call and another MoD policeman turned up. What was surprising was he said they knew we were coming, but they wished we'd let them know. 'How did you know we were coming?' Chris Choi and I asked. He just replied: 'We get to know about these things; we get our information.' When we again asked him how he knew we were coming, he simply said: 'I'm not going to discuss those sort of things.'

"The MoD chap then asked for some identification. Chris Choi didn't have any at all and all I had was my credit card. I showed it to the guy. He looked at it and said: 'Oh, yes. I know your name.' 'Oh, really?' I replied. I started laughing and said to the camera: 'Did you catch that? He knows who I am.' But this is similar to conversations I've had with other staff at Rudloe; they all seem to know who I am."[18]

By far the strangest saga in the Rudloe affair came in late 1996, when the official file relating to the 1962 UFO encounter of Anne Henson that had been investigated by the Provost and Security Services vanished from the shelves of the National Archive. Claims and counterclaims circulated: The file was lost somewhere in the photo-ordering department, the MoD had removed it due to the fact that the P&SS report had been declassified in error, it had gone missing during inventory, it had been confiscated on behalf of Rudloe Manor, and so on. Ultimately, it did resurface—albeit only (and somewhat conveniently) when questions were raised by Ieuan Wyn Jones, an elected Member of the British Parliament.

When I spoke with the Sandman about the mystery of the missing file, he claimed to know only peripheral details of this aspect of what turned out to be an extensive surveillance operation of Matthew Williams and me. He stated: "The file wasn't really removed to stop people being able to read it—although this is, I suppose, what the effect of its removal turned out [sic]. The main reason it was taken off the shelves was twofold: first, so it could be provided to the Director of Security and Provost Marshal at the MoD, so that he could make an estimate of how damaging this file was to their stance that the Provost & Security Services had no UFO role to play. And second, and this was very important, there were references in the file to departments that the MoD really wasn't sure they wanted the public to know about—Air Intelligence departments, their titles, and so forth—and so it was reviewed to see what departments could be revealed and what couldn't, or what should have been revealed and what shouldn't. It did the rounds at the MoD with a number of people for a while."

He continued, "But when the Director's office saw that the file showed that his boys were going around the country interviewing and watching UFO witnesses—which was something even Nick Pope's little office never had the budget to do—it was obvious that their cover and denials were blown. And, so, the file did the rounds at the MoD of the people who were really involved with the bigger P&SS-UFO studies and they decided to just ride-out the storm, claim that this was just a once-in-a-lifetime example of the P&SS having UFO links, and hope that this satisfied everyone.

"The big concern they had, though, was how this one document in the file—that should never have got passed the censors—was declassified in the first place. That led to big questions and some people in the declassification-of-records offices were hauled over the coals over it." The Sandman stated that both Matthew Williams and I had been under a limited amount of surveillance when we both began our investigations into Rudloe at roughly the same time in 1994, but that this same surveillance operation intensified when "the file thing began."[19]

For Williams, the surveillance would hit an all-time high after he actually succeeded in physically penetrating the Government's underground world in July 1997.

13

CLOSE ENCOUNTERS OF THE
UNDERGROUND KIND

According to rumor, very deep below RAF Rudloe Manor there exists a series of tunnels and caverns. These, supposedly, are home to an off-limits chamber in which are stored the remains of three-to-twelve alien bodies that were recovered from a UFO that crashed on British soil during the Second World War. As was the case with many of these types of stories, the bodies were humanoid but small in stature with large bald heads and huge black eyes. Supposedly the bodies were cryogenically preserved within a series of missile-like containers.

To everyone who had an interest in the Rudloe-UFO saga, this was a fascinating story. For Matthew Williams, the discovery of this invaluable evidence was the ultimate prize to be won. "The information I obtained, most of which came from official sources, suggested we're talking about hundreds of square miles of tunnels under Rudloe," Williams told me. "These apparently link up Rudloe Manor with Colerne Airbase; the weapons storage facility at Copenacre; Monks Park, which is a weapons storage facility for the Navy; the Defense Communications Network; and the Corsham Computer Center. There are two points of access to the publicly accessible tunnels very near Rudloe Manor. One's at the underground quarry center at Corsham. You can put on a hardhat and a lamp and go for a walk, and have a look at the areas where they took the Bath

Stone out. There are other tunnels, less sophisticated, but which are longer and more intricate. These are the ones which the professional cavers seem to like. It's some of these tunnels which seem to have a connection point with the military ones. As it's been described to me, [over] long distances in the tunnels, there are infrared security cameras which are positioned just to monitor anyone getting too close."

I asked Williams, "How active are the tunnels?"

He replied, "It's been intimated to me that there's an area for emergency housing down there, and that's one of the locations where the Royal Family would go in a national emergency. But I've been told that the tunnels which have been made good, which Rudloe themselves are using, is [sic] fifteen miles in length. And in the central hub, there's a labyrinth of tunnels to allow people to have offices, buildings, storage areas, etcetera. Now, I've taken photographs while flying over Rudloe Manor in a light aircraft, and the pictures clearly show many structures in the facility which have lift shafts; and the size of the lift-shafts: you can easily drive vehicles into them."

Matthew Williams explained to me that during the course of his Rudloe research he had come into contact with a number of the private groups in the area whose hobby was caving. "They're experts in the mines," he said. "The caving clubs know the whole area. On a number of occasions, they reached an area where the military tunnels start, and on one occasion there was somebody there—a military man. He asked what they were doing, and they replied: 'We're the caving club.'

"He then said, 'If you're interested, perhaps we can get you a tour.'

"From the way I understand it, on occasion, at their discretion, the military will allow people to see a little bit more of the tunneling system if they have a valid reason. I suppose it's good for public relations. Now, some time later, they were contacted by someone from Rudloe Manor who then made them a formal offer and said: 'Come along; we'll take you down.' They met with a person of a certain rank and they were taken down an elevator shaft and down into various tunnels where there was heating and lighting, corridors and space, and so on. They were also taken on a tour of the old quarry area, which is supposed to be more of a derelict area, because it's where the quarrying was finished and there was no clean-up operation afterwards.

"Although they had a good tour, it was made clear that there were other parts of the tunnels which were out of bounds due to the high security which existed there. Apparently the police who looked after the heavily restricted areas operated independently from the normal RAF Police who patrolled Rudloe Manor, and the two didn't liaise in any way or fashion. These other guys weren't military police, but were a separate security force; and the people who worked at Rudloe Manor didn't know what went on in that higher-security area. They only knew that it was a lot more up to date; it was a lot more well developed, was a lot deeper underground, and was controlled by the Home Office."[1]

It was in late July 1997 when the UFO rumor mill began to churn wildly. It was widely reported within a number of UFO publications and at places where the flying saucer faithful gather, that Williams—along with Richard Conway of the British UFO Research Association—had "broken into Rudloe's underground base." This was not correct, however. In reality, the intrepid pair had focused their attention on nearby Monks Park. Still partly a working quarry at the time, Monks Park had previously served as a Royal Navy storage depot before being occupied by Leafield Engineering, who made and stored components for the defense industry and commercial users. There were rumors that Monks Park had direct underground tunnel links to Rudloe that could be accessed—if one knew where to find them. The official surveillance of Williams reached an all-time high after his penetration of Monks Park.

Williams told me, "I was in the area of Monks Park with UFO research colleague Richard Conway, and we decided to take a look at the facility. I was aware that there was a lone guard at the facility. We climbed the Y-Fork security fence at the back of the site and made our way, out of sight of the guard, around the facility. We observed lift-shafts which were locked and secured.

"We found that many of the buildings were open and unsecured and we moved through them, finding that most were empty and disused. Then we came across a warehouse building which was full of crates and boxes. On the sides of the boxes were stapled-on plastic wallets, with pink folded slips inside. The slips were professionally printed manifests for the contents of the crates. The company that had produced the slips was 'Logistical Services' and the logos used on the top of the paper were a Navy warship and submarine. The prints were made in July of 1997. It appeared that the warehouse we were in was a loading bay. We moved further into the warehouse and spotted a tram access-way. It seemed to go downwards and the tram was not present.

"Upon closer inspection, both Richard and myself were able to look over the safety barrier down into the depths of the underground storage area. To our surprise, there were lights on at the end of the long, descending tram corridor. The tram could be seen at the end. Looking at the wall, we could see the controls for the tram. I suggested that we try and go underground on foot by walking down the rail tracks for the tram. Richard was reluctant, but I reminded him that this was the whole reason we came here. And after some coaxing, Richard agreed to descend into the tunnel.

"The steep-angled descent of the tramway was made harder by the fact that there were lots of wires and floor obstructions. We carefully made our way down the corridor towards the waiting tram. Being aware of certain objects that looked like they could be trip-switches and alarm sensors, we navigated around these carefully. It took us five minutes to get to the bottom of the tunnel. Looking back upon the way we had just come from, the entranceway seemed like a small speck behind us. Climbing up and over the tram to allow us access to the facility, we got our first look at the underground tunnels.

"What we saw made our mouths drop. My heartbeat got more excited at the fact that I was at the doorway to a potentially massive, underground facility, tunnels all around me and nobody to be seen and stop us going in. It seemed too good to be true. Richard climbed to the point where I stood. We observed how modern it looked and how clean—even the rock-face walls were painted. There were forklift trucks sitting around at various places in this high-loading bay in front of us. We both pondered if we should go in and what our chances were of getting caught. I managed to convince Richard that we would be safe and that the facility seemed empty of people. In a few moments, Richard's feelings understandably changed.

"As I took a step inside the tarmac of the base, I jumped as alarms sounded. Now, in the distance, we could also hear klaxons, and sirens were going off. I turned and caught Richard's glance. Almost instinctively, Richard had turned and was already starting to climb out of the tram to make an escape up the corridor. I stopped him and said that we had a better chance of hiding in the underground facility and said it was our best chance to escape. I pointed out to Richard that by the time we got to the top of the entrance tunnel we had just come in through, there would be security waiting for us. By going in,

UFO researcher Matthew Williams prepares to enter the British Government's underworld in search of UFO secrets.

we had the chance of hiding and perhaps finding another way out. He agreed with me—reluctantly—so I said: 'Let's Go! Run!'

"We both leapt off the tram and started running along corridors. The lighting on the ceiling changed from fluorescent tubes to orange, red or green lamps. This gave the atmosphere of the tunnels the most eerie effect. We ran and ran, taking lefts and rights along various tunnels. As we ran, I said the best idea was for us to try and lose ourselves in the tunnel system, perhaps even to hide. As we ran and looked and took photos, I realized that we could easily lose our film, so we decided not to give up the film voluntarily. As we ran, we were getting deeper and the tarmac roads were getting longer. We found ourselves passing long off-reaching storage bays hundreds of feet deep, full of containers and crates. We passed too many of these to take in what they were full of. We passed bays with markings for various MoD departments, and even one bay which had the sign 'CIA' written on it. We didn't stop to look at what was contained within, and later on forgot to go back there. We eventually came to a large theater of storage bays. We ran to the end of a bay and turned along another. Surrounded by wooden boxes stacked up to 20 feet around us—and in the dark of this obscure storage bay—me and Richard hid next to some cardboard crates.

"I said that we would need to wait at least two hours to allow any security to have checked the facility and hopefully given up. I set my watch timer. The air temperature was a stark contrast from the blistering sunny weather outside. Our two hours passed slowly and Richard pondered on the fact that there was so much stuff stored down here, that we were bound to be picked up by security guards. Thoughts of: 'would we ever make it out alive?' crossed Richard's mind. I thought that this was nonsense and assured Richard that nothing would happen—that was too much like conspiracy theory. Still, I could understand how Richard was feeling as this was his first trip to a base with me, let alone getting into the fabled underground facilities. This must have been a shock to the system. I must admit that I was quite enjoying the whole thing, so I made light of the situation and ribbed Richard about the situation we were in. In the end, Richard did make the valid point that I jumped out of my skin when those alarms went off.

"Eventually, our two hours passed and after hearing many clicks and imagined footsteps, we emerged from our hiding place to find out where we were. Having a very good route-finding memory, I was confident I could find our way back. We got to a main roadway and saw some maps on the wall. After studying these maps and photographing them, I looked for exits. For the next two hours, we walked around the tunnels, visiting different exits. Most of them led to the 'Kingston Mineral Quarry.' All of the doors were alarmed and had infrared sensors on them, along with high-powered, magnetic door-locks. I decided that trying to get out of one underground facility into another was not a good idea.

"We then decided that perhaps the easiest route would be back up the main entrance shaft. We got near it and located the offending infrared devices that we tripped on the way in. They were posted at many locations—so many, in fact, we wondered how we hadn't tripped them earlier. I decided that we had no chance of getting past these, and so we had to retreat. Just before we started to attempt to sneak past the devices, both myself and Richard quite clearly heard gunshots echoing down the tunnel-way. We could differentiate shotgun fire and also semi-automatic rifle fire. This certainly excluded this escape route from being used.

"We were stuck now and it seemed like to attempt to leave via any exit could mean capture. Just then we found a long sloping staircase that led to the surface. We walked up it slowly, and nearly at the top we were stopped by an infrared sensor that was registering our presence with a frail yellow light. The light sequence was yellow, amber, and red—amber or red would mean alarms going off. We moved very slowly away from the sensor. So, yet another escape route was out of the question to use. As we retreated we then heard voices of many people laughing and joking, and diesel vehicles moving around past the doorway that we had been attempting to reach. It seemed like we would have walked right into the hands of security, perhaps even into the security guards' building, if we had left via this route.

"Now we left and started to scour many parts of the base that we had overlooked in hope of finding other escape routes. By now we had been underground for five hours. It was nearing 10:00 p.m. and we still had no idea of how to leave. In the time we had been down underground, we had photographed many areas and had run out of 35mm film. It was at this point that I remembered passing a sign-posted exit, which did not appear on the underground maps. We decided to have one final look to see if we could get out. Expecting all sorts of alarms and infrared sensors we slowly made our way through the passage that led to the exit way. We were confronted with a metal, spiral staircase, which was anchored into the rock. Knowing that we were at least 200 feet underground, we expected a long climb—and certainly got it.

"Finally we reached the top of the stairs and I halted Richard as I spotted some alarms. This seemed like the way out but I could not see any way of passing the alarms without setting them off. Freedom was just one emergency-door away. We had no real way of knowing where we would be above ground. We made a run for it, setting the alarms off a second time. Bursting through the door into the darkness, we were able—fairly quickly—to adjust to the darkness enough to be able to see our way back to our entry fence. We scaled the fence quickly and jumped. I twisted my ankle when I landed and was then in excruciating pain. Richard ripped his hands on the barbs.

"As we composed ourselves from our less-than-successful fence-hopping attempts, behind us we heard gunfire. These were shotguns. We didn't look back to see where the shots were coming from. As we ran, I was slowly able to overcome the pain of my ankle a little more, which was just as well, because—to top it all off—we then got stampeded by a herd of Friesian cows who were almost trampling us as we ran. That was all we needed. I had to stop running and turn to face the cows and shout at them to make them turn away. This gave away our location, but, thankfully, we didn't have far to go. We got in the car and drove away through a route I knew would bypass any major roads. The next day we got our photos developed and distributed copies. So quite an exciting day.

"The follow-up to this is that I went up to the Guard-House at Monks Park and was given a cock-and-bull story about the base being nothing to do with the MoD anymore. As I knew otherwise, I kept pushing and in the end got the admission that the base had been sold to a private company that was an MoD contractor, and some MoD 'stuff' was stored there. The guard seemed to know more than he was saying, although one thing he did say was that there were entranceways from the base to Rudloe Manor's underground facility, but to the best of his knowledge, those were sealed up. As I and Richard remember, the boxes we saw contained possible component parts for weapons and electronics equipment, including satellite gear.

"Like a scene from *The X-Files*, I couldn't help but think that somewhere in amongst all those hundreds of thousands of boxes there could be a part of a UFO or some secret weapon designed by the MoD. The truth may still be down there."[2]

Williams's excursions into the Government's underground world were not over. "Near Rudloe Manor [is] the Corsham Computer Center," Williams added. "This is very high security and we penetrated that one too—I did this for a *Sightings* TV show and we got quite far in. The guys filming it said they had never had so much excitement. I love taking TV crews into dangerous situations. The guards foolishly opened one of the security doors by mistake; they must have thought we were service personnel when they saw us on the CCTV. When we got inside they realized their error and came and got us. One of the guards locked himself inside a security compartment in his rush to get us; he typed in the wrong code on a keypad. We filmed all of this. I can't help but feel a bit proud."[3]

Some within the British UFO research community, and indeed within the Government, took the view that Williams and Conway were simply living out "*X-Files* fantasies" by "wildly breaking into the Royal Air Force's underground storage areas in search of dead space aliens and photographing anything that moved—or didn't," as the Sandman described the situation. Other elements of the Government took a different and far more serious view of this. Only weeks later, questions would be asked at an official level about Williams's intentions—including even whether or not he was utilizing his UFO research as a cover for working with none other than the Irish Republican Army.

14

THE BRITISH ROSWELL?

In December 1996, along with Irene Bott, the then-President of Britain's Staffordshire UFO Group, I became embroiled in an intriguing, alleged UFO crash account. The official world seemingly placed both of us, as well as the prime witness to the event, under some form of surveillance by military sources. It all began in 1991 when the late UFO author and premier collector of crash-retrieval accounts, Leonard Stringfield, had revealed that he had been provided with the details of a reported UFO crash on the British mainland in early 1964.

Stringfield's source—S.M. Brannigan—claimed that at the time in question he was stationed aboard a "specially rigged LST, a flagship (AKA 'spy-ship')" that was attached to a naval amphibious force at an unspecified location in either the Caribbean or the Atlantic. Brannigan's specialty was the translation of intercepted Soviet military transmissions, and he recalled one particular instance when an amazing coded message was received at the ship's "crypt-machine room."

The message was given to Brannigan and he set to work on translating its contents. Almost immediately he realized that this was no ordinary interception. It told of a UFO over-flying Europe that, for reasons unknown, malfunctioned and plummeted to Earth. Whether by accident or design, as the UFO descended, it broke into two parts—the chief section of which crashed in a large area of forest in central England known as the Cannock Chase, near the town of Penkridge, Staffordshire, while the "remains" hurtled on until they slammed into the ground somewhere in West Germany.

As Brannigan continued his work, more information came to the fore. U.S. Air Force Intelligence was implicated in the recovery—and not just of the UFO. Three dead personnel had also been found. As the enormity of the event became apparent, other U.S. forces became involved, as did various elements of NATO.

Interestingly, despite the crash having occurred in the mid-1960s, Brannigan was still fearful about revealing too much information. As Stringfield noted: "Brannigan admitted there was more to the incident, involving coded information, that he preferred to keep confidential. The Brannigan disclosure, while sketchy, may spotlight only the tip of the iceberg as to the scope of military crash/retrieval operations in foreign lands. If such incidents are to be secreted, it is my suspicion that U.S. special retrieval teams have been, and still are, prepared to 'go into action' into any crash location within its sphere of military or economic influence such as was exercised with NATO in the 'artifact' retrievals in England and West Germany."[1]

The details of the case as provided by Stringfield were admittedly brief. Irene Bott and I made a breakthrough five years later in the summer of 1996. Bott was the President of Britain's Staffordshire UFO Group that was based in the town of Rugeley and only a few miles from where the alleged crash at Penkridge occurred. Keen to promote her group's activities in the area, Bott gave an interview to the nearby *Burntwood Post* newspaper and revealed details of the incident that had been related to Stringfield by his source, Brannigan. Several days after publication of the interview, Bott received a letter from Harold South who lived in the nearby town of Brownhills.

According to South, not only did he know the location of the crash site, he had witnessed the recovery of the object by the military and, as a result of this, was both interrogated and warned to stay silent by the local police. On 11 December 1996, Bott and I visited Harold South at his Brownhills home. On our arrival, South told us that barely an hour earlier, he had received a somewhat disconcerting telephone call from the Ministry of Defense Police that had almost caused him to cancel the interview. However, he ultimately advised us that he would proceed as previously arranged. In a tape-recorded interview, South began:

"It was about quarter to ten on a morning, a weekday. Either February or March 1964. At the time I was working as a washing machine repairer. My area was north of Cannock and I'd been over there to drop off a part before starting my calls. I was driving my van towards Penkridge from Cannock. About two miles after Cannock, I came to a roadblock: it was manned by Army, Police, and Royal Air Force personnel. The Police were shepherding the traffic, but the military were standing by. I didn't see any arms, but they had batons, truncheons. I looked over to the right and there was a RAF aircraft transporter in a field—a unit and trailer. I thought: Oh, it's an aircraft they're transporting. But it was funny, it being in a field.

"Being a railway enthusiast, I always used to carry a camera in the van and at any opportunity I got to see anything of railway interest, I could immediately go and snap it. I thought: I'll get a shot of this. But before I had a chance—we were stuck in the roadblock— the police came over and said: 'You'll have to make a diversion.' I said: 'What the hell's happening?' I wasn't in a very good mood; I'd already been held up through dropping that part off. I headed back to Cannock, but me being a nosy person, I stopped the van about half a mile up the road and sneaked back across a couple of fields."

As he approached the field via the seclusion of Cannock Chase forest, South developed the impression that all was not as it should have been. Keeping his distance for a while, he saw that the field was by then swarming with people—some in Royal Air Force uniforms, others in Army fatigues. Most interesting of all was a team of people "who looked like scientists" who were closely examining specific areas of the field. "There were about four or five that were digging a hole; I should imagine there were about twenty or thirty in the field, altogether."

South edged closer, careful at all times not to give away his position. It was then that he was able to obtain a clear view of the

RAF transporter vehicle. Next to it was a mobile crane adorned with Army insignia. But that was nothing compared to what was stretched out on the transporter's trailer. Straining for a better look, South noticed that a large object had been lifted on to the trailer and had been partially covered by a tarpaulin. He continued, "I noticed something very unusual about the load."

Far from resembling a conventional aircraft, the object appeared to be triangular shaped. "Of course, a million things went through my mind," he added. Anxious to obtain some form of record, South had wisely remembered to take his camera with him from the van and managed to secure "a couple of snaps." Unfortunately, his decision to photograph the mysterious vehicle caught the attention of the police contingent coordinating the roadblock. South headed for his van and exited the area with the utmost haste. His actions, however, had not gone unnoticed.

South continued, "I got back [home], put the van in the garage, and my mother said: 'You've got to report to Bloxwich Police.' I thought I'd better not go to the police station in the van, so I got my motorbike and went to the station and I was ushered upstairs. In this room was a police inspector by the name of Reid, a PC by the name of Robert Bull, and a female plain-clothes person taking notes. They started questioning me, asking me what I was doing around there at the time. They said I was observed taking photos of an incident at Penkridge and they wanted the film. Meanwhile, while I was being held, they'd got a search warrant to search my home, and the officers that went there told my mother they were looking for a stolen camera.

"My mother—being a bit naïve—said: 'He's got a camera. But he hasn't stolen it; it's in the van.' She gave the camera to them, and they gave her a receipt. Been about midnight, I should imagine, that I was released from the police station. The police didn't even mention the object; they just wanted to know what I was doing out there and why I had a camera with me. Then shortly afterwards, about three weeks, the camera was returned to me by post. It was in a parcel postmarked Melksham, Wiltshire. There were a few RAF bases around there.

"I only got the camera back and not the film—but they did put a new film in. Me, being a bit nosy, I started asking people in the area if they knew what had happened. First, I heard that there had been some UFO activity in the area; on the motorbike club night at Hednesford [a nearby town] I was asking one or two of the people. I didn't mention anything about what had happened to me, but they said there had been some UFO scares. I was also told that there was a rumor going around that a UFO had crashed and had been retrieved by the military."

"When me and Nick arrived here," Bott said, "you mentioned that you'd just received a call from the Ministry of Defense Police. What was all that about?"

South looked somewhat concerned, but nevertheless was keen to secure our opinions.

"This was about a quarter of an hour after you phoned," South

While investigating an alleged UFO crash in the Cannock Chase forest, England (pictured), researchers Nick Redfern and Irene Bott uncovered evidence of a surveillance operation on the prime witness of the event.

explained. "The phone rang, I picked it up and said: 'Who is it?' 'The MoD Police,' they said."

The call had flustered South; however, he said that the nature of the call had "to do with a complaint" and "they gave me a number I was to call them back on. But I didn't."

"That's the number, is it?" inquired Bott, pointing to a sheet of paper on South's desk.

"Yes," he replied quietly.[2]

"Can I dial 1471 [the British equivalent of *69, that, when dialed, provides the number of the last incoming call]?" asked Bott. South nodded. Sure enough a number was available—it was different from the one that South had been requested to call by his mysterious Ministry of Defense Police source. Intriguingly, the number was a Midlands, UK-based operator-controlled service under the control of the military.

Tape-recorded questions raised by Bott revealed that the military operator was responsible for channeling calls both to and from military establishments in the Midlands area. In other words, the call to South could have come from any number of military locations in the general vicinity, and since any such calls would be routed via the operator's office, dialing 1471 would reveal only the operator's number and not the original source of the call.

Fortunately we also had the number that South had been asked to call. Once again, Bott dialed.

"Guardroom," said an unidentified, male voice.

"Hello," said Bott, "Could you tell me what this number belongs to, please?"

"This is the guardroom."

"The guardroom?"

"Yeah."

"I'm a little confused," said Bott. "I'm dialing a number that was given to a gentleman at this address to ring."

"Can I have your name, please?" asked the unidentified voice.

Bott wavered: "Well…I'd like to know why he would be getting a call."

"I wouldn't know," the voice replied. "Nobody's called from here in the last twenty minutes. I've been here. Where are you?"

Bott replied, "Well...I'm in Brownhills. You're where?"

"Lichfield," came the reply. "This is the Army base at Lichfield."

"So you're at Whittington?" asked Bott.

"Yes, that's right."

"What's your name?" Bott pressed on.

"My name's Mr. Law, from the MGS."

"MGS: what does that stand for?"

"Ministry of Defense Guards Service."

"Ministry of Defense Guards Service," Bott repeated, her voice echoing incredulity. "Oh, gosh, it gets worse."

Mr. Law laughed, but was keen to stress: "The call hasn't come from here."

"Okay," said Bott, "because of the line of work I'm in, I can't tell you too much, but it's very weird nevertheless." The conversation was terminated.[3]

For ten minutes Bott, South and I sat musing upon the implications of the morning's events. At 9:00 a.m., Bott had telephoned South on her cell phone to advise him that she and I were on our way to interview him about his recollections of a strange craft retrieved from a Staffordshire field in 1964. And, within fifteen minutes of her call, someone from the Ministry of Defense Police was on the phone to him. The possibility that this was mere coincidence seemed remote in the extreme. Why would the Ministry of Defense Police be telephoning a retired washing machine repairer in his seventies?

All three of us agreed that there had to be a connection with the events of early 1964. But several questions remained: Was the call to South from the MoD evidence that my activities and Bott's were being monitored? Was it South that was being watched? Or could it be that all three of us were the subject of official scrutiny and surveillance? What was so important about that decades-old incident that warranted apparent on-going MoD involvement more than thirty years later?

As incredible as it seemed, it did indeed appear that someone, somewhere, knew that Bott and I had made arrangements to meet with South. Since the only contact with South had been via Bott's cell phone, this was disturbing and suggested the presence of some form of eavesdropping operation. Perusing the Interception of Communication Act of 1985, I learned that domestic telephones are supposed to be monitored only with the express permission of the Government's Home Secretary. However, in an "urgent case" a senior civil servant could issue a warrant. Interestingly, while there were 843 official warrants issued for the interception of telephone calls in 1992, in the following year the British *Daily Express* newspaper learned that no fewer than 35,000 calls were tapped by the Government Communications Headquarters (the UK equivalent of the U.S. National Security Agency) at Cheltenham during the period 1 January to 31 December 1992.

As 1996 drew to a close, Bott and I mulled over the experience with Harold South and his strange call from the Ministry of Defense Police. It seemed almost as if a game was being played. When speaking with South, the MoD made no attempt to block their telephone number (it was uncovered in seconds via the 1471 call-back system), and South was even supplied with a number to call at Whittington Army Barracks. There seemed only one conclusion: somebody in the Intelligence or defense community wanted to let us know that, by probing into the complexities of the Penkridge crash, we had opened up a sensitive can of worms.

If the intent was to simply keep everything under wraps, why didn't someone pay South a visit and request his silence? Had this occurred, and had South merely told us that he had changed his mind about talking, then neither of us would have been any wiser. But by letting us know that South's decision to talk had sparked renewed interest on the part of an anonymous agency, was the intent really to put us off from uncovering the truth? Or was it possibly a subtle attempt to alert us to the fact that the case was one of profound significance?

Another question surfaced. If the call to South was indeed an attempt to convince the two of us that the case was valid, was the call officially sanctioned or was the call from a sympathetic insider who was trying to subtly break the case open without compromising his or her identity? No conclusive answer was ever forthcoming, and all that was left were additional questions: Who was South's mysterious caller? Why was South treated in such a strange fashion at Bloxwich Police Station? And, most important of all, what was that mysterious craft recovered by the military more than thirty years previously from a Penkridge field?

Clearly, it was not standard practice to hold a member of the public against that person's will (and not convicted of any charges) simply because that person happened to photograph an aircraft. In addition, while air-accident investigators do on occasion solicit photographs and movie footage of aircraft crashing to Earth that were taken and filmed by the public, this is largely to assist in any follow-up investigation.

In Harold South's case, the object had crashed some hours before he had come across it. The implication was obvious: South's film was confiscated not because his shots would aid the investigation team in determining how the vehicle crashed, but because he had photographed something that the military wanted kept under wraps.

In view of this, could the object have been some form of experimental aircraft? Taking into consideration the unique shape of the aircraft, the testimony to Leonard Stringfield from S.M. Brannigan, and the on-going interest in the incident on the part of the Ministry of Defense more than thirty-two years later, this possibility can only be considered extremely unlikely. An intriguing footnote to this incident is a letter contained within the now-declassified UFO files of the Ministry of Defense from 1966 and written by an American UFO researcher named Robert S. Suter of Savage, Maryland.

It was on 27 April 1966 that Suter contacted the MoD seeking to obtain "verification of a persistent rumor here in the USA." The rumor referred to nothing less than an unidentified flying object that had been "shot down" over the UK "several years ago" and that allegedly contained "the remains of a once living organism."

Predictably, Suter received a reply from the Ministry of Defense denying any knowledge of such an occurrence, yet the timing of Suter's letters was interesting. The letter referred to the retrieval of a UFO within the UK "several years ago," and the incident at Penkridge had occurred approximately two years prior to Suter contacting the MoD. Was this, perhaps, the first reference to the Penkridge crash to turn up in officially declassified files? And was there a connection between the bodies reportedly recovered at Penkridge and the "once living organism" described by Robert S. Suter?

If an answer to that question is known, it remains buried within the vaults of the Ministry of Defense.

15

PENETRATING THE PLEASURE DOME

In my first book, *A Covert Agenda*, I mentioned a small (but nonetheless intriguing) body of evidence pertaining to the collation and investigation of UFO data on the part of the sprawling Government Communications Headquarters at Cheltenham (GCHQ).[1]

Although GCHQ actively and forthrightly denies that any such claims have a basis in reality, time and again snippets of information surface, suggesting that behind the official stance there exists an incredible story just waiting to be uncovered. First and foremost is the striking fact that GCHQ works closely with its American counterpart, the National Security Agency—an agency with a rich history of involvement in the UFO puzzle.

GCHQ has the daunting task of supplying numerous agencies and departments within both Government and the Military with Signals Intelligence-based data. This, in itself, accords with the requirements of the British Government's Joint Intelligence Committee—the function of which is to produce a weekly survey on various aspects of Intelligence operations (known as "The Red Book") for senior sources. For its part, GCHQ secures a great deal of its Signal Intelligence data from intercepted overseas communications, and for this purpose controls the Composite Signals Organization that operates from locations within the United Kingdom and abroad. In 1947, the governments of a number of nations—specifically the United Kingdom, the United States of America, Canada, New

Zealand, and Australia—signed the UK/USA Agreement that was designed to allow the aforementioned nations access to a variety of Signals Intelligence data for mutual use.[2]

It is also a matter of record that GCHQ's collation and analysis of Signals data is undertaken with the National Security Agency. Harry Chapman-Pincher, a renowned expert on British and worldwide security issues said, "The United Kingdom provides territorial facilities for intercept installations for the National Security Agency, which runs in close harness with Britain's counterpart, Government Communications Headquarters."[3]

In view of the now-admitted wealth of Signal Intelligence-derived UFO data held on file at the NSA's headquarters at Fort George G. Meade, Maryland, the idea that elements of GCHQ would never be exposed to similar material appears most unlikely. But how could material that would confirm this be uncovered? The answers are now slowly beginning to surface, thanks to the research of Robin Cole, an industrious investigator who lives almost on the doorstep of GCHQ.

Cole's diligent investigations have led to a surprising number of revelations: that GCHQ has a large and impressive library that contains a considerable number of books on UFOs; that GCHQ was implicated in the study of military-originated UFO encounters as far back as the early 1950s; and that GCHQ was involved in the investigation of an intriguing UFO incident that occurred off the East coast of England in October 1996, when unknown aerial targets were tracked on Military radar and seen out at sea by the crews of several boats and ships.[4]

Cole is unsure which department within GCHQ was implicated in the 1996 affair, but he was able to determine that the investigation was coordinated from one particular part of the GCHQ complex known as the Oakley Installation. When the encounters over England's East coast took place, two new and decidedly impressive structures (nicknamed by the staff as The Pleasure Dome and The Barn) were developed. Both had been constructed with the benefit of a multi-million pound budget.

"The Pleasure Dome has acquired its nickname because the higher your status, the higher up you work inside the building, thus giving the employee a more panoramic view across Cheltenham and creating a nicer environment to work in," stated Cole. "The Barn covers sixteen and a half thousand feet and comprises two floors on the south and three on the north. This contains so many computers that a special chiller unit was built to keep them all cool. Both sites are as big underground as they are above ground, as far as square working footage is concerned, with enough room at the [nearby] Benhall site—known to the employees as The Funny Farm—that lorries can be driven in to unload equipment and supplies, thus allowing both to remain in complete operation should war break out."

Strangest of all was the series of events that occurred back in 1997 when Cole published a booklet outlining his findings on the GCHQ-UFO connection titled *GCHQ and the UFO Cover-Up*. Like so many UFO researchers before him, Cole had attracted the close attention of certain officials. "GCHQ have a copy of my report," he stated. "I don't know how they got hold of it, but it wasn't from me, and they obtained it before it went on general release. I know that much."

Had GCHQ asked Cole about the sources of the information contained in his report?

"No. Not directly, anyway. I did get a telephone call from somebody who works there and they said, 'Very interesting, your report; it's good stuff. Obviously, I can't comment as to its accuracy, but who was it that gave you the information?'

"I said, 'Well, that's confidential information.' They then said that they only wanted to know so they could approach the source and get a bit more information. I thought: I'll bet you would!"

But, as Cole explained for the first time, "Before I put my report on general release, I had proofreaders' copies done for the members of the group—I only felt it was fair that the members knew about the information before anybody else. I'd like to know if the copy GCHQ have is a finished copy or a proofreaders' copy. If they've got a proof, then I know that someone within our group handed it to them—

which wouldn't surprise me. As I said, we've got a few members in the group who work for GCHQ. The only way that GCHQ could possibly have got hold of a finished copy is to have got into my flat and taken a copy."

But was that really feasible? "There have been a number of…I don't like talking about it because people think that you're losing the plot or getting paranoid. But, yes, there have been instances where things have gone missing, things have been moved, and I tend to have a set place for everything. I suppose the most significant thing is that, just after publication, I held the master copy of the report in my flat, with the photographs—color photographs—all pasted up in an envelope on a shelf. I went out to do a new print run about four weeks later, got the report out, and the photos had vanished. Luckily, I'd made backup copies, which I'd disseminated to various people. I'm glad now that I did, because I hunted my flat high and low. But there have been other occasions like this.

"Just after my report was published—1997—I was interviewed with regard to its contents by Central Television. They picked up on it straight away and did a damned good piece which was shown on both the evening and late-night shows. Well, the following morning the phone rang. 'Mr. Cole?' said a voice. I said, 'Yes.' 'This is Detective Sergeant Tim Camp from Cheltenham CID [the Criminal Investigation Department of the British Police Force]. Can we come and have a chat with you, please?'

"Well, I was obviously a bit stunned as it's not every day that you get a call from CID, and I said 'Yes. But why exactly?' 'Oh, nothing to worry about Mr. Cole,' they said. 'We'd like to ask you one or two questions.' I said, 'Anything specific?' Camp replied, 'What do you know about a group called Truth-Seekers?' "

As it transpired, Truth-Seekers was the brainchild of UFO investigator Matthew Williams, who published a conspiracy-based magazine under the name of *Truth-Seekers' Review* from the mid-to-late 1990s.

"Well," continued Cole, "I wondered what they wanted and just said, 'Okay, I know about Truth-Seekers.' 'That'll do for us. Can we come and have a chat?' I said, 'Yeah, sure. When would you like to come?' 'Can we come now?'

"As it happened," Cole explained, "I wasn't doing much so it wasn't really a problem. But then it dawned on me: I'd only got their word for it that they were who they claimed to be. Well, I have a friend named Trish who works at Police headquarters in the Incident Room. I called her and explained what had happened and asked if she could get over to my flat to check this guy out when he arrived. In the meantime, I surreptitiously set up a tape recorder in my living room, so that when D.S. Camp arrived, I could get the entire conversation down on tape. Well, then, of course, he and a colleague arrived.

"I opened the door, but the two guys didn't give their names; instead they just came in and sat down. I said, 'Sorry, you are...?' 'Detective Sergeant Tim Camp.' His colleague stayed silent. 'As you know, Mr. Cole,' he said, 'we'd just like to ask you one or two questions about Truth-Seekers and what you know about them. It's

While researching the UFO secrets of the British-based Government Communications Headquarters, investigator Robin Cole was placed under deep surveillance by officials.

nothing to worry about; we were just concerned that they might be a front for an IRA [Irish Republican Army] group and we have to check these things out.'

"We chatted about Matthew and his actions at Rudloe Manor and so on. And then they got around to me. 'What do you do? Who do you work for? What's your interest in the UFO phenomena?' I told them, they seemed satisfied and got up to leave. But just at this point, Trish arrived, and it turned out that she did know them; so they were legitimate police officers.

"Now, after they had left, I phoned Matthew and said, 'Look, I think I've dropped you in the shit, mate. I'm really sorry.' Matthew replied, 'I don't know why they're questioning you about me, because I've already been stopped several times by the Ministry of Defense Police at Rudloe and I've always given them my business card. So I don't understand why they're questioning you, when they could just as easily come and see me.'"

The story, however, was not over for Robin Cole.

"On the following day, I telephoned Cheltenham CID and asked to speak with D.S. Camp—I just wanted to make sure that I hadn't said anything which was going to get Matthew into hot water. When I asked for Detective Sergeant Tim Camp by name, the guy in CID said, 'We don't have a Detective Sergeant by that name working here.'

"At that point, I heard the guy say to one of his colleagues, 'Who the hell's Detective Sergeant Tim Camp?' I could hear mumbling and then this chap came back on the line, 'Detective Sergeant Camp isn't with CID; he's with Special Branch.'

"Eventually, I got through to his colleague—D.S. Camp wasn't available—and he basically said, 'Don't worry, Mr. Cole, we've got all the information that we wanted to know.' This got me thinking. Why is Cheltenham Police's Special Branch interested in a UFO investigations group which, at the time, was based in South Wales and whose activities revolved around RAF Rudloe Manor in Wiltshire? It didn't add up. Well, I now have a strong feeling that Special Branch were using Matthew as a front to check me out—to see if I had Nazi banners on the wall or anarchy signs on the front door.

"The reason I say this is because, just recently, I learned of a radio presenter in the north of England who was interested in doing a piece on GCHQ and asked people with knowledge to contact him. Lo and behold, the next day, Special Branch was around to question him. So, I find this all a little too coincidental. And it does suggest a direct link between (a) UFOs; (b) GCHQ; and (C) Special Branch."

In mid-2000 I contacted Cheltenham Police regarding the visit made to Robin Cole's home to discuss the activities of Matthew Williams. Several days later, I received a telephone call from Cheltenham Police informing me that the only comment that Detective Sergeant Tim Camp of Special Branch was prepared to make to me was one of "no comment."

As fascinating as Cole's revelations were, additional evidence revealed that his attempts to blow the lid on the GCHQ's secret UFO activities attracted the keen attention of the Security and Intelligence services. It appears that the surveillance of Cole's activities began months prior to the publication of his report in 1997. In other words, from the very day that he began looking into exactly what GCHQ knew about UFOs, Cole was being carefully watched and scrutinized. Cole cites one example of this extreme surveillance:

"I had just got home after a Sunday night out. I had some stuff to dump in my office and didn't switch the light on. I put the things down and just glanced out of the window. Well, outside my window there's a streetlight and beneath this was a white van. At first I just registered that the van seemed out of place. You know what it's like; you tend to recognize the various cars and vehicles in your own street. But then I thought: well, it wasn't there when I came in ten minutes ago. Why is it outside my flat under the streetlight? As I looked at it, I noticed that on top of the van were these two, weird, silver domes one behind the other—as if they were a part of the roof, built in. I thought that was odd, particularly when it occurred to me that where they were parked was also right next to the telephone junction box. At that point, I grabbed my camera and put the light on in the office. But as I did that, the van suddenly started up and went quickly down the road. Well, a couple of weeks later, the van turned up again. This time, I ran down the steps outside my flat and dashed into the road; and again the van started up and shot off. But it was enough for me to get details of the van's registration and make, which was a Bedford. Then I set about trying to trace the van.

"It so happens that I got a friend, a retired police officer, to pass the details on to a serving officer who put the details through the police computer." [Note from the author: the names of the retired and the serving officer are both known to me, and their positions within the Police Force have been confirmed. However, as the misuse of the Police National Computer is considered an extremely serious offense, I have agreed to omit their names.]

"Well, a few days passed. But on getting home one evening, I found a few messages on my answer-phone from [the retired police officer] in a very excited state. As it was about 11 o'clock at night, I thought: it's too late to phone him now, I'll give him a call tomorrow. I went to bed, but at 12:15, the phone rang. It was him.

"He said, 'That vehicle, you were right to be suspicious about it. The registration regarding who actually owns it is blocked, but the address that it's registered to is a Ministry of Defense post office box in Wiltshire.' This was heavy stuff. But I've not seen the van since—and this was March 1997. But this was real proof that I was under some sort of surveillance."

Heavy, indeed, particularly since Wiltshire was the home of RAF Rudloe Manor, whose covert involvement in UFO investigations just keeps on cropping up time and again. In addition to detailing the story of how he began his investigations of the link between UFOs and GCHQ and the apparent surveillance of his activities, Robin Cole had an equally bizarre account to relate concerning the acquisition of the aerial photograph of GCHQ that appeared on the front cover of his *GCHQ and the UFO Cover-Up* report. "I rang GCHQ up and told them that I was a freelance writer. I said that I was working on a piece about GCHQ and the possibility of the staff there having their trade union rights restored—this was heavily in the news at the time. 'Can I come along and take some photographs?' I asked.

"GCHQ responded by saying that they wouldn't allow that, but they did have their own photograph which they would allow me to use. Now, they didn't say that right away; I had to phone them on several occasions. Well, they wanted to post the photo to me, but I didn't want them to do that because they'd have a record of my name and address. In response to that, I said that I needed the photo that day to finish the article. 'Can I come and collect it?' I asked. That was okay; they had no problems with me doing that. So, I jumped into a suit, walked up to the main gates and up to the security booth and said, 'Hello, I've come to collect a photo.' 'Ah, you're the journalist, aren't you?' the chap said, adding while pointing his finger, 'You want to speak with those two guys sitting over there in the white Rover.'

"I walked over to this car, somebody presumably pressed a button, and down came the electric window of the car. It looked like the classic spy scene. The guy in the passenger seat was just looking forwards and the other one was looking straight at me. I repeated, 'I've come to collect a photo,' and they passed me this brown envelope. I didn't really know what to do at that point and just said, 'Oh, thanks,' and walked off and up went the window of the Rover with no further words said."[5]

It is clear that Robin Cole had hit upon a very raw nerve. Never before had anyone in the UFO research community conducted so intricate an investigation of GCHQ and its UFO-related activities. And the response was nothing less than direct surveillance of Cole by covert operatives from within GCHQ, Special Branch, and the Royal Air Force. Cole told me that, even to this day, he still feels a degree of concern for his safety. He has every right to. One thing, however, now seems certain. GCHQ, like its U.S. counterpart the NSA, is a veritable hotbed of UFO activity.

But what was the real story behind the extraordinary surveillance of Cole's activities?

According to the Sandman, "Here's the rub: nobody in Government actually disputes that there may be real UFOs. In fact, when we were being briefed on people like Cole, Williams, you, and Bevan, it became very clear to us that there were unexplained cases that couldn't even be solved when they had been studied. But Special Branch and GCHQ weren't really that concerned that there were odd things flying about because they were like ghosts: they were weird, but they never did us any harm, never attacked us like a sneak attack we might have expected from Russia back then. They were more concerned that this chap Cole—like your friend Matthew [Williams] at Rudloe—was using his UFO research at GCHQ as a clever cover to find out names of people working at the base and details of operations, and that he might be in league with anti-establishment people, or even overseas countries looking for a way into GCHQ's world, who worked there, project names, and so on.

"That's exactly why [Detective Sergeant Tim] Camp was sent out—to check Cole out and see if he was legitimate in just looking for UFO information. And also to find out if, as we still thought, Cole, you, Williams, Bevan, Conway, and all the rest were all a part of some group secretly doing work for some foreign group looking for information on Rudloe, GCHQ and so on.

"That Cole was a friend of yours and Williams—who was also a friend of Bevan and Conway—and that you were all in contact with each other, and were all hanging around together, and were all wandering around outside military bases taking pictures, didn't really help take away the suspicions, either," he added wryly. "They really had it in their heads—as I did back then—that you really had all been recruited by some foreign power to find out military and defense secrets, and that the UFO side of what you were up to was just the smokescreen."

16

MYSTERY MUTILATIONS

Perhaps the most bizarre example of official surveillance of a person embroiled in the UFO and Fortean communities concerned British-based Jonathan Downes. Although primarily known as a cryptozoologist and the Director of the monster-hunting Center for Fortean Zoology, in the mid-to-late 1990s Downes wrote regularly—and extensively—for a whole range of newsstand UFO-related publications that existed at the time.

Stated the Sandman: "Downes is, as you well know, the chap best known for his Yeti and Loch Ness excursions. But as with you and your people and the UFOs, there was some concern that this was just a ruse—or partly, a ruse, at least. Downes was well acquainted at the time with a number of people in Ireland that we were interested in. The Downes thing was very low-key and didn't last long, but he was watched for a while, purely to see if he was working with certain Irish people. But there was nothing to it, just this chap [Downes] talking with chaps in Ireland who were his friends, but who we were watching and who were also interested in those monster pursuits."[1]

The scenario of Special Branch monitoring Downes's activities purely because he happened to have friends in Ireland sounds wholly outrageous; however, it is a scenario that Downes himself can corroborate: "It was a Friday lunchtime in early May 1996. [My ex-wife] Alison and I were beginning to suspect that we had strayed into a particularly far-fetched and badly scripted episode of *The X-Files*.

We were sitting in the departure lounge of Plymouth Airport, waiting to put Tony ["Doc" Shiels, a renowned Irish monster-hunter] on his plane back to Ireland, after one of his occasional visits. Suddenly, the airport lounge seemed to be full of security guards. There were only about half a dozen men in uniform, but there were a number of rather sinister-looking men in black suits, wearing sunglasses, and looking quite menacing.

"A man in plainclothes, who introduced himself to Tony as a senior police officer, came over to us. I was engaged, at the time, in assembling my tape recorder so I could tape an interview with Tony. But at the sound of the words: 'Mr. Shiels, can I see your boarding pass?' which was accompanied by the practiced flash of a warrant card in a leather wallet, [I was] prompted to put my tape recorder away very quickly. They conversed in low voices. I didn't try to overhear their conversation, but I gathered that Tony had shown the policeman all the relevant travel documents, and that all was in order.

"I decided that this was the right time to go to the lavatory. Sitting in the thin-walled, Formica-lined cubicle, I was effectively invisible, and so could overhear snatches of a conversation between one of the Men in Black and someone else over a walkie-talkie. I only heard some of what they said, but the words 'Special Branch' were mentioned on several occasions. I was also shocked to hear my own name. Slinking out as soon as the coast was clear, I rejoined Alison and Tony. They told me that, with no notice whatsoever, Tony's plane had been canceled. I began to feel somewhat scared. The policeman came over to talk to Tony again, and the public address system asked Alison, as the owner of our van, to report to the Information Desk. She was asked to move our van on the grounds that it was causing an obstruction. It wasn't. And Tony was told that his flight would now be departing three hours late. The Men in Black were still milling around. I just sat there feeling very paranoid.

"I still don't know to this day what it was all about. The harassment, such as it was, continued all afternoon, but we were, by this time at least, in such a state of advanced paranoia, that even innocent occurrences were open to vicious misinterpretation. Was the target of this activity me or Tony? Were the motives magical, ufological, or, as seems more likely, political? Or was Tony guilty of being Irish in the wrong place and at the wrong time? [It was] a week when security at all airports and military bases had been stepped up because of a rumored IRA blitz to coincide with the 80th anniversary of the Easter uprising."[2]

The Sandman elaborated on the situation concerning Downes: "There was another thorny angle with the Downes thing, too. Downes, as I think you know, went to school with Hewitt—[Major] James Hewitt, who was [Princess] Diana's lover for a while. Well, there was a big cat case that Downes was looking into in the 1990s that, in a roundabout way, actually linked the Marines with Hewitt, with big cat reports, with Diana, and even with the Marines keeping watch on Diana and Hewitt's affair. Again, the concern was that Downes would use this big cat investigation with the Marines link and the Diana-Hewitt link as a ruse—a ruse to learn more about Diana's affair with Hewitt, pump his Marine source for more information on Diana and Hewitt, and pass it on to people that would—or at least could—then exploit it as part of a destabilization of the monarchy. No one really knew who these people might be or even if they really existed at all. And eventually it was never shown to be, and Downes really was just looking for the cats. But we had to look; we thought it was justified in looking [sic]."

Evidence does exist to demonstrate that, in the 1990s, Downes was indeed speaking with a former British Royal Marine who was involved a secret operation to monitor the love affair of Major James Hewitt and Princess Diana. He also happened to have knowledge of Britain's big cat mystery. As Downes himself revealed, "For many years, there have been persistent rumors of a government and military cover up regarding the big cats seen on Exmoor and Bodmin. I have tended to disregard these reports as merely paranoid conspiracy theorizing. I had never been able to see any real reason why any such cover up would or should take place. But a telephone call I received several years ago gives a reason why such a cover up might have taken place.

"I am taking a totally neutral position as regards this report," stressed Downes. "The caller seemed plausible enough, although extremely paranoid. He was also obsessed with Princess Diana and was claiming that when he had been a Royal Marine he had been part of a detachment of security services sent to protect Her Royal Highness while she was paying illicit visits to the home of her lover Major James Hewitt—who I happened to go to school with—in the Devon village of Bratton Clovelly. It must be said, in his defense, that he told me this some weeks before the liaison became public knowledge. It was certainly the first that I had heard of the scandal that was later to rock both the nation and the monarchy.

"I mention this only because it does, to a certain extent at least, establish his bona fides as a Royal Marine and presents some corroboration for the story that he was to tell me. My informant claims that when the Royal Marines made their well publicized and apparently fruitless hunt for the Beast of Exmoor in the mid 1980s, that he was a sergeant in charge of one of the small reconnaissance parties. He also claims that the Marines were also searching for the beast in another unspecified location in the South West. He further claims that the search was not the primary aim of the exercise, but that security implications forbade him from telling me what the Marines were really doing there."

Downes elaborated, "Over my last decade as a Fortean pundit I have met a number of ex-military personnel, or more accurately people claiming to be ex-military personnel, who have told me that something unpleasant to do with national security has happened on Exmoor over the last twenty-five years. But the main claim of my mysterious caller is that three animals were shot at unspecified locations, and that at least one was shot on private ground by a party who were not only trespassing but who had not been given permission to carry firearms. He claimed that a relatively junior officer had panicked and that the cover up had been perpetrated further up the chain of command in order to 'save face.'"[3]

"So that was our concern," reiterated the Sandman, "that someone had said to Downes something along the path of 'See what you can learn from this Marine chap on Hewitt and Diana, do it under a cover of your big cat investigation that this soldier knew of, get the information to us, and we'll expose their affair.' But when we learned that Downes was an ardent Royalist and that both his father, who was the deputy governor of Hong Kong, and his brother, a vicar in the Army, had been decorated by the Queen, we knew we were barking up the wrong tree completely on this one. But there were some on the team that thought we should keep watching [Downes]."

And, according to the Sandman, "One of the other reasons why Downes was watched was because someone—and I don't believe we ever actually got to the bottom of who it was exactly—leaked to Downes, some years before, a wad of Police reports on animal mutilations that he began looking into. Here, the worry was that this was a type of dangling carrot by someone; have Downes be given the documents [sic] as a type of enticement by someone or some group. Then, he would be blackmailed by this group who would say something like, 'You have been given classified Police reports. Work for us or we will turn you over to the Police.' Then, Downes— because of the blackmail fear—would be forced to work for whoever it was that wanted to use him."[4]

In the mid-1990s Downes was indeed provided with seemingly still-classified British Police reports on animal mutilations that had UFO overtones to them. The story essentially began on 11 April 1977, when no less than fifteen wild ponies were found dead at Cherry Brook Valley, Dartmoor, by Alan Hicks, a Tavistock shopkeeper. Hicks had been crossing the moors with his children. It was not until mid-July that the media began reporting on the incident in-depth. Newspaper articles at the time demonstrated that the story traveled as far as South Africa; however, consider the following extract from the *Western Morning News* of 13 July 1997:

"Fears that the mystery deaths of fifteen ponies near a Dartmoor beauty spot were caused by visitors from space were being probed by a Torbay team yesterday. Armed with a Geiger counter, metal detectors and face masks, four men are investigating what leading animal authorities admit seems a 'totally abnormal happening,' and are hoping their equipment will throw a new light on the three-

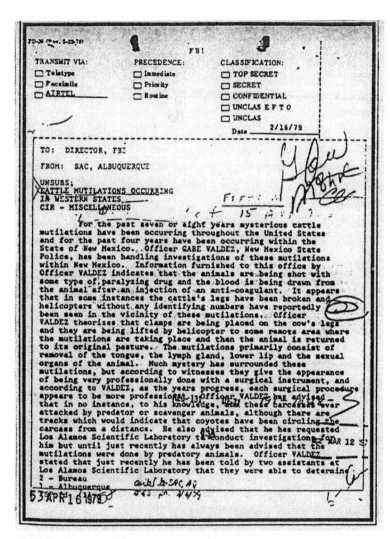

A U.S. Government document on mysterious animal mutilations that have been linked with UFOs. Researchers of the phenomenon have been subjected to widespread surveillance.

month-old mystery. While other investigators have looked for signs of malnutrition, disease or poisoning—or even gunshot wounds—the four men are seeking proof that extra-terrestrials were responsible for the deaths. 'If a spacecraft has been in the vicinity, there may still be detectable evidence,' says the Team Leader, Mr John Wyse, founder of the Devon UFO Center. His team is investigating the Postbridge mystery because the ponies' deaths have similarities with unsolved cases in the United States. Many of the Dartmoor ponies—all found within a few hundred yards of each other in the Cherry Brook Valley below Lower White Tor—had broken bones.

"'Horses and cattle have been found in the United States in strange circumstances with the bones smashed or the bodies drained of blood,' said Mr. Wyse. 'Our members have already made a preliminary investigation and we know the bodies are now decomposed, but there may still be some evidence of an extra-terrestrial visit.'"[5]

The *Western Morning News* also quoted the secretary of the Livestock Protection Society as saying "I still suspect that something dramatic happened—something very strange indeed. No one can give any logical explanation. One theory is that the ponies died of red worm—but that does not explain the broken necks and legs."[6]

Over the course of the next few days, further possibilities were explored. A second source from the Livestock Protection Society stated: "My theory is that the ponies were in a very enclosed valley. There was a waterfall at the head of the valley, and they may have been caught in a sudden burst of water and knocked against the boulder."

The Dartmoor Pony Society felt that the ponies had probably died on various parts of the moors and had been simultaneously dumped together by a farmer unwilling to bear the cost of their burial. A spokesperson of the Livestock Protection Society responded thus: "One wonders if the people who say this sort of thing can possibly have been to the valley and seen the distribution of the ponies or the terrain."

Numerous other theories were postulated at the time but the trail went cold until 1991 when Jonathan Downes began to probe the case. Downes succeeded in tracking down some of those quoted by the newspapers some fourteen years previously. Curiously, Downes detected a distinct reluctance to talk. Even more bizarre, one of those individuals (who adhered to a non-paranormal explanation) remonstrated a research colleague of Downes's for "pestering her day and night" with endless telephone calls, when, in fact, the only contact had been a solitary call.

As Downes noted, this apparent telephone surveillance and harassment was highly reminiscent of John Keel's experiences. Keel stated in his book, *The Mothman Prophecies*: "I kept a careful log of the crank calls I received and eventually catalogued the various tactics of the mysterious pranksters. Some of these tactics are so elaborate they could not be the work of a solitary nut harassing UFO believers in his spare time. Rather it all appears to be the work of either paranormal forces, or a large and well-financed operation by a large and well-financed organization with motives that evade me." [7] It was also highly reminiscent of the experiences of Greg Bishop cited earlier.

Interestingly, in the following year—1992—a friend of Downes, Ian Wright, came across another dead pony on the moors and in the same vicinity. This time the animal had been systematically disembowelled. That same year was also highly significant for another reason—as will now become apparent. One spring afternoon, Jon Downes was deep in conversation with a police officer from Middlemoor Police Station, Exeter. The subject of that conversation was the so-called big cat sightings (such as the notorious Beast of Bodmin and Beast of Exmoor) that have been reported throughout Devon and Cornwall for decades. Was Downes aware, the officer inquired, that at Newquay Zoo in the late 1970s a series of grisly mutilations of animals under extremely strange circumstances had occurred? Downes replied that he was not aware of the incidents. Fortunately the officer was able to put Downes in touch with the one man in a position to discuss the facts: the head keeper at the zoo at the time in question.

Downes wasted no time in tracking the man down. Elderly and in failing health, he confirmed to Downes the basics of the story: very strange deaths had occurred at the zoo. Wallabies, swans, and geese had been beheaded, but more significantly, their corpses had been totally drained of blood.

"There was no blood left in the animals at all," the zookeeper informed Downes and added, "I had the area UFO compositor—or whatever he called himself—come down, and the suggestion was that it was beings from outer space who came down and needed the blood—or whatever else it was that they drew out of those animals—to survive. It never developed any further than that. I believe that they got a radiation count in the wallaby paddock at that time."

Was the culprit ever located? "No," replied the zookeeper. "But the same thing was happening all over the world. I can tell you that."

Downes advised me that the zookeeper, it must be stressed, was not an adherent of the extraterrestrial hypothesis. Rather, he suspected black magic and a witch coven. As he conceded, there was also talk of big cats seen in the area. At that stage the conversation was terminated. Downes, however, felt that the man was keeping something back and resolved to address the matter at a later date. Regrettably, he did not get the chance. Forty-eight hours later, the man was dead. Although the death seemed to have only been as a result of the man's failing health, to this day Jon Downes finds this whole saga—and the timing of the man's death—particularly strange and disturbing. But more was to follow.[8]

In 1994 Downes received a package of documents that consisted of, among other things, a secret police file on the animal killings at Newquay Zoo in 1978. Downes is reluctant to reveal precisely how and from whom this material came into his possession, though he has been willing to share the relevant papers with me. The first police report of 2 October 1978 reads thus:

"Over the past months a number of incidents have occurred at the Newquay Zoological Gardens at Trenance Gardens, Newquay. These incidents were thought at first to be unconnected and possibly due to the incursion of a marauding animal, but as will be seen this has now been discounted. On the 3rd June 1978, a wallaby was discovered to have been beheaded in it's [sic] paddock. This was found by staff when first opening up the premises in the early morning. The head of the animal was not found but the point of severance was unusually clean cut.

"On the 17th August 1978, a black swan was found to have been beheaded also. The head and neck were missing, but the body of the swan was unruffled, showing no sign of a struggle. No blood was to be found at the scene. Later the neck was discovered in undergrowth on the premises, but the head was never found. The point of severance was again very clean. Between these dates, a Chinese goose, which is a fairly large species of goose, was removed from its enclosure and it's [sic] carcass, minus head was discovered stuffed between a loose wooden fencing panel on the outer security fence. This was jammed tightly in a very confined space. At this spot the security fence was completely intact."

Interestingly, the report continues that, "The upper part of the body was missing and there was no trace of blood at the scene. Marks in the grass showed signs of someone or something having flattened the grass and several particles of meat were visible." At that stage in the proceedings, an autopsy was deemed the most profitable course of action. From the police file comes the following:

"An examination of the remaining carcass in the presence of the Zoo's Consultant Veterinary Surgeon, W. Clifton Green of Edgecombe Gardens, Newquay, and his assistants, brought the unanimous verdict that the carcass had been dissected by a human being rather than an animal as the skin around the wound was clean cut, and there were no teeth or claw marks visible on the carcass. The backbone had been deeply severed between the missing vertebra and some of the internal organs were missing."

Also forwarded to Downes was a copy of the official report on the dead wallaby: "The hind quarters of the wallaby were presented for examination, the anterior half of the carcass being absent. No external marks or injuries were present on the remaining skin. The carcass had been transected through the lower lumbar region at the level of an invertebral space, through the anterior part of a lumbar vertebral centrum. The left articular process was broken but no other gross damage was present. The rest of the carcass appeared to have been clearly transected by a sharp appliance, the wound edges were even and clean. No evidence of bite wounds were present, nor was there any indication of interference with muscular tissue. The bladder and rectum were absent from the pelvis, but the pelvic girdle and skeletal system of the hind legs appeared undamaged. At the time of the examination, there was no evidence of any great haemorrhage having occurred at the time of incision. Nor, judging by the transection, was there any struggle. It is thus possible that the division of the carcass occurred after death, and was not its cause. The subject inflicting the damage is uncertain, but the possibility of human involvement cannot be excluded following this post-mortem."

Notably, the removal of the rectum, bladder, and the lack of "any struggle" are all common factors present in the North American animal mutilations of the 1970s. Perhaps most bizarre of all was a further report concerning "something" that "attempted to gain entrance to the lion's cage" at night. It hardly needs to be stressed that only someone very foolhardy or near indestructible would dare venture into the cage of a lion. And yet, incredibly, something did. Investigation outside of the cage, the report states, revealed prints that were thought to possibly be those of a large cat of some type. Yet the modus operandi behind the killings suggested a degree of sophisticated intelligence—something that left this particular aspect of the affair somewhat murky. And most significant of all: "The method of killing would indicate that the culprit is an extremely strong 'person' or that some form of drug was used to pacify the animals. If tissue samples were available, then the drug, if used, could be detected."

This particular comment fits almost perfectly with a similar statement that can be found in the aforementioned FBI records. From an FBI document of 16 February 1979, comes the following: "...the animals are being shot with some type of paralyzing drug and the blood is being drawn from the animal after an injection of an anti-coagulant. It appears that in some instances the cattle's legs have been broken and helicopters without any identifying numbers have reportedly been seen in the vicinity of these mutilations..."

Note, too, the reference to the cattle's legs being broken—a characteristic very reminiscent of the 1977 pony deaths on Dartmoor. More than twenty years on, the mysterious animal deaths of 1977 and 1978 remain just that—a mystery. However, Jonathan Downes has also been given access to additional papers that ask a number of interesting and perhaps highly relevant questions to the whole affair. "Any mysterious disappearances over the relevant period?" "Any reports of unusual aircraft or incidents?" "Have the local population reported any loss of livestock?" Whoever posed the questions also raised the issue of an abandoned mine near the zoo and whether it could have served as a "possible refuge." A refuge for who or what was never expanded upon, and whoever the manipulators in the Downes affair were, they have long since vanished back into the murky shadows from which they originally surfaced.

17

THE SPYING CONTINUES

One of the Sandman's most notable claims is that a year after Simon & Schuster made plans to publish Nick Pope's book *Open Skies, Closed Minds* (that was a first-person account of Pope's time as the Ministry of Defense's "real Fox Mulder" as his publicist described him), Pope was placed under surveillance by Special Branch. "The MoD boys anticipated that [Pope's] book would make waves—and they were right. So if it was needed, a plan was put out there to see if there was any way of discrediting him."

The Sandman stated that one of the routine operations put into place was to intercept the contents of Pope's garbage container outside of his house. "This is something done regularly by Special Branch and the Yard," said the Sandman. "We'll go through it all, throw out the cornflake boxes and the tea-bags and look for evidence of anything else that might be useful to use against that person."[1]

Additional testimony surfaced that suggested this claim of surveillance of Pope was not as outrageous as it sounded. And, incredibly, that testimony came from Nick Pope himself. As Pope explained to me, it was the day after the Easter Bank Holiday in 1995, and as was his usual routine, he had placed his garbage bin outside of his house ready for collection. However, as the previous day had been a Bank Holiday, the garbage was due to be picked up one day later than normal.

"I'd forgotten this," Pope told me, "and put mine out on the normal day. You know how it is when you put your rubbish out, everyone thinks: what does he know that I don't? So, it ended up that in our little bit of the close, everyone had put their rubbish out because I had got the wrong day. But when I got back home in the evening, my rubbish had been collected but everyone else's was still standing there. I mentioned this to one or two people, who said, 'Well, you know, it's obvious. Some agency has been collecting your rubbish as part of a surveillance operation, and has been doing it on the official collection day so as not to arouse suspicion, But like you, on this occasion they got the wrong day. They collected your rubbish thinking the real collectors would be along soon, and you'd never notice.' Now, at the instigation of a friend, I wrote a sarcastic little note, and put it in the next batch of rubbish."

"What did it say?" I asked, amused and intrigued at the way this was progressing.

"Well, I wrote: 'To whom it may concern: Bet you didn't think they'd have you doing this when you joined up. Bet you thought it would be more glamorous, lots of running around with guns. Still, everyone has to start somewhere. Apologies for the remains of the Indian takeaway!'"

So who did Pope think was responsible?

"If it was anything sinister, I think it was probably journalists, as opposed to anything more spooky. This hasn't happened to me since, but it's been suggested to me that this is because of my note. It rather sort of smoked them out."[2]

Was the whole matter as innocent as Nick Pope believed, or was there more to it? I contacted a number of people while pursuing this admittedly odd affair, including Matthew Williams. While working with the Personnel Division and later the Criminal Investigations Unit of the British Government's Customs & Excise, Williams had been involved in operations that mirrored exactly the claims of the Sandman and the experience of Nick Pope.

As Williams told me, "If there was someone who was under surveillance, we would find out from the local council which day was 'bin day,' then we'd turn up very early in the morning on that day and collect the rubbish just like the bin-men would. Doing it the same day as the official collection usually means you don't create suspicion. The whole contents of the rubbish would then be brought back to the offices, and then there was the task of having to go through it all. But the thing is, this was standard practice for many government departments. And a lot of those departments would send their 'cream' over to us to be trained.

"Normally, during surveillance operations, you'd be given background information on the person you were investigating; however, occasionally orders would come down from on high to carry out a surveillance of someone's house or place of business, or whatever. In these cases, you would never know on whose behalf you were carrying out the surveillance. Or why. You would just report back to whoever it was that had requested the surveillance. These operations were known as 'Secret Squirreling' operations, and they would basically allow the security services to carry out their investigations without getting their hands dirty.

"The whole thing is, it could mean that those directly involved in carrying out surveillance on people in the UFO community aren't the security services, the Men in Black, or MJ12, but are just some local civil servant who doesn't really know what he's investigating—that keeps everything really secret."[3]

There were other occasions when British authorities seemed determined to destroy the credibility of Nick Pope. On 14 November 1999, the *News of the World* newspaper published an article written by Ian Kirby, a political correspondent. He claimed that the Ministry of Defense was planning to release all of its information on UFOs in February 2000. According to the *News of the World*, not only would this see the release of "photos and details of every UFO investigation in the past 30 years," it would also involve the MoD making public "plans by military experts for action in the event of an alien invasion of London."

Ian Kirby further stated that Defense Minister Peter Kilfoyle had examined the documents in question. It was claimed that Kilfoyle was "not convinced about the existence of aliens." Nevertheless, Kirby was informed by a source that, "These files are of huge public interest. They paint a fascinating picture of how UFO reports were investigated—and what would happen if aliens ever did land in Britain."[4]

After I carefully read the article I telephoned the MoD's press office for comment. Identifying myself (truthfully) as a journalist working full-time for a national Sunday newspaper at the time, I asked if the *News of the World*'s story was indeed correct.

"Nonsense," came the reply. "We are not planning any sort of big release of UFO files next year at all. Files will be released every January at the Public Record Office in the same way that they've always been. But this story that appeared in the press is incorrect."

"So, do you know where the story did originate?" I pressed.

Astonishingly, the press officer informed me that "You can get a good indication from the fact that Nick Pope has a new book to promote"—a reference to his then-recently published first novel, *Operation Thunder Child*. In other words, the MoD was laying the blame for this account squarely on Nick Pope.[5]

My next step was to telephone Pope—the alleged whistleblower himself—and I engaged him in what was a decidedly curious conversation worthy of an entire episode of *The X-Files*.

"Well…I can see why they might think that. The timing couldn't have been better," Pope began, "but there are a few other things going on as well," he replied in a typically tight-lipped bureaucratic style.

"Like what?" I queried him.

"Oh well, you know. There still might be more to this story. Something may happen with the Freedom of Information Act; people are planning to use the FOIA to get this material and when I can tell you more, I will."[6]

Notably, Pope also told me: "There are one or two things about the Ministry's stance over the last few years that have caused me to question things perhaps a little bit more than I did previously. I do think that there's a little bit more going on than perhaps I previously thought. I have to be very careful with every single word I say, because I know that every word, every sentence, every nuance, will be picked over by ufologists, the Ministry of Defense, and a number of other agencies."

"Excuse me, a number of other agencies? What do you mean by that?" I pressed.

"I mean, a number of other agencies," was his tight-lipped reply. Pope has steadfastly declined to elaborate upon this revelation. But the enlightening fact that his "every single word" was being "picked over" by "a number of other agencies" adds further weight to the allegations that even those in the official world with UFO interests - such as Pope himself - are watched closely by the all-seeing eyes of Government.

Faced with claims from the MoD that they believed him to be the source of the *News of the World's* information, Nick Pope released a statement outlining his position: "It has been suggested in certain quarters that I was the source of the story in the *News of the World*

Elements of British Intelligence monitored author Nick Redfern after he investigated claims that alien bodies were held at Porton Down— a secure facility in England that has undertaken defense research into biological and chemical warfare.

and that my motive in planting the story was to generate publicity for my latest book, *Operation Thunder Child*. Let me make it absolutely clear that this is not the case. Although I was briefly quoted in the piece, these quotes must have been lifted from an old article. There was, of course, no mention of my book. Nobody from the paper spoke to me, and indeed the first I knew about this article was when the *Daily Mail* telephoned me on the Sunday morning that the story ran, and asked if I had seen it.

"The *Daily Mail* then commissioned me to write a general piece about the sorts of cases detailed in the MoD's files. I was careful not to get drawn into a debate about whether or not these files were going to be released, and my article used the phrase 'If, and when, they are made available publicly.' Following the initial story in the *News of the World*, I was understandably keen to mention my book if I could. It is not for me to say whether or not there is going to be an official release of all the MoD's UFO files.

"There is already a steady release of these files each year under the terms of the Public Records Act, and although the current policy may change in light of the Freedom of Information Act, it would be premature to speculate on these changes before the terms of the Act have been agreed. Ufologists are understandably excited about the forthcoming FOIA, and are doubtless planning to blitz the MoD with requests for UFO data. It is possible that speculation about what UFO material may be obtained using the FOIA has played a part in generating rumors of a mass release of the files."[7]

There is no reason to doubt that, in his statement, Pope was being anything less than entirely truthful. However, Pope was being extremely charitable when he stated that the UFO stories he was blamed for spreading had originated in what he vaguely and weakly termed "certain quarters." Let us not obscure the facts: Those "certain quarters" were Pope's own colleagues at the Ministry of Defense, who were informing writers and journalists (myself included) that Pope was, to put it bluntly, concocting bogus UFO stories to promote his new novel. Not a nice tactic, but one that does support the claims of the Sandman that plans had been put in place to discredit Pope, if it was deemed necessary.

Although there can be little doubt that researcher Andy Roberts has laid to rest nearly all of the questions relating to the rumors that a UFO crashed on the Berwyn Mountains, North Wales, in January 1974, stories relating to this strange affair continued to surface. The most sensational allegation came in 1996 from a British Army soldier whose identity was obfuscated by researcher Tony Dodd who first heard the story. According to the soldier, three nights before the events of 23 January 1974, a number of alien bodies and several still-living, extraterrestrial creatures were recovered from the mountainside by an elite team of military personnel and were transferred under tight security to an official installation in the South of England called Porton Down, the British Government's biological and chemical defense research establishment.

Porton Down has not been without its share of controversy. Much of it focused on two issues: biological and chemical experimentation performed on animals (such as dogs and primates), and similar research performed on military "volunteers" from the 1950s onward. In fact, history has unfortunately demonstrated that a number of personnel used in the trials and experiments developed serious health problems.[8]

According to the Sandman, the roots of the story that alien bodies were found on the Berwyn Mountains can—like other aspects of the alleged UFO crash—be traced back to the ultra-fascist group, APEN. He stated specifically that the tales concerning alien bodies taken to Porton Down were in reality carefully constructed by the members of APEN around 1975:

"The reason was to try and create a really strong UFO case that would have the UFO faithful flocking to APEN's door and then these people would—APEN hoped—be recruited into their ranks as part of this right-wing indoctrination plan for a group along those lines. So, APEN were responsible for spreading the tales—limitedly, at least, around 1975 in North Wales. They actually had people, stationed in town there, just spreading gossip about bodies being found and the Porton link. The idea was specifically not to leak the body stories to the UFO groups, but to spread them around the North Wales villages, so that if UFO investigators went to these villages and asked about the Berwyn case, and the villagers said something like, 'I heard tales about bodies being found on the mountain,' that would look impressive and it wouldn't look like it came from within the UFO research. Then APEN would allude to the groups that they had more on this case, and people would then really be knocking on APEN's door and getting pulled in.

"But, of course, when we shut APEN down, all you had left were these fragments of tales that APEN had spread around North Wales about bodies and Porton, and that no one had really heard outside of the North Wales' people.

"Now, here's where it got really odd," said the Sandman. "In 1995, one of those APEN chaps was over in Northern Ireland. We were still watching this chap as he was by then linked with some very heavy-duty Irish terrorist groups. Not the IRA, but I'm legally unable to say to you what group it was. But what happened is that we were listening to this chap forging links with this terrorist cell in Belfast. This cell was trying to find out about biological warfare operations at Porton Down, virus research, and things like that. The plan was that they wanted to try and recruit an insider at Porton, who might be sympathetic to their cause, and in a worst-case picture, actually get materials into the hands of the terrorists that could be used as a biological attack on London.

"Well, everyone was very concerned, but at this stage the most advantageous thing to do was just sit and listen and try and get a handle on all the players before we made any arrests and then hopefully arrest everyone at once. But this APEN chap said he had an idea, and he proceeded to tell the Irish group about APEN and how they had spread bogus UFO tales back in the seventies and set up this APEN organization as a way of recruiting people to an extreme right-wing group, and doing it all behind a UFO smokescreen. He also told them how they even added a story about alien bodies being taken to Porton to really make it sound juicy and really to try and convince people to come on board with them.

"The Irish people found this very interesting and they all came together with a plan: why not re-launch the tale about the alien bodies being taken to Porton? Then, see which researchers look into it—and that finally turned out to be mainly you and master Williams. The plan would then be to try and recruit you and Williams to do their work for them, or maybe even blackmail you, if they could find anything. Then, in a way similar to that of Bevan, if your research into activities at Porton attracted official interest, you can say, 'Well, we're just looking into this alien body story.' It would be good cover. And it was about this time that another level of this investigation began with us specifically watching you and Williams to see where you were going with the [alien body] story and if you had been recruited into their ranks."[9]

That the Sandman's story is likely correct can be substantiated for a number of reasons. From mid-1996 until 1999, both Matthew Williams and I dug deeply into the aliens-at-Porton-story. Also, we did find numerous people who worked at Porton Down in 1974.

Not only that, but from the age of approximately eighteen and until I left Britain for the United States in 2001, I was (and still am—albeit from a different perspective now that I live on the other side of the world) deeply involved in the work of animal-rights organizations in Britain. This included taking part in proactive demonstrations, passing out leaflets and pamphlets at organized rallies, and generally trying to get the word out to the public about the various experimental atrocities that were carried out on innocent animals at Porton Down, among several other locations.

"You were a real headache for us," sighed the Sandman. "We had a file on you anyway already because of your animal demonstrations and all that, and we knew that you were looking for—and finding—people that worked at Porton in '74 when the [UFO] crash supposedly happened. And some of us were split; on the one hand, there was the concern that you were doing all this work as a cover for working with these APEN people and their contacts who wanted solid information on Porton and what was going on, and who they might be able to recruit there. But some of our other boys wondered if you were using the [alien body] investigation as a cover to collect information on people that worked at Porton, and that you would then give this information and these names to your friends in the animal groups."

Ironically, the Sandman stated: "Very few of us really thought, at the time, that you and Williams were just looking to find the truth about the [alien body] story and nothing else and that it was all innocent. Everyone was paranoid that there was more to it."[10]

There is no doubt that my research into Porton Down and the alien body allegations, along with my friendship with Matthew Williams, was of concern to officials. It was shortly after Simon & Schuster published my book, *A Covert Agenda: The British Government's UFO Top Secrets Exposed*, in September 1997 that my path crossed directly with Special Branch. I was sitting in my office when the telephone rang.

"Is that Nicholas Redfern?" asked a male voice.

"Yeah, it is. Who's that?" I replied.

The voice on the other end identified himself as a representative of Special Branch and added, "We've seen your book and you have a chapter in there on Rudloe Manor. We'd like to speak with you about this."

"Really? And you're from Special Branch?" I asked in a mocking tone, fully expecting this to be a ufological wind-up by a friend. It was not. To cut a long story and an even longer phone conversation short, two days later, there was a knock at the door. I opened it and was faced by two men with the unmistakable look of plainclothes police officers. Both were probably in their mid-forties, with short, cropped hair.

They provided what appeared to be the correct identification and I invited them in. I listened to what they had to say, answered an array of questions, and slowly absorbed what was certainly one of the most bizarre experiences of my life. I had prepared myself for a typical "good cop/bad cop" scenario. But nothing could be further from the truth. The two were to-the-point but cordial, almost apologetic at times and without any shadow of a doubt embarrassed to be involved in what all three of us conceded was a truly weird situation.

"We only want to ask you about your research into Rudloe Manor and your friend, Matthew Williams," they said in a fashion similar to the questions posed to Robin Cole at Cheltenham. "What's your motivation? What are you looking for at Rudloe and where does Mr. Williams stand and have a role in this?" they asked.

I gave them a detailed history of the rumors concerning Rudloe Manor and UFOs. I related the odd tale of the missing file at the National Archive. I told them that I had found numerous military personnel who had confirmed the Rudloe stories to me on-the-record. And I informed them that in a very strange move, the MoD—quite out of the blue—had admitted in 1995 to researcher Chris Fowler that Rudloe had indeed acted as the "coordination point" for UFO reports for the entire Royal Air Force up until 1992.

"And you believe that there are or were secret flying saucer investigations going on there?"

"Well, yeah, I do actually," I said. "Have the Government and the MoD been truthful on the Rudloe story? I'll tell you—and prove to you—that they haven't."

"So you have problems with authority figures and you distrust Government."

"Yes, I do, actually, and with a lot of justification, I think."

Questions were then asked about a number of issues: my political beliefs; my longstanding connections with animal rights organizations; why I was investigating the claims that alien bodies had been taken to Porton Down; what I was doing hanging around Porton Down in July 1997 and writing down the license plates on the cars of the employees that were heading toward the facility; and whether I considered UFO research to be an area that the Security Services had a right to suspect was full of "potential subversives." I responded that if the Ministry of Defense was of the official opinion that UFOs were of no defense significance, then by definition, research into UFOs and UFO researchers themselves could not be considered subversive or threatening.

"So your only interest in Rudloe and Porton Down is the flying saucer story?" I was asked.

"Well, what else would it be?" I replied, completely unaware of the assertions of the Sandman at that time.

"Do you think Mr. Williams is legitimate about only looking for flying saucers?" they inquired.

"Yeah, I do. Why?" I replied bluntly.

The pair exchanged glances and a remarkable theory was outlined to me: "We are looking into allegations that some people in the flying saucer research groups are being used as front operatives for terrorist groups, animal rights groups, and extremist organizations."

The story related to me was that two possibilities were under consideration within the corridors of power: That some UFO researchers in the United Kingdom were being unwittingly directed to undertake in-depth investigations of sensitive military establishments on behalf of anti-establishment groups that were carefully spreading bogus UFO tales to the research community as a form of "bait;" and that some UFO investigators in the United Kingdom were wittingly conducting research into such installations for anti-establishment sympathizers under a carefully executed cover story of carrying out "studies into flying saucers."

"So, you mean that when these people hang out taking pictures at these places like Rudloe and British Aerospace at Warton, looking for crashed UFOs and alien bodies, they're really there to get the latest on the base and give the details to our enemies?" I pressed.

"That's it in its basic, simplified form, yes. And we just want to know if you think your friend Mr. Williams is involved."

"Of course he's not involved," I replied firmly. "Some of the old guard in the UFO subject don't like Matt because of his approach, but he gets results and I can tell you he's a good guy. He's into UFOs, he's into freedom of speech, direct action, and asking questions when they need to be asked and looking for answers when those answers need to be found. But there's nothing wrong with that. I do exactly the same."

"Okay, sir; thank-you for your time." The interview was over and we all headed for the front door.

I would see one of them on two more occasions—both in 1999 and in the immediate aftermath of the publication of my book, *Cosmic Crashes*. Again the line of questioning was cordial, focused upon certain players in the UFO research community with politically linked backgrounds, and my views concerning the possibility that they, too, were witting or unwitting players in a terrorist-related mind-game. Special Branch also wanted to discuss with me another individual: none other than Matthew Bevan. The questions were predictable, and I answered in the affirmative to all of the following: "Did you meet Matthew Bevan in the company of Matthew Williams?" "Did you subsequent to that meeting conduct a lengthy interview with Bevan?" "Are you going to publish that interview in its entirety?"

At the time, I suspected that all of these questions, which spanned 1997 to 1999, were because I had tapped into a genuine black box of data on crashed UFOs, dead aliens, and who knew what else. The words of the Sandman, however, would suggest that the reasoning behind the official concern was far stranger than if aliens really had crashed landed on the Berwyns and were hidden away in some Hangar 18-style facility at Wright-Patterson Air Force Base, RAF Rudloe Manor, or Porton Down.

In late 2000 Matthew Williams was arrested by the British Police Force for causing criminal damage to a field in Wiltshire, England. He admitted creating—under cover of complete darkness—a highly elaborate "pictogram"-style Crop Circle that many researchers of the phenomenon assert cannot be made by human hands.

Since then, Williams has been variously described as a Crop Circle hoaxer, an outright liar, a charlatan, and, most absurd of all, a Government agent dispensing disinformation, specifically designed to muddy the waters concerning who or what is responsible for the Crop Circle mystery. The real story behind Williams's involvement in the Crop Circle controversy is far stranger.

It should be stressed that Williams does not consider himself to be a hoaxer of Crop Circles. Rather, he is of the opinion—as are a surprisingly large number of people who make such formations— that his actions are directed or manipulated by a higher power or intelligence. While many researchers of the Crop Circle mystery scoff at Williams's assertions that the elaborate crop formations are all made by people, it is truly ironic that the British Intelligence community firmly believed him—and it was that belief which led to his Crop Circle activities becoming the subject of an official investigation. And for the answer as to why Matthew Williams's Crop Circle-making activities attracted the interest of British Intelligence and Special Branch, we have to travel back in time to the height of the Second World War.

In early 1941, Sir David Petrie was appointed the first Director General of the Security Service, MI5, and was given substantial resources to restructure the organization, whose origins date back to 1909. As a result, MI5 became one of the most efficient agencies of the War. After the defeat of the Nazis in 1945, it was learned that all of the Nazi agents targeted against Britain had been successfully identified, and in some cases recruited as double-agents, by MI5—something that contributed to the success of the Allied Forces landing in Normandy on D-Day, 6 June 1944.[11]

A number of files pertaining to M15's wartime activities have been declassified and are now available for public inspection at the National Archive, Kew. One deals with MI5 investigations of what are intriguingly described as "markings on the ground."

According to the report: "This account is not concerned with the activities of fifth columnists such as sabotage, capturing airfields and key points, and harassing the defending army, but in the methods used in communicating to each other and to the enemy. Reports from Poland, Holland, France and Belgium showed that they used ground markings for the guidance of bombers and paratroops (and of lights by night)."

The report continued: "Such ground markings might be the cutting of cornfields into guiding marks for aircraft, painting of roofs and the inside of chimneys white, setting haystacks on fire, and laying out strips of white linen in pre-arranged patterns. For guiding and giving information to advancing troops they would conceal messages behind advertisement hoardings and leave markings on walls and telegraph poles."

Most notable of all, from interviews conducted with Allied personnel who had taken part in the hostilities in Poland, MI5 had determined that one of the ways that Nazi spies were communicating with German Luftwaffe pilots was by "beating out signs," twenty meters in diameter, "on harrowed fields or mowing such signs on meadows or cornfields." Crop circles, in other words!

As a result of finding such curious formations across wartime Europe, MI5 began to check cornfields throughout the British Isles for any evidence of similar activity. In a section of a report titled "Examples of Ground Markings Investigated," a still-anonymous MI5 employee wrote:

"Field, north of Newquay, Cornwall: Aircraft noticed, in May 1940, strange marking in this field and it was photographed. Enquiries were made and it was found that the lines were formed by heaps of lime used for agricultural purposes. The farmer concerned was above reproach and removed the lime heaps."

A second report followed: "Field at Little Mill, Monmouthshire: In May 1941 a report was made that an unusual mark was visible amongst the growing corn. Near one of the gates was a mark in the form of the letter G, some 33 yards long. This mark had been made by sowing barley transversely through the grain."

MI5 added: "Air photographs were taken and it was seen that the tail of the marking pointed towards the Ordnance factory at Glascoed. The farmer, a man of good character, was interviewed, and admitted that he had sown the field himself. He explained that he had sold the field in April. Shortly after, having a drilling machine nearby which had a small quantity of barley seed in it, and wishing to empty it as he had to return it to the farmer from whom he had borrowed it that night, he turned his team of horses into the grain field and drilled it into the ground thickly to get rid of it. He did this because it is extremely difficult to remove the grain in the machine by hand, and to sow it was the quickest way of getting rid of it. He agreed to plough up this part of the field. As a satisfactory explanation had been reached, the case was carried no further."

And the reports kept on coming: "Field, near Staplehurst, Kent: In October, 1943, aircraft saw a faint white circle on the ground.

Enquiries were made, and it was discovered that before the war the field was used as an emergency landing ground by Imperial Airways; the mark was made by them, and they paid a small yearly rent to the farmer. At the beginning of the war the mark was obliterated in some way, but this had worn thin. Steps were taken to obliterate it again."[12]

It is quite clear from examining the contents of these now-declassified files that MI5 thought that the wartime Crop Circles across Europe and the similar formations found on the British mainland were the work of Nazi spies, and the designs were intended to convey a specific coded message to German bomber-pilots.

It is also illuminating to note that most of the Crop Circles in the British Isles have been found in the county of Wiltshire, which also happens to be home to a whole range of sensitive installations and establishments, including the aforementioned Porton Down, Salisbury Plain, Boscombe Down, and RAF Rudloe Manor.

Could it be that Government interest in today's Crop Circle mystery parallels that of its wartime counterpart? Is there a belief within the Intelligence community that at least some of the Crop Circles might be coded messages left for subversive groups intent on disrupting activities at Porton Down, Boscombe Down, Rudloe Manor, and Salisbury Plain? As unbelievable as this might sound, we now have official documentation at our disposal showing that this is exactly what MI5 had concluded was occurring during the Second World War.

According to the Sandman, it was precisely this belief that led to continued interest in Matthew Williams's activities. "I've told you about how you and Williams were being watched in 1996 when the two of you began investigating the tales about alien bodies taken to Porton Down. That was a real example of how we feared this Porton research of yours was a cover for something else. Well, in that same year, there were Crop Circles turning up right around Porton Down. So, yes it's quite true that there was a low-key, official study of the Circles done to see who was making them. But the main reason for this was because MI5 had institutional memory of something similar being worked on during the [Second World] War, and so that's what was considered here—the scenario that these were coded messages for subversives.

"Now it gets interesting," said the Sandman. "Who moved down from Wales to live in Wiltshire in 2000? Young master Williams. And to where did he move? To Devizes, the heart of Crop Circle land, and just a relatively short drive to Porton, Boscombe, and Rudloe. Then Williams got mixed up in making Crop Circles in the area, and we already knew he—and you—had an interest in Porton. So there was that nagging worry again: was this chap making these things as part of some odd plot that involved leaving coded messages, possibly for pilots of light aircraft, that might be engaged upon for various reasons at Porton? There was a pressing need to get answers."[13]

Another reason why this angle was pursued was because none other than Jonathan Downes—who was already under surveillance—had also been looking into links between Crop Circles and Porton Down, as Downes told me in 2000: "I am aware that midway through 1996 on land adjacent to the Government's chemical and biological research establishment at Porton Down, Wiltshire, a Crop Circle was found. When it was first seen, the circle was still in the process of being formed and had actually been surrounded by both troops and police who had cordoned off the area."[14]

The Sandman continued: "So, Downes was looking at Porton with a Circles connection. And you and Williams were looking at Porton with the alien body story. Then, when Williams admitted to making Circles, there was a good chance he could be arrested for criminal damage to the farmer's field—and he was. But the real motive was not so much to get Williams convicted. That was just the first stage. The real intent was to confiscate his computer. The plan was to say—if he told the press and they asked—that his computer was being confiscated because we wanted to see if there were any Crop Circle designs on his computer that matched Circle creations that had popped up elsewhere in the Wiltshire fields; and that if we did find plans on his computer, then we could say we're going to get this chap prosecuted for making those, too. But that was never the real motive. The real motive was to get our hands on his computer to see if we could learn more about his motivations with you, with Bevan, with his Rudloe research and really check into what was stored on his hard-drive."[15]

After Williams's arrest, the Police's Computer Crime Unit—deeply involved in the Matthew Bevan caper—did indeed confiscate Williams's hard drive, and for a period of several months. The idea that the British Police Force's Computer Crime Unit would need to review Williams's hard drive for a period of several months to search for evidence of Crop Circle chicanery seems unlikely—and absurd. What seems more likely is the scenario suggested by the Sandman: that this was a chance-in-a-million for British authorities to access the secrets they believed were stored on Williams's computer. That would vindicate their suspicions that Williams's UFO research was simply a ruse for more controversial actions. The fact that the same people who arrested Bevan confiscated Williams's computer makes this scenario far more likely, too. As it transpired, the Police's search uncovered nothing at all of an incriminating nature, and Williams's hard drive was eventually returned to him—albeit after a lengthy and drawn-out battle.

My final personal contact with Special Branch came in late 2001. After writing an article for Mark Birdsall's *Eye Spy* magazine on David Shayler, the MI5 whistleblower, I received a telephone call from a highly concerned Birdsall, informing me that he had been visited at his home in North Yorkshire by "two lads from the Metropolitan Police." Birdsall advised me that the officers informed him that while publication of the article was not deemed to have harmed the national security of the country, there was a pressing need on their part to obtain the tape recording of the interview I had conducted with Shayler. For a while I mused upon this—and did nothing.

Shortly after I moved to the United States, I was contacted by a representative of Special Branch who advised me that I must hand over the tape, like it or not, even if he had to fly to the United

States to acquire it. Based upon what I was told, I was left with little choice, and I did indeed hand over the original recording. In answer to a follow-up question, I naturally denied making—or hiding—any copies of the tape. But I was not the only UFO researcher to be of interest to officials at the dawn of a new century.[16]

In January 2005, it was announced that Federal prosecutors had formally dropped charges against a man who had exposed a "buried surveillance network" surrounding the infamous Area 51 in Nevada. Some say that a number of crashed and recovered UFOs that are currently being "back-engineered" by the U.S. Government reside there.

Chuck Clark had been charged in 2003 with a single count of malicious interference with a communications system used for the national defense of the United States. Prosecutors held him responsible for the disappearance of one of the wireless motion sensors buried beneath the desert land that surrounds the secret base. In a "deal with the government," Clark agreed to enter a one-year term of "pretrial diversion" and to either locate and return the lost device, or financially reimburse the Air Force.

"He paid for the missing sensor, and complied with the conditions of his pretrial diversion and the case was dismissed," said Natalie Collins, a spokesperson for the U.S. Attorney's Office in Las Vegas.

Along with fellow Area 51-watcher, Joerg Arnu, Clark had been mapping the sensors using a handheld frequency-counter to detect their unique radio transmissions. Together they dug up as many as forty of the devices, made a note of their three-digit codes, then reburied and tested them.

The sensors were marked "U.S. Government Property," and in some cases, were planted miles outside of Groom Lake's fence line on public land, rather than on Government-owned land. On 12 March 2003 one of the sensors "went missing," said the Government, and FBI and Air Force agents descended upon Clark's trailer home in Rachel, Nevada. As part of the settlement deal, Clark was barred from interfering with any of the sensors or otherwise breaking the law, and was obligated to keep the court informed of his whereabouts during his year of supervision.[17]

Midway through 2005, the story of a London-based computer hacker named Gary McKinnon hit the headlines in a situation that eerily paralleled that of Matthew Bevan almost a decade earlier. Thirty-nine-year-old McKinnon, an unemployed former computer engineer, was "seized" by the Metropolitan Police's extradition unit at his Wood Green home. He was accused of causing the U.S. Government no less than one billion dollars of damage by breaking into its most secure computers at the Pentagon and NASA in search of classified UFO data. A terrified McKinnon was told that he was likely to be extradited to the United States to face eight counts of computer crime in fourteen states and could be jailed for up to seventy years.

Prosecutor Paul McNulty alleged that McKinnon, known online as Solo, had perpetrated "the biggest hack of military computers ever." The charge sheet alleged that he hacked into an Army computer at Fort Myer, Virginia, where he obtained codes, information, and commands, before deleting approximately 1,300 user accounts.

Friends said that McKinnon was "desperate" to prove that the American Government had mounted a huge cover-up to hide the fact that aliens had visited Earth. Andrew Edwards, who had known McKinnon since their days together at Highgate Wood Secondary School, said: "Gary told me all he was doing was looking for proof of a cover-up over UFOs. He's been interested in UFOs for some time and believes the Americans are holding back information—although he didn't find any proof."

McKinnon's attorney, Karen Todner, stated that McKinnon—who had originally been indicted in 2002—was disappointed it had taken the authorities this long to bring him to court, adding: "This decision for extradition is driven by the American government. Mr. McKinnon intends to contest this case most vigorously. Of particular concern to him is the treatment of other British nationals under the

American judicial system, which inspires little confidence. We believe that as a British national, he should be tried here in our courts by a British jury and not in the U.S."

In July 2005 in an interview with Britain's *Guardian* newspaper, McKinnon stated: "I'm walking down the road and I find I can't control my own legs. And I'm sitting up all night thinking about jail and about being arse-fucked."

When asked by the *Guardian*, "What was the most exciting thing you saw?" Mckinnon replied, "I found a list of officers' names, under the heading Non-Terrestrial Officers. It doesn't mean little green men. What I think it means is not Earth-based. I found a list of 'fleet-to-fleet transfers,' and a list of ship names. I looked them up. They weren't U.S. Navy ships. What I saw made me believe they have some kind of spaceship, off-planet."

"The Americans have a secret spaceship?" asked the *Guardian*.

"That's what this trickle of evidence has led me to believe," McKinnon replied.

"You know," he told the *Guardian*, "everyone thinks this is fun or exciting. But it isn't exciting to me. It is terrifying."[18]

As director of the National UFO Reporting Center in Seattle, Peter Davenport has spent the last eleven years filing accounts and eyewitness reports of UFO sightings. In August 2005 journalist Emily Burton revealed that "During a classified meeting on the East coast several years ago, with a government agency Davenport is not at liberty to identify, the exact scope of the government's involvement in their own UFO research was partial revealed."

According to Davenport: "They identified themselves, ... and they said, 'Peter, we know who you are. We have visited your website extensively.' And they said, 'You appear to us to have information that we are very interested in.'"

Burton elaborated that "They wanted to know more about a UFO that had been seen near a commercial airliner. After a four-hour meeting, they thanked Davenport and told him, 'Out of our sense of gratitude, we're going to tell you what our position about UFOs is in the U.S. government,' he said.

"The officials told Davenport: 'Number one: we know that UFOs are real. Number two: we know that UFOs are what they appear to be. Namely: sophisticated craft under intelligent control. There's no doubt of that,' they said. 'And number three, we in the government are a bit worried about them.'"

"Clearly," said Davenport, "the U.S. Government—from my vantage point I think I can say this safely—is doing everything in its power to quash interest in the subject of ufology in general. And in individual cases that are dramatic and well documented, and evident to a large body of people. Now, is that conspiracy or is that policy? I'm not sure I can answer that."[19]

CONCLUSIONS

So what can we say about this decidedly strange affair that apparently motivates Government, Military, and Intelligence agencies in both the United States and the United Kingdom to subject numerous figures within the UFO research community, UFO witnesses, and even alleged alien abductees to periodic (or perhaps even continual) surveillance?

With regard to such characters as George Adamski and George Van Tassel in the 1950s and 1960s, it is very clear that the UFO angle of the FBI's surveillance was secondary to the fact that—at the height of the Cold War and McCarthyism—both men were presenting their UFO data in a highly political fashion. Adamski even stated that Russia would one day dominate the world and that any visiting aliens were most likely communist in nature! In other words, official surveillance of both men is exactly what we would have expected to see from an agency as diligent—and perhaps even as paranoid—as the FBI certainly was in the 1950s.

Similarly, the fact that in the mid-1970s the mysterious APEN were intent on utilizing the UFO subject as a convenient cover as part of their plans to create a new ultra-right-wing political group within the United Kingdom makes it hardly surprising that they were subject to both official scrutiny and ingenious manipulation by Special Branch.

The same can be said about Paul Bennewitz. The all-too-successful attempts of the Military and the Intelligence world to not only stop his investigations into classified activities at Kirtland Air Force Base, New Mexico, but to also drive him to nervous collapse by concocting horrific, bogus UFO tales are understandable, albeit overwhelmingly unforgivable. In its collective mind, the official world was just protecting its Military secrets from a man who had not only wrongly perceived those secrets to have extraterrestrial origins, but who was intent on telling the whole world what he had uncovered.

The issue of Military agencies apparently monitoring purported alien abductees suggests that extraterrestrials—or at least non-human entities from some other realm of existence—could very well indeed be with us, and officials are highly concerned by both their presence and their motivations. Or maybe this is just a cover for the Military's own activities.

And what of the situation in the United Kingdom during the mid-to-late 1990s and beyond, that saw me, Matthew Williams, Matthew Bevan, Robin Cole, Jonathan Downes, and others all subjected to surveillance by Special Branch? Was it purely because of our UFO interests? According to the Sandman, no. The UFO angle was secondary to the official concern that our combined UFO research was a carefully executed cover for far more nefarious activities, such as collecting data on Military installations and new technologies to be forwarded to potentially subversive groups.

That the theory was not just outlandish, but totally without foundation, is irrelevant. For officials, even if this was a remote possibility, it had to be investigated. And it was investigated. The important thing about this story is that we do not have to rely on wild conspiracy theories or unsubstantiated data to support it. Much of the data that is cited within the pages of this book that focuses upon official surveillance of UFO researchers in the United States is gleaned directly from U.S. Government files declassified under the terms of the Freedom of Information Act.

As for the situation in Britain, although the Sandman has certainly made some provocative statements, he is only responsible for putting the pieces of the puzzle together. For example, that both Robin Cole and Matthew Williams were of deep interest to Special Branch is something that can be completely supported. When Cole was visited by Special Branch representatives in 1997, he had the foresight to surreptitiously tape record the conversation, thus proving for posterity that questions were being asked about their activities.

Likewise, the story and surveillance of computer hacker Matthew Bevan is a matter of official record; and my own experiences with Special Branch are known to a number of additional individuals, including Jonathan Downes and *Eye Spy* magazine editor, Mark Birdsall. And Downes's own, somewhat unnerving, experiences with Special Branch can be attested to by Downes, himself.

Perhaps the most important question is: why is the Sandman talking? Although there were reportedly no less than twenty people working on the British surveillance operations of the 1990s—a large enough number that would arguably offer some protection for any potential whistleblower not wishing to be identified—the Sandman was the only one also involved in the APEN saga of two decades previously. In other words, his identity has to be known at an official level. And with this observation, he not only concurs but elaborates: "Back in the APEN days and even in the nineties, UFOs were a force in Britain. There were magazines everywhere, and there were groups; people were doing things. Doing things in the field, I mean, not just on the world wide web. But today, it's all come a cropper and over with. Even young master Williams hasn't poked his nose into Rudloe for years. [Robin] Cole doesn't do his group anymore, Downes has washed his hands of UFOs, as has Bevan with his computers, and you live on the other side of the world. At a pro-active level of people running around military bases, taking pictures, breaking in at Monks Park, it doesn't happen anymore.

"So, we made a decision to have someone—me—reveal the background, the history, the story, to a conduit—you—without having to come right out and say it officially. That way, you get it published, and we can send out a signal to any subversives that might try this in the future—recruiting UFO fellows—that we know their game. That was the problem before; we kept it all so deeply hidden that these people kept trying it on—recruitment, that is. Or I should say more accurately that we thought—and some still do—that this is what was going on. But making it not exactly an official sign or official statement of what went on also gives us plausible deniability, too, as the Yanks say, if we need it."[1]

UFOs may indeed be among us. They may perhaps even have alien origins. And as a UFO researcher, writer, abductee, contactee, or just an intrigued outsider, you may well be the subject of official interest on the part of one or more Government agencies. As I have demonstrated time and again, the reason for that official interest and surveillance usually has more to do with politics, so-called subversives, and perceived anti-establishment groups, than it has to do with little green men.

Then again, perhaps things are not quite as they seem. Perhaps aliens really did make contact with George Adamski. Perhaps a flying saucer did crash on the Berwyn Mountains. Perhaps there really are alien bodies buried deep below Wright-Patterson Air Force Base in Dayton, Ohio. And perhaps this is the real reason for the official surveillance of the UFO community, and the claims of the Sandman are merely an ingenious, diversionary ploy designed to lead us away from the alien truth.

Or, alternatively, perhaps some people within the UFO research community are not all what they appear to be—as certain colleagues of the Sandman no doubt still believe—and their research really is acting as a convenient cover for collaboration with dark and sinister forces. As *On the Trail of the Saucers Spies* has demonstrated, when it comes to UFOs, nothing is quite as it seems.

ACKNOWLEDGEMENTS

I would like to offer my sincere thanks to the following for their contributions to *On the Trail of the Saucer Spies*: First and foremost, Patrick Huyghe and Dennis Stacy and everyone at Anomalist Books; for interviews and information, Chris Fowler, Robin Cole, Jonathan Downes, Jenny Randles, Richard Conway, Nick Pope, Anne Henson, Neil Rusling, the Sandman, Matthew Bevan, Greg Bishop, Andy Roberts, David Clarke, and numerous others; Matthew Williams for the interviews, photographs, and for the use of material from various editions of his *Truth-Seekers' Review*; and the many and varied official agencies that have declassified their official files on the subjects cited within these pages.

NOTES

Introduction:
1. *Have You Checked Your File Lately?* Robert Durant. Published privately, 1992.

Chapter 1: The Early Years
1. *The FBI Files: The FBI's UFO Top Secrets Exposed,* Nick Redfern, Simon & Schuster, 1998.
2. U.S. Air Force Public Affairs Office Fact Sheet, 1988.
3. *Body Snatchers in the Desert: The Horrible Truth at the Heart of the Roswell Story,* Nick Redfern, Paraview-Pocket Books, 2005.
4. *CIA's Role in the Study of UFOs 1947–90,* Gerald Haines, *Studies in Intelligence,* Vol. 1, No. 1, Central Intelligence Agency, 1997. See also: www.cia.gov.
5. *Incident at Aztec,* Nick Redfern, *Fortean Times,* No. 181, March 2004. *Behind the Flying Saucers,* Frank Scully, Henry Holt, 1950. *UFO Crash at Aztec,* William Steinman & Wendelle Stevens, UFO Photo Archives, 1987. *Clearwater Sun,* 27 October 1974. *Fate,* February 1988. *Official UFO,* December 1975.
6. *UFOs and the National Security State, An Unclassified History, Volume One: 1941–1973,* Richard M. Dolan, Keyhole Publishing Company, 2000.

Chapter 2: Contacts of the Cosmic Kind
1. www.integratron.com

Chapter 3: Who Goes There?
1. *George Adamski—The Untold Story*, Lou Zinsstag & Timothy Good, Ceti Publications, 1983.
2. *Flying Saucers Have Landed*, Desmond Leslie & George Adamski, Werner Laurie, 1953.
3. *Aboard A Flying Saucer*, Truman Bethurum & Mary Kay Tennison, DeVorss and Co., 1954.
4. *The Saucers Speak!* George Hunt Williamson & Alfred C. Bailey, New Age, 1954.
5. *The White Sands Incident*, Daniel Fry, Horus House Press, Inc., 1992.
6. *Messengers of Deception*, Jacques Vallee, Berkeley, 1979. *Deceptions*, Jacques Vallee, Souvenir Press, 1988.
7. *The Hughes Papers*, Elaine Davenport and Paul Eddy with Mark Hurwitz, Sphere Books, Ltd., 1977.
8. *Extra-Terrestrials Among Us*, George C. Andrews, Llewellyn Publications, 1986.
9. *Situation Red: The UFO Siege*, Leonard H. Stringfield, Sphere Books, Ltd., 1977.
10. *UFOs: Operation Trojan Horse,* John Keel, Souvenir Press, Ltd., 1971.

Chapter 4: Here Come the Men in Black
1. Lecture given by John Keel, 1988.
2. *They Knew Too Much About Flying Saucers*, Gray Barker, University Books, Inc., 1956.
3. *Flying Saucers and the Three Men*, Albert Bender, Saucerian Books, 1962.
4. *They Knew Too Much About Flying Saucers,* Gray Barker, University Books, Inc., 1956.

5. National Archive file: AIR 2/17527. Interview, 11 September 1999.

6. *The UFO Silencers*, Timothy Green Beckley, Inner Light Publications, 1990.

7. *From Out of the Blue*, Jenny Randles, Global Communications, 1991.

8. Interview, 16 October 1995.

9. Interview with Nick Pope, 29 March 1994.

10. *Far Out*, Vol. 2, No. 6, 1994.

Chapter 5: Watching the Watchers

1. *Unconventional Flying Objects Sighted; And Portions Recovered By [First Name Deleted] McLean, Friona Texas*, U.S. Air Force Office of Special Investigations, 13 November 1952.

2. *Focus*, 30 September 1989.

3. UFO Crash/Retrievals: The Inner Sanctum, Status Report VI, Leonard Stringfield, published privately, 1991.

4. *CIA's Role in the Study of UFOs 1947–90*, Gerald Haines, *Studies in Intelligence*, Vol. 1, No. 1, Central Intelligence Agency, 1997. See also: www.cia.gov.

5. *Above Top Secret*, Timothy Good, Sidgwick & Jackson, 1987.

6. Citizens Against UFO Secrecy, Bulletin, 1990.

7. *Harmonic 33*, Bruce Cathie, Reed, 1968. *Harmonic 695*, Bruce Cathie, Reed, 1981. *The Bridge to Infinity*, Bruce Cathie, America West Publishers, 1989.

8. National Archive files AIR 2/17983 & AIR 2/17984.

9. *Casebook on the Men in Black*, Jim Keith, I-NET, 1997.

10. Ibid.

11. www.ufoevidence.org/documents/doc839.htm.

12. *Flying Saucers—Serious Business*, Frank Edwards, Lyle-Stuart Books, 1966.

13. *Swamp Gas Times: My Two Decades on the UFO Beat,* Patrick Huyghe, Paraview Press, 2001.

14. Ibid.

15. *UFO,* Vol. 18, No. 2, April/May 2003.

16. *UFOs and the National Security State: An Unclassified History, Volume One: 1941–1973,* Richard M. Dolan, Keyhole Publishing Company, 2000.

17. *Swamp Gas Times: My Two Decades on the UFO Beat,* Patrick Huyghe, Paraview Press, 2001.

18. Interview, 16 March 1996.

19. *Controlled Offensive Behavior—USSR,* Defense Intelligence Agency, 1972.

20. *Situation Red: The UFO Siege,* Leonard H. Stringfield, Sphere Books, Ltd., 1977.

Chapter 6: Cosmic Kidnappers

1. *The Interrupted Journey,* John G. Fuller, Souvenir Press, Ltd., 1980.

2. *Missing Time,* Budd Hopkins, Ballantine Books, 1989. *Intruders,* Budd Hopkins, Sphere Books, Ltd., 1988.

3. Interview, 8 May 2005.

4. *Glimpses of Other Realities,* Linda Howe, LMH Productions, 1997.

5. *Project Beta: The Story of Paul Bennewitz, National Security, and the Creation of a Modern UFO Myth,* Greg Bishop, Paraview Pocket Books, 2005.

6. National Archive file: AIR 2/16918.

7. National Archive file: AIR 2/17984.

8. *Clear Intent: The Government Cover-Up of the UFO Experience,* Lawrence Fawcett & Barry Greenwood, Prentice-Hall, 1984.

9. *Abducted!* Debbie Jordan & Kathy Mitchell, Carroll & Graf, 1994.

10. *Alien Encounters,* No, 19, 1997, Nos. 24 & 25, 1998.

11. *MILABS: Military Mind Control & Alien Abduction*, Helmut Lammer & Marion Lammer, IllumiNet Press, 1999. *If Not...Then Why All This?* (Video; for details see: www.anw.com/ml/index.htm.)

12. *Into the Fringe: A True Story of Alien Abduction*, Karla Turner, Berkeley Books, 1992. *Taken: Inside the Alien-Human Abduction Agenda*, Karla Turner, Kelt Works, 1994.

13. *Wake Up Down There! The Excluded Middle Collection*, Edited by Greg Bishop, Adventures Unlimited Press, 2000.

14. Interview with Irene Bott, 14 May 1998.

15. Interview, 14 August 2003.

16. *MILABS: Military Mind Control & Alien Abduction*, Helmut Lammer & Marion Lammer, IllumiNet Press, 1999.

Chapter 7: In Search of APEN

1. *On the Trail of the Phantom 'copter*, David Clarke, published privately. *Out of the Shadows: UFOs, The Establishment and the Official Cover-Up*, David Clarke & Andy Roberts, Piatkus Books, 2002.

2. www.met.police.uk/so/special_branch.htm.

3. *On the Trail of the Phantom 'copter*, David Clarke, published privately. *Out of the Shadows: UFOs, The Establishment and the Official Cover-Up*, David Clarke & Andy Roberts, Piatkus Books, 2002.

4. Special Branch file: 37/74/94. Memo, Chief Superintendent, "B" Squad, Special Branch, 22 March 1974. Memo from Chief Superintendent to Commander (Ops), Special Branch, 20 March 1974.

5. *Fire on the Mountain*, Andy Roberts, published privately. www.flyingsaucery.com. *Out of the Shadows: UFOs, The Establishment and the Official Cover-Up*, David Clarke & Andy Roberts, Piatkus Books, 2002.

6. Ibid.

7. Interview with Jenny Randles, 28 March 1997.

Chapter 8: Enter Sandman

1. Interview with the Sandman, 16 March 2004.

2. *Quest International*, Vol. 8, No. 3, 1988. *Contact UK*, Report, 20 August 1978.

3. *Clear Intent: The Government Cover-Up of the UFO Experience*, Lawrence Fawcett & Barry Greenwood, Prentice-Hall, 1984. www.nicap.dabsol.co.uk/cuban1.htm.

Chapter 9: Beta and Beyond

1. *Project Beta: The Story of Paul Bennewitz, National Security, and the Creation of a Modern UFO Myth*, Greg Bishop, Paraview-Pocket Books, 2005.

2. Interview with Greg Bishop, 22 March 2005.

3. *Body Snatchers in the Desert: The Horrible Truth at the Heart of the Roswell Story*, Nick Redfern, Paraview-Pocket Books, 2005.

4. CIA's Role in the Study of UFOs 1947-90, Gerald Haines, Studies in Intelligence, Vol. 1, No. 1, Central Intelligence Agency, 1997. See also: www.cia.gov.

5. *Project Beta: The Story of Paul Bennewitz, National Security, and the Creation of a Modern UFO Myth*, Greg Bishop, Paraview-Pocket Books, 2005.

6. *Pentagram*, 23 November 1988.

7. *The Excluded Middle, Virtual Issue*, Greg Bishop, 2000.

8. *Wake Up Down There! The Excluded Middle Collection*, edited by Greg Bishop, Adventures Unlimited Press, 2000.

9. *Central Intelligence Machinery*, Her Majesty's Stationery Office, 1993.

10. Letter to the author from Clive Neville, Ministry of Defense, 10 May 1989.

11. Letter to the author from Nick Pope, Ministry of Defense, 11 October 1993.

12. Interview with Nick Pope, 29 March 1994.

13. Conversation with Mary Seal, 4 February 1993.

Chapter 10: Deep Throat or Disinformation?

1. *Above Top Secret*, Timothy Good, Sidgwick & Jackson, 1987.

2. Interview with Jenny Randles, 28 March 1997.

Chapter 11: Hacking the Hangar:

1. Letter from United States' Senator Barry Goldwater to Shlomo
Arnon, 28 March 1975.

2. *Situation Red: The UFO Siege,* Leonard Stringfield, Sphere Books Ltd, 1978.

3. Ibid.

4. *Body Snatchers in the Desert: The Horrible Truth at the Heart of the Roswell Story,* Nick Redfern, Paraview-Pocket Books, 2005. *The Roswell Incident,* Charles Berlitz & William Moore, Granada Publishing Ltd, 1980. *Crash at Corona,* Stanton T. Friedman & Don Berliner, Paragon House, 1992. *The Truth About the UFO Crash at Roswell,* Kevin D. Randle & Donald R. Schmitt, M. Evans & Company, Inc. 1994.

5. *UFO Crash/Retrievals: The Inner Sanctum,* Leonard Stringfield. Published privately, 1991.

6. *The UFO Crash/Retrieval SynDr.ome,* Leonard Stringfield, The Mutual UFO Network, 1980.

7. *UFO Crash/Retrievals: Amassing the Evidence,* Leonard Stringfield. Published privately, 1982.

8. *Second Look,* Vol. 1, No. 7, May 1979.

9. *Far Out,* Vol. 1, No. 3, 1993.

10. *UFO Crash/Retrievals: Amassing the Evidence*, Leonard Stringfield. Published privately, 1982.

11. *Dateline NBC*, 27 October 1992. *UFO*, Vol. 9, No. 3, 1994.

12. Ibid.

13. *UFO Crash at Roswell*, Kevin D. Randle & Donald R. Schmitt, Avon Books, 1991.

14. Interview with Matthew Bevan, 12 April 1998.

15. *Breakthrough*, Whitley Strieber, Harper Collins Publishers, Inc., 1995.

16. Interview with Matthew Bevan, 12 April 1998.

17. *Alien Liaison*, Timothy Good, Random Century Ltd, 1991.

18. Interview with Matthew Bevan, 12 April 1998.

19. Interview with the Sandman, 25 July 2005.

Chapter 12: Rudloe Revelations

1. Royal Air Force Provost & Security Services Brochure, 1994.

2. Letter to Martin Redmond, Member of Parliament, from Nicholas Soames, Defense Minister, 27 October 1996.

3. *Quest International*, Vol. 8, No. 3, 1998.

4. *Above Top Secret*, Timothy Good, Sidgwick & Jackson, 1987.

5. *Alien Liaison*, Timothy Good, Century, 1991.

6. Ibid.

7. Letters to the author from Jonathan Turner, 17 & 21 September 1994, and 10 May 1995.

8. Interview with Anne Henson, 2 February 1998.

9. National Archive file: AIR 2/16918.

10. Letter to the author from Air Commodore J. L. Uprichard, Royal Air Force, Director of Security and Provost Marshal (RAF), 4 May 1994.

11. Interview with Nick Pope, 29 March 1994.

12. Letter to Chris Fowler from Kerry Philpott, Ministry of Defense, 14 December 1995.

13. Letter to the author from Group Captain J. Rose, RAF Rudloe Manor, 28 February 1996.

14. Interview with Matthew Williams, 17 January 1997.

15. Letter to the author from Flight Lieutenant A.F. Woodruff, RAF Rudloe Manor, June 1994.

16. Interview with Matthew Williams, 17 January 1997.

17. Letter to the author from Jonathan Dillon, 16 May 1994.

18. Interview with Matthew Williams, 17 January 1997.

19. Interview with the Sandman, 12 February 2005.

Chapter 13: Close Encounters of the Underground Kind

1. Interview with Matthew Williams, 17 January 1997.

2. *Truth-Seekers Review,* Vol. 2, No. 16.

3. Ibid.

Chapter 14: A British Roswell?

1. *UFO Crash/Retrievals: The Inner Sanctum, Status Report VI,* Leonard Stringfield. Published privately, 1991.

2. Interview with Harold South, 11 December 1996.

3. Interview with Mr. Law, 11 December 1996.

Chapter 15: Penetrating the Pleasure Dome

1. *A Covert Agenda: The British Government's UFO Top Secrets Exposed,* Nick Redfern, Paraview Special Editions, 2004.

2. *Open Government,* Her Majesty's Stationery Office, 1993. Crown copyright. Reproduced with the permission of the Controller of Her Majesty's Stationery Office.

3. *Their Trade is Treachery,* Chapman Pincher, Sidgwick & Jackson Ltd, 1981.

4. Full Incident Report, British Coast Guard, 5 October 1996.
5. Interview with Robin Cole, 29 September 1997.
6. Interview with the Sandman, 8 January 2005.

Chapter 16: Mystery Mutilations

1. Interview with the Sandman, 8 January 2005.
2. *The Owlman and Others,* Jonathan Downes, CFZ Publications, 2004. *Monster Hunter,* Jonathan Downes, CFZ Publications, 2005.
3. *Strange Secrets: Real Government Files on the Unknown,* Nick Redfern, Paraview-Pocket Books, 2003. *Monster Hunter,* Jonathan Downes, CFZ Publications, 2005.
4. Interview with the Sandman, 8 January 2005
5. *Western Morning News,* 13 July 1977.
6. Ibid.
7. *The Mothman Prophecies,* John A. Keel, Tor, 2002.
8. *Monster Hunter,* Jonathan Downes, CFZ Publications, 2005.

Chapter 17: The Spying Continues

1. Interview with the Sandman, 14 January 2005.
2. Interview with Nick Pope, 4 January 1999.
3. Interview with Matthew Williams, 25 October 1997.
4. *News of the World,* 14 November 1999.
5. Interview with the Press Officer, Ministry of Defense, 14 November 1999.
6. Interview with Nick Pope, 14 November 1999.
7. Statement circulated by Nick Pope, 20 November 1999.
8. www.mod.uk.
9. Interview with the Sandman, 10 January 2005.
10. Interview with the Sandman, 11 January 2005.
11. www.MI5.gov.uk.
12. National Archive files: WO 199/1982 and KV 4/11.
13. Interview with the Sandman, 10 January 2005.

14. *The Planet on Sunday*, 19 December 1999.

15. Interview with the Sandman, 10 January 2005.

16. *Eye-Spy Magazine*, See: www.eyespymag.com.

17. www.securityfocus.com/news/10373.

18. *Daily Telegraph*, 28 July 2005. *Sydney Morning Herald*, 13 July 2005. *Guardian*, 9 July 2005.

19.http://www.kentuckynewera.com/articles/stories/public/200508/20/04w5_news.html.

Conclusions

1. Interview with the Sandman, 13 February, 2005.

INDEX

Printed in the United Kingdom
by Lightning Source UK Ltd.
125660UK00001B/333/A